February 5, 2020
Love always,
Ruth
ONE
NURSE UNIVERSE
D1230782
RECOLLECTIONS FROM THE BEDSIDE
Susan Turnage RN

Cover Illustration: Nicholas Brucker

First published by Dog Ear Publishing
8888 Keystone Crossing
Suite 1300
Indianapolis, IN 46240
www.dogearpublishing.net

ISBN: 978-145757-064-3

This book is printed on acid-free paper.
Printed in the United States of America

DEDICATION

To my Grandmother, Mary Rock.

In her arms, I was her Zurka.

That was always good enough.

For you, Nannie.

Oi yoi yoi yoi

ACKNOWLEDGEMENTS

To my classmates, the 1972 graduates of Hahnemann Hospital School of Nursing, a very special thanks. We did not comprehend what a stellar education we were receiving and what powerful nurses we would become. Gratitude for your camaraderie and collaboration.

To the tribes of nurse sisters and brothers that mentored and supported me along my career path, thank you for all the positive hours we shared and the advice you gave. I heard it. I used it. I shared it. Thanks for the hilarious and soul restoring mealtime discussions.

Special thanks to my editor, Cheryl Cease Williams. Your observations, recommendations and occasional shoves were invaluable.

To my treasured sons, Gustav and Nicholas, thank you for your love and goofiness. Your encouragement led to this book. If my memoir is made into a movie after my demise, please be sure they get Cher to play me.

To my husband for his quiet vigilance during the writing of this book, thank you. Time evaporates for me when I write. If not for him, my yoga students would have experienced an uncounted number of teacher no-shows.

***

And to each and every one of my patients, endless gratitude.

Together we laughed, cried, bent the rules, found our way through the darkness and always had hope.

We are like angels with just one wing,
together we fly.

CONTENTS

ON RAMP

When digging through my satchel of stories for this book and organizing them to publish, I felt held back by the reading strategy of one member of the Nearly Normal Readers Group, NNRG, of which I am a founding member. This member would read the book's first paragraph, then (1) pronounce the entire book unreadable trash and quit the read or (2) continue to read. Over the 19 years we have been meeting, her abrupt judgments served to enliven many of our discussions. Sometimes she dismissed books that were considered by the literary community to be classic treasures.

Once the gauntlet of "trash" was thrown by her however, the rest of us could usually find a paragraph, phrase, concept, or word she could agree was of value. It made for fun meetings.

For those of you, like her, who may also hold a book at a reverent distance before committing to the read, I offer you an enticement for reading my book.

Annually, Gallup examines honesty and ethical standards among various professions. In 2018, nurses topped the list of Very high/High at 84% (Gallup, December 3-12, 2018, gallup.com). Nurses have topped the list every year since 1999, except for 2001. After the fall of the World Trade Center towers, firefighters took the top spot – deservedly so. (In case you wonder who was at the bottom of the list in 2018, it was Members of Congress, with 8%).

So!

Stories from an honest and ethical professional. I hope this is invitation enough.

One inspiration to bring you with me behind the bedside curtain came from a few sentences in the preface of the book, *What the Dog Saw and Other Adventures*, by Malcolm Gladwell.

> "What is the first thing that we want to know when we meet someone who is a doctor at a social occasion? It isn't "What do you do?" We know, sort of, what a doctor does. Instead,

> we want to know what it means to be with sick people all day long. We want to know what it *feels like* to be a doctor, because we're quite sure that it doesn't feel at all like what it means to sit at a computer all day long, or teach school, or sell cars. Such questions are not dumb or obvious. Curiosity about the interior life of other people's day-to-day work is one of the most fundamental of human impulses,…"

I finally put pen to paper when my son, Gustav, who, after hearing one of my stories said, "You gotta write this stuff down, Ma"

***

Nurses have long been pigeon holed in a distant land of body fluids and odors, prompting the oft-stated phrase, "Oh! I could never be a nurse. Ewwwww!"

These stories reveal my 'day to day' nurse life. What it meant and means to me, to be a nurse, tending the sick and dying. What I saw, felt, smelled, heard, and touched.

Nursing is much more than secretion and excretion management. It is a calling, my calling.

You hold in your hands a few of the proud and not so proud moments of my life and nursing career. I expect you will laugh, sigh, cry, and perhaps suppress a gag.

If you discover a passage you find especially disgusting, flag it. You may then use it as a quick remedy for lingering dinner guests you want to clear from your domicile.

You're welcome.

With love,

Nurse Susan

1

BAPTISM

"MEN!," Miss Cook bellows for attention from the center of the open men's ward. "The student nurses will be bathing some of you today."

Ms. Cook, my Fundamentals of Nursing instructor, had the job of teaching us the procedure for bathing a patient in the hospital bed. A salty veteran nurse who had seen it all, as she liked to tell us, Ms. Cook sighed a lot when she looked at us. Her face read hopelessness at the quality of women and men (only two) entering nurse's training in 1969.

On Day One of bathing an actual patient, we wake early. Ms. Cook escorts a dozen of us from the dormitory classroom to the men's ward of the hospital. It is 6:30 AM. Nervous, we huddle at the nurses' station like penguins on a tiny iceberg, our light gray student uniforms freshly ironed, freshman nursing student caps perched on our heads. The student nurse caps resemble a large, upside down, white cupcake paper, trimmed with a thin black velvet ribbon.

Ms. Cook stands surrounded by four large rooms, each holding six occupied beds and open to the wide central hall via an open archway. Every privacy curtain is pulled back. All the men stare at her in silence. It's obvious a few of them have seen her before, some look apprehensive, others wear creepy smirks. This does not help us relax. Some of us have clinical experience, but many do not.

Her rigid posture conveys, to us and to the men patients, that she demands the procedure be followed exactly as taught. Our eyes bug out; we knew she treated us like newly enlisted recruits – but the patients, too?

A couple of expected cat calls and leers ensue, but she aborts them with The Look. Some men appear to be silently praying, *not me, not me*. I begin to shake. Ms. Cook calls out student names and points to a bed for each. She calls my name twice before I can move my legs to my patient's bedside.

I am standing face to face with a very short and stocky black man. We fix our eyes on each other. He is sitting up with the head of the bed elevated. To my distress, he looks more frightened than I feel. We both jerk our heads as we hear a final shout from Ms. Cook, "And make sure you wash the groin area."

Before either Mr. Smith or I faint, I quickly pull the fabric privacy curtain around his bed. I rush to his shoulder and whisper earnestly, "I swear to God not to wash or look at your groin if you swear to God to lie to Ms. Cook and tell her I did." He slumps in relief and nods. He whispers to me he has been admitted to the hospital for complete bed rest following a heart attack. For his heart to heal, he is not allowed to feed or bathe himself.

Mr. Smith is very distressed at having someone bathe him beside his wife. I tell him not to worry, we will get through this fast and easy. What a lie! My hands shake as I grab the metal wash basin and rush down the center hall to the utility room. Basin water steaming, towels in hand, I return to him, and we plot our performance.

I tell Mr. Smith this is my first time at the hospital bedside as a student nurse, and he tells me he is on his first week of three weeks of bed rest. In a joint effort to establish camaraderie, we agree his heart must be getting stronger to survive both a Ms. Cook verbal assault and the prospect of being bathed by a white, 17-year-old student nurse.

We whisper our plan as I wash his chest, arms, back, and legs. He tells me he has a genetic disorder, Achondroplasia, a disorder of bone growth, the most common form of dwarfism. This is his first time in a hospital, and he misses his wife, hates all the noise, and can't wait to get out of, what he dubs, this dreadful bed.

I tell him I have never seen a naked man in my life, except for briefly when my Dad's bathing suit was knocked to his knees by furious surf lashing at a Wildwood, New Jersey beach when I was a child. He tells me not to worry, I will do just fine. I understand what he is telling me. He means I will do just fine some other day on some other male patient. I am relieved and grateful for his collaboration and his support.

"Now turn away," he urges as I hand him the soapy washcloth so he can tend to his privates. I turn away and for good measure clench my eyes shut. I guess he washed his groin, we don't talk about it. I hand him a rinsed cloth and the towel with my back still turned, and we are done with the bath. I hand him two patient gowns, and he wraps up carefully to maintain privacy.

As I finish rolling him side to side to change his sheets, we hear Ms. Cook whisk open a curtain a few beds away and bark at a patient, "Did Ms. Wade wash your groin?"

At the sound of those few words, our eyes bug out and lock. He pats my fingers and nods. I nod once in response. I finish making his bed, run the basin back down the hall to the utility room, dump it out, and quickly return to put all the supplies away. We are ready. I pull the curtain back and smooth it. I stand next to him near the head of the bed. My gray-and-white student nurse uniform now has big wet spots all over the front. Hair that has escaped from my ponytail sticks out here and there in disarray. As he stares straight ahead, I watch for the approach of the groin Gestapo.

Standing at the foot of my patient's bed, Ms.Cook booms, "Did Ms.Yonchek wash your groin?" With confidence he tells her not only did I wash his groin but I brushed his hair and teeth, too. Oh God, I forgot about his hair and teeth. He heard some other patients say that when I was away to empty his wash basin. What a great partner in crime.

"Good," she croaks through thin, tight lips. As she stomps off, I give Mr. Smith the hairbrush and get water for his teeth. We congratulate ourselves, mouthing, "Ha, ha, ha." And, "Weren't we clever to fool Ms. Cook?" And, "Aren't we so tricky?" The two of us are giddy with the relief of sharing the success of that first bath.

I return to bathe Mr. Smith two more mornings that week and three days the next week. True to our first day, I do the pits, he does the parts, but I have grown in confidence and even offer him a back rub after his bath, which he gratefully accepts, explaining how the hard rubber mattress has been giving his back fits.

Each time we are together, Mr. Smith and I never tire of recounting our first meeting. He explains how he told his wife and family about our covert operations, how he always refers to me as "My Nurse." I can't help but beam. Both of us know how much I appreciated his help with my first male bed-bath.

During the rest of Mr. Smith's hospital stay, our relationship continued to evolve. I taught him what I knew about eating healthy and doing gentle exercises like walking. I encouraged him to take his medicine, to get his blood pressure checked, and to come back to the clinic for check-ups. What Mr. Smith taught me, in return, was that more often than not, I would learn more from my patients than they would learn from me.

I spent a total six weeks on the men's ward. Mr. Smith was discharged over a weekend, so I did not get to say goodbye and tell him to behave and all that ceremonial patient/nurse separating that concludes a connection such as ours. It didn't feel right not to say goodbye and thanks at the time, but sometimes that is just how things work out.

My next clinical rotation took me to the women's ward. I had come a long way since I conspired with Mr. Smith to pull one over on Ms. Cook. Well past my embarrassment, washing private body parts had become as second nature to me as scrubbing elbows and hands. I continued to thrive as a student nurse and began to sense the comfort of my healing hands brought to my patients.

Then I learned how life can be full of wonderful surprises. One early afternoon, near the end of my six-week clinical rotation on the women's ward, I hear a man's voice calling loudly from up at the nurses' station. "Hey! Is My Nurse here?" As I'm tending a patient, I peer around the curtain beside her bed to see Mr. Smith in his real clothes. I pop out and wave excitedly. He strides toward me. He tells me he had come to the hospital heart clinic for a checkup and wanted to say hello and check on me.

"How did you find me?" I ask in amazement. This was an 18-floor hospital, and I could have been anywhere. "I've been hollering on every floor for you," he says as he laughs.

We talk, catching up. He is feeling good, he says, as is his wife and family. His wide grin tells me he thinks I am doing good, too.

* * *

Bathing a stranger is a profoundly intimate task. A procedure that derailed a few nursing students early in training, like those whose parents sent them to nursing school for a good paying job.

In the 1960s in my community, women who sought a working career mostly became a teacher, nurse, secretary, or hairdresser. And often, it was the parents who had the final say. We all knew on the first day of nurse training who had the calling and who did not. Of 72 students who started training, three students left the night after the bed bath lesson. As the nursing procedures became increasingly complex and invasive, like inserting an NG tube down someone's nose into their stomach, more students bailed – too much gagging and retching. We would conclude three years of our Hahnemann Hospital training with 54 competent and skilled graduate nurses.

The way to learn how to bathe someone is to bathe someone. To this purpose, Ms. Cook led a lab classroom demonstration and bathed a junior student nurse volunteer to show how it is sequentially and properly done. With relief, I see our model "patient" got to keep her underwear on. Just watching, my heart beat fast as I thought *just get through it, just get through it.* "It" was not just Ms. Cook demonstrating the bed bath on another student nurse. "It" was me trying to remember the exact order of the procedure so I could demonstrate it under Ms. Cook's maniacal eagle eye.

Watching Ms. Cook bathe one of my not-quite-naked peers in that cold, fluorescent-lit skills lab made my palms clammy and lungs tighten even though I had done hundreds of bed baths at the nursing home. Her hands sped from basin to body, never a drop of water landing in any unintended place. Not a spot of water on her starched white uniform. Her short graying hair never budged beneath a perfectly placed white nurse's cap. All the while she moved, so did her mouth, chopping out words like a bull horn auctioneer. An absolute model of efficiency without a speck of the healing touch. It could have been a sink of dirty dishes instead of a breathing human under her hands.

Miss Cook scared me half to death with her stark behavior. Nothing like the kind, compassionate and funny nurses I had worked with as a candy striper or nurses aide.

My fear made me pay careful attention. The bath moved from face to neck to arms. Ms. Cook cloaked body parts with towels and a flannel bath sheet until it was their turn for scrub, rinse, dry. Then expertly covering the clean front parts and rolling the patient side to side while changing the sheets at the same time, she proceeded to wash the back side of the patient's body. My mind compared the scene to a bus being washed. Therapeutic touch it was not.

One truth about this demonstration, which we students would discover later, was that in our actual training hospital, there would be no extra towels. There may or may not be a flannel bath sheet. A washcloth, once procured, was wrung out and hidden in the patient's bedside cabinet for the next day, as it was too iffy to chance that a fresh one would be available. Especially on the wards, the hospital floors that served Philadelphia's indigent population, clean linen was in very limited supply. The bed-bath procedure supplies we learned to use in class and what we actually got in the hospital were different realities; the staff nurses taught us that part. "Ha, good luck with that," they would hoot when we naively asked for a full set of sheets, towels, washcloth, and flannel bath blanket for our patient's bed.

In our hospital procedure manual, you could find specific steps and supplies needed to bathe a patient. There is a sequenced and stark list. Gather all the supplies you will need and place them near the bed. Test the bath basin water with a thermometer or your elbow to be sure it is not too hot. Wipe the face and neck with a warm soapy cloth, rinse and dry same. And on it dryly goes from head to toe.

But this is not a bus wash, it's a fellow human being, and there is an art to bathing that person, a learned art. Combine soothing hands with warm water and you generate a healing power that can have a profound effect on relieving pain and suffering. It's not just about hygiene. A kindly delivered bath can slow the breathing and heart rate, and the blood pressure will come down as the patient relaxes. When done by an experienced, gentle, and competent nurse, the bath is a restorative therapy.

* * *

Every three months during the next two years of my nurse's training, Mr. Smith would visit the hospital's heart clinic for a check-up. Without fail, he would holler on every floor for me. Eventually, my classmates got to know him and would tell him where I was. Mr. Smith followed me through pediatrics, obstetrics, neurology, and psychiatry. When I could not come out of the operating room or ICU, he would leave a finely printed, unsigned note for me, always with the same words. "I'm doing good, I hope you are doing good."

The women's ward, site of my second rotation, was directly above the men's ward. It was efficiently dubbed, "Six." Identical in layout to one another, each with its series of rooms opening to a central hallway, both wards served the same indigent populations, men on the fifth floor, women on the sixth. The canvas curtain hung around each bed provided only visual privacy. You could smell and hear everything, even the scraping noise of curtains being opened and closed, from one end of the ward to the next. The bathrooms and dirty utility room were a substantial distance from the bedside, all the way at the end of the ward. The linoleum floors throughout echoed the foot fall of "clinics," our white leather, lace-up nurses' shoes. We were required to shine them at least weekly. Not only were the monstrous hospital beds with their rubber-coated mattress covers ancient and bulky, they also smelled bad. The hand cranks that elevated the head or foot of the bed made a clunking racket when pressed into use, and many of the beds refused to work at all. Rarely was there an empty bed for more than an hour or two. The ward was always filled with patients and very busy nurses around the clock.

The distance down the long hallway to the bathrooms or utility hopper seemed to lengthen if you had to give a warm soap suds enema to a patient and then get them to walk 50 feet to the bathroom. It was horrible for them, but given the geography, there was nothing any of the nurses could do to make the trek any shorter or less prone to mishap.

Then again, there were always bedpans. On the men's ward, it became street theater for the patients to watch a nurse carry, very carefully, a towel-draped, loaded bedpan from the bedside to its final destination in the dirty utility room.

"Hey, looks like you're spillin' that!" one man laughingly hollered toward me as I walked the covered bedpan, brimming with its smelly contents, slowly to its destination.

In response, I opened my eyes wide and headed right for him, feigning a stumble and saying, "Woah, look out! I am carrying a big load." That got a big laugh from the gallery, and that patient never made another peep when I passed by him on my many bedpan trips back and forth.

The first bed-bath patient I encounter on my women's ward rotation was not new to the student nurse body. Her chronic health issues and frequent hospital stays had kept her permanently on the bed-bath roster for student nurses. My classmates liked to call her Mother Earth, as in old as dirt.

As I introduce myself, her Don King clump of white hair bobs, and she demands, "I want my bath in the chair!"

I quickly agree. "Fine with me."

Her vigorous verbal proclamation was followed by spasms of coughing. Her emaciated body slumps low in the center of the bed. Road maps of blue veins course just under her translucent skin. I get the reason for her nickname. Even though she is in her late 60s, she looks ancient. My Mom's phrase, "She looks like the wrath of God," comes to my mind. I don't think she weighs more than 60 pounds. She moves slowly, wincing often.

I collect bathing supplies and pull the curtain around the bed. I draw the water super-hot so by the time I get to use it, it still will be really warm for her. I help her slide to standing from the bed and slowly lower her featherweight body into the large, vinyl-covered bedside chair. I am afraid I'll break her in half and am not sure how to hold her without causing pain.

Suddenly she coughs into a tissue and thrusts it under my nose. "Not bloody today," she victoriously announces, the mucous-filled tissue nearly touching my face.

I pull back slightly. *Diminished vision,* I think, telling myself I need to watch her movements. *That specimen almost hit me in the chin.*

Moving from the bed to the chair causes her to cough more. She manages to rasp out, "Where's the other girlie?" I imagine she has met a parade of student nurses and has formed attachments. Now, here comes a new one. I explain that, just like me, her girlie started on a different ward today.

"Bah," she snorts, setting off another spasm of coughing. She is bringing up a lot of secretions.

I know the drainage must come up and out to clear her lungs, but I also know it must be exhausting her. She is right, it isn't bloody. But there are volumes of it.

I pass her a washcloth and, after she cleans her face, I take the soapy cloth to her back. Her ribs resemble Venetian blind slats with the skin drawn in between each bone. I use one finger to wash between each rib. The slow movements of the warm washcloth rinse relax her. Her head drops forward, and her breathing quiets. The warm lotion backrub soothes her, and she leans into my hand. I cover her back with a flannel sheet and place the soapy cloth on her chest. She raises her head and pinches a nipple between her thumb and index finger, lifting a flabby thin breast. I wash under it, rinse, and dry. She lets it go, and it slaps against her rib cage. The sound makes me jump and drop my jaw.

She cackles. "That's what happens when your titties get old!" She coughs, laughs, and claps her bony hands.

I freeze in astonishment. My mind slides away into some backwater thought about growing old. *Really? Will I look like this?* I wonder. That ballast shifts my thoughts to consider my face on this little elf body.

She delights in my response and pushes the towel off her thighs. Her hands press against the skin just above her knees. She drags that loose thigh skin up to her hips. Down to the knees, back to the hips. Her eyebrows jump up and down as she gazes into my face. She is comical to watch. I unfreeze and giggle. I shake my head and quietly finish her chair bath.

As I push the curtain open and shove it back to the wall, the patient in the next bed rolls her eyes at me and says, "She does that stuff to all her new nurses."

* * *

Fifteen years after learning the bed-bath procedure from Ms. Cook in that skills lab, I discover for myself how powerful and soothing a hospital bed bath can be.

It is late evening as I lay on a hospital gurney, with sweat, blood, and oily exhaustion covering me. Just an hour before, after a day and a half of labor and a lot of bleeding, doctors had wheeled me to the operating room (OR) for an emergency C-section to deliver the baby that was stuck in my pelvis. I had given birth to a healthy son, who is a little dehydrated, but perfect in every way.

Lying there in a daze I hear a voice at my bedside that says, "You'll feel better after a bath." Too exhausted to open my eyes, I snap, "I don't want a bath, leave me alone." I am totally spent, annoyed at being bothered. Apparently, this nurse has heard the same rude response before. She ignores me and puts a warm, wet washcloth over my face. I melt and fall silent. I let her have her way with me. She gently washes my face. She scrubs my neck, rinses it, dries it, and rubs lotion onto my skin. She places a warmed, white, flannel blanket lightly over my head and neck. I float into a fuzzy white tactile world, my vision, hearing, smelling, and taste all subdued.

Working silently, she draws out one limp arm at a time and, with amazing speed and competence, scrubs them until they feel as though they are glowing. Without any effort from me, she props me onto my side and washes my back and bottom with gentle thoroughness. Enveloped in a cocoon of relaxation, I can sense that as she cares for me, she is changing the bedding, too. Then her hands arrive at my stomach. The palms of her hands push hard, kneading my belly, coaxing my equally sluggish uterus to respond and shrink. My privates and legs receive a vigorous washing, and by the time she rubs lotion onto my legs, I feel boneless, as though weightless and adrift on a lake of soft warm air.

I have entered a realm of total peace. I lay magnificently paralyzed and serene. My arms and legs do not exist. I have no pain, no idea of time, no concept of place, no need of anything. I do not know who this angel nurse is nor how she managed to move me from that gurney to my bed. Her healing hands have taken away the ghastly, bloody, and painful surgical ordeal, delivering me into motherhood.

After she leaves, I sleep for 24 hours. I awaken restored and ready to begin the next chapter of my life.

2

BAND-AIDS®

"Watch out for the big cracks," yells Eileen, who just tripped over the uneven concrete pavement of the alley. Her shoe skates stay on and she doesn't fall.

A dozen children strong, we skate around the end row house, arms swinging, and up the Brill Street sidewalk. Once we reach the other end of the row houses, we cut back through to the alley and do the same loop over and over. It's a Philadelphia playtime ritual for 5 and 6-year-old children in the late 1950's.

I am skating smoothly until somebody hollers, "Race!" I push to the front of the group too fast, and my skates bump over a big crack. I fall down with a thump, first onto my hands and knees, then all the way to my side. Everybody keeps going, as if they don't hear me hollering, "Hey! Wait!"

I push up on my elbows and watch them disappear. My hands feel hot and are skinned but are not bleeding. Both my knees are bleeding. Again. The scabs from yesterday or the day before having been ripped off. I remove my skates and go back inside the house.

Quietly I walk past Mom asleep on the living room sofa. She hates to be disturbed during her morning naps. Softly I tiptoe up the steps to the linen closet for a Band-Aid®.

I count the steps as I go up. Fourteen. Counting helps me check that nothing has changed. I always count. I started counting everything as soon as I learned numbers.

I open the white wooden closet door and reach for the metal box of Band-Aids. I shake the Band-Aid tin. It sounds like there are plenty. I tiptoe back down the steps, holding onto the railing. Fourteen steps, just like before.

Mom's eyes are still closed.

Once in the kitchen, I sit on the floor, scoot backward under the round table and rest my back on the wall. This is my private first aid area.

Both my knees are skinned and bloody. Dried blood spots go all the way down to my lacy white anklets. My thumbs push the Band-Aid box lid. Pop, it opens. I push it closed. Click. Pop, click. Pop, click. Three times. I always do it this way. I open the tin again and pull out one Band-Aid for each knee. Slowly I breathe in the smell, holding the Band-Aid under my ski jump nose.

I love the smell of Band-Aids. They smell like all better.

No matter how big the booboo is, I am only allowed one Band-Aid. Mom says if I ever use a whole can of Band-Aids again on one leg sore, I will never get another Band-Aid from her as long as I live.

Once, before the one Band-Aid rule, I covered my knee and shin, all the way down to my ankle with a Band-Aid parade. I thought it looked like a really good job. Mom had a big fit. I cried.

Slowly, I tear the short end of the paper wrapper, then pull the red string, slicing open the wrapper down its long side. Pulling out the Band-Aid, I smell it again. So good. The two paper tabs pull away easily. I take my time and place it over the oozy open sore, gently pressing the sticky sides down. It hurts a little. Then I do the other knee. I close the Band-Aid can and scoot back out from under the table. Paper tabs and wrapper go into the kitchen trash can; I remember to keep my foot on the pedal that opens the lid until it softly closes. Mom hates the slam it makes if you let it go too fast.

I tiptoe back upstairs. Fourteen. The Band-Aids go back in the linen closet. Down the steps, holding the railing. Fourteen. Back outside!

Even though I keep wishing that Mom would kiss my knees and make them better, I am content to go to my private clinic and take care of my own self.

* * *

I am age 6 and in second grade at St. Bartholomew's Catholic School. My classroom has ten desks in a row and eight rows across. We sit in alphabetical order. My last name begins with Y, so I am next to last in the last row.

No matter what happens, it is very important to Sister Mary Immaculate that we do not laugh. She says laughing is another thing that makes the Blessed Virgin Mary cry. Any child who laughs must sit in the cloakroom for the rest of the day. The cloakroom smells like there are a thousand dirty wet dogs in there.

Today Sister says we all need to line up in ones, not twos, and go to the cafeteria. We will see a nurse to get our polio vaccine sugar cube and a needle. There will be no talking, laughing, or crying in the line, so as not to upset the Blessed Virgin Mary.

I squeeze my lips into a tight circle, so I don't talk. I look down so I don't see my friends Tony or Peter or Dennis making faces at me. Tony can puff up his nose like the seals at the zoo, which makes me laugh. He is fast at turning his face back to his regular face though, so I am the only one who gets into trouble for acting up. It seems like he never gets caught being silly.

The sun is coming into the cafeteria through the big windows up near the ceiling, making it so light and warm in there. Lines of students come in from every door; some of the big kids from eighth grade are there, too. Many long rows of wooden tables are set up with lots of little white paper cups at one end. Inside the cups, I see pink sugar cubes. On each table, white metal trays with a painted black edge are piled with needles. There is a nurse beside every table, sitting in a chair.

I am quiet. Everyone is quiet.

We step forward slowly. I keep my hands in the big kangaroo pockets on the front of my plaid dress under my white pinafore, so I don't accidently touch anything. When I get close enough, I see how it works. First, you get the needle. Then, you get the sugar cube. I stretch my neck to watch what happens during the needle part. For some kids, a moan slips out but no crying.

Oh goodie! You get a Band-Aid over the needle spot.

I stare at the nurse as I move closer and closer. I take in her white uniform dress with no dirt on it and the clean white nurse's cap on her curly brown hair that has been tied back in a ponytail. She has a silver, stretch-band wristwatch, like Mom's. I notice her white hosiery and polished white shoes. As I get nearer, I am breathing fast with nervous excitement and smell the cotton balls that have been dipped in alcohol. I feel my heart thumping, because I am afraid to get the needle.

The nearer I come, the more the nurse seems to glow in the sunshine, so clean and pretty. I look down at my plaid dress and white pinafore and back to her uniform. I want to wear a white dress like hers. I see my red Mary Jane shoes and her polished white ones.

When my turn with the nurse comes, I look up into her face. She is smiling. When her hands gently touch me, they are soft and warm. The cool alcohol cotton ball sends a trickle down my tiny arm to my elbow. It surprises me, and I jump. She whispers that I will be OK. I watch her face and never feel the needle. The Band-Aid goes on, and her hands give my arm a little squeeze as her thumbs slide over the Band-Aid tabs. She rolls the sugar cube into my mouth from the cup and pats my head. In a soft voice she says, "good girl." She even smells good, like the Ivory soap at Nannies' house.

Stepping away from her side, I feel puffed up like one of those little brown sparrows I see on the power lines outside our kitchen window. I feel so happy.

I know right then and there that someday I will be a nurse, as kind and clean and gentle as this one.

***

At age 16, I had the opportunity to work as an aide in a nursing home in Northeast Philadelphia. It was here that I met Jean, a nursing student at Villanova University. Jean fed my interest with descriptions of her nursing classes, making me hunger to hear more. When she invited me to visit her on campus, I jumped at the chance. What I saw there, girls studying for a college degree in nursing at a vibrant and alive campus, only strengthened my resolve. I was determined to pursue a nursing degree right here at Villanova, if they would have me, and felt nothing could stop me.

I decided one evening to announce my plans at dinner. With great enthusiasm, I told my family the dream that began the first time I stuck a Band-Aid on my own bloody knee: I was going to go to college to become a nurse. Proof that hope springs eternal despite the suffocating weight of history, I expected a round of applause, maybe even Mom saying she was proud of me.

Nothing.

Then, in a low and measured tone, Dad growled, "If you think I will waste my money for you to throw it away at college, *you're nuts*. You'll never amount to anything but a mother with a bunch of kids."

My chin dropped. I swallowed tears and gulped to keep from crying. I sat there with my disappointment until I could feel it slowly lighting an ember of fury in the pit of my stomach. Maybe Dad could bully Mom by holding her purse strings, but he would not bully me. Somehow, I would get my own goddamn money.

Still, I had no one to ask to borrow money. My beloved Nannie lived on a small pension and spent frugally. I knew nothing about obtaining a loan, and the 85 cents an hour I was earning as a nurse's aide at the nursing home wouldn't get me far.

But I was determined. After doing some research, I found that college may have been beyond my meager means, but a hospital school of nursing tuition conceivably was within reach. I would need about $900 total tuition for three years of nursing school.

At some point in my calculations, I remembered Dad telling us he had been saving for our weddings.

I bided my time for a few weeks and on a night when the dinner-time tension between my parents seemed less thick, I took the plunge.

"I will never marry," I announced to my family, adding that I would like to use my wedding money to pay for nursing school. Dad said if that's what I wanted, it would be fine, but that was that, I would never get any more money from him. His $300 wedding money plus a $50 check from a Future Nurses Club award was enough to pay first year tuition and put me firmly on my path.

I applied to and was accepted by three local nursing schools. I chose Hahnemann Hospital in downtown Philly where, praise the Lord, staying in the dorm was mandatory. At 17, I was out of the house. And except for a few holiday visits, I never went back. As promised, I never received another penny from Dad. I didn't need it. Over the next three years, I worked two and sometimes three jobs at once, often late into the night, to pay for the rest of my tuition.

From the beginning, I took to nurses' training with a passion. Two summer stints as a candy striper at Philadelphia General Hospital and my continuing nurse's aide job had begun to shape my clinical aptitude. Slowly and surely, my studies and then my nursing practice began to mend what my childhood experiences had broken inside of me. As time passed, my self-worth grew, crowding out my father's declaration that I would never amount to anything. I wasn't healed, but I was getting better. My future seemed bright and full of possibilities.

3

GAG ORDERS

The instant gag. Everybody has at least one aversion that generates an immediate grabbing of the stomach and, sometimes, an unstoppable, unwelcome spasm that returns evidence of your last meal into your lap.

It can occur with furious speed.

For my sister, it has always been hair in a clogged shower drain. Even wearing rubber gloves, she is unable to de-clog a drain without tears, gagging, and the appearance of severe emotional trauma. Knowing this, cleaning her shower drain is the first thing I do upon arrival at her house for a visit.

This is how it went down the last time I was there.

"Hey, Joan." I call her at work, reporting in. "I'm here, the rental car's GPS found your house fine. The airport was not too busy."

"What's that noise?" she asks. There is no, "Hello." No, "Great, you made it."

"I just unscrewed the shower drain stopper." I am squeezing my phone against my shoulder, making it hard to speak clearly. "I'm cleaning out the drain." *I am such a good sister,* I think, mentally patting myself on the back.

"How did you find the screwdriver so fast?" she continues.

"I couldn't find your toolbox," I grunt, "so I'm using one of your butter knives."

Click.

It might be a clogged drain for my sister, but for me it's something that tends to make a career in nursing a little more difficult -- if not downright unpleasant. Dentures. Even writing the word here makes me gag.

The appearance of dentures in any patient's bedside table denture cup sends shivers down my spine and causes instant waves of gagging 100 percent of the time. Even wearing two layers of disposable gloves when touching and cleaning my patients' dentures does not prevent me from shuddering and retching, tears welling up in my eyes. I hide this from my patients by keeping my back to them or standing at the head of their bed and out of sight. If there is such a thing as a denture phobia, I have it. I am sure I am in good company and that there is a support group out there somewhere for me.

An aversion like mine is one of the many reasons nurses who work together and know what is best for their patients become a community of collaborators. I will tidy up any body fluid mess, clean a trach, and give an enema in exchange for another nurse helping my patients with their dentures.

It's also one of the reasons I love pediatrics.

I have no idea how I developed this specific reaction to dentures except possibly from my Uncle Tom, who delighted in popping his top dentures loose at Thanksgiving dinner, rolling them 360 degrees in his mouth, and dropping them back into place. The accompanying gravy-colored drool that ran down his chin made Aunt Sue shout at him to stop. I believe alcohol was a factor in him displaying his talent. Lucky for me, it is not a common aversion among nurses, giving me a lot of backup.

There are some days, though, when secretion or excretion events can wreak unexpected results even in the most seasoned of us nurse types. Not once in three years of nurse training was there a class discussion on how it may be possible for you to encounter a patient care scenario that could cause you to unexpectedly toss your cookies. We had no recommendations on the topic of managing the nausea or instant vomiting that could occur, given just the right circumstances. It never crossed my mind that I would fall prey to an uncontrollable and unanticipated physical reaction while tending an ill patient.

Until it happened.

Twelve-year-old Beverly and her twin brother, Robert, were patients on the pediatric unit where I worked as a new graduate nurse. I was 20 years old and living in my own apartment above a radio and TV repair shop in Germantown, Pennsylvania. Life was amazingly great. I had a job and a boyfriend and no one to tell me three soft pretzels from the street corner cart did not constitute dinner.

Beverly and Robert came to the hospital with identical injuries resulting from a car accident. They had been back-seat passengers during a night-time car trip in an old jalopy that had no seatbelts. Their father was the driver. In the middle of the front seat sat their father's girlfriend. Next to her sat their mother. According to Beverly, a fight between her mom and her dad's girlfriend erupted while they were driving around. When the dad leaned over to intercept the slap fest between the two women, he lost control of the vehicle, drove off the road, then went down a steep hill and into a tree. Dad and his girlfriend were killed. Their mother had multiple fractures and internal injuries, none life-threatening, but she was profoundly injured. The front bench seat broke free and landed on Beverly's and Robert's thigh bones, snapping them up near their hips.

To treat the broken femurs, both Beverly and her brother were put in Spica casts. A Spica is like a medical straight jacket, a plaster cast that goes from toes to armpits. A cross bar between the thighs is plastered to the cast to permanently separate the legs. This keeps the top of the femurs in their hip sockets and the bones immobilized so they can heal. A hole is cut out at the crotch to allow for bowel and bladder elimination. The cast stays on for months and requires constant hygiene care. Keeping a Spica cast clean is a priority to prevent both the development of sores from wet plaster and gauze against the skin and the strong odor that a soiled cast can generate. Even so, the cast always gets soiled over time, no matter how meticulous you are in your efforts to prevent it.

Because Beverly was sweet, chatty, and adorable, all the nurses loved to care for her, and we fought to have her assigned to us. On day shift, there were 12 staff nurses on this pediatric ward, and Beverly had a new nurse every day. Our head nurse, Miss Hebel, gave all the nurses under her supervision a chance to care for as many patients with different disease states and injuries as possible. She wanted us to be efficient, knowledgeable, ethical, and well-versed nurses. She had devoted her life to nursing, and we all held her in high regard. Her mentoring was priceless. I did not know it then, but Miss Hebel was one of the top five nurses I would ever work with. Her knowledge base was phenomenal, and her ability to help you think and see and knowledgeably smell was extraordinary. She inspired all of us to emulate her dedication to nursing and learning. What a gem to have as a head nurse so early in my career.

Since the twins required months of care, Beverly was my patient about once a week. With so many new and inexperienced graduate nurses caring for Beverly, a terrible oversight took place during her hospital stay. None of us noticed that Beverly had not had a bowel movement in some time.

When I greeted sweet Beverly one morning, her usual grin had been replaced by a grimace. She had a tummy ache and when asked, she could not remember when she had last gone Number Two. Miss Hebel helped me scour the nurses' notes in Beverly's chart. Ten days had passed since the last notation of a bowel movement. An "as needed" order for a suppository every three days for no bowel movement was not noted as given, either. It was a forehead slapper. This was highly unusual for our unit; apparently, it was something we carefully managed . . .until we didn't.

This is a terrible and dangerous occurrence. It was an unacceptable lapse in Beverly's nursing care, and I did not need Miss Hebel to tell me that. Long-term care patients usually have a calendar at the bedside or in their chart with the bowel movements noted on it. If there had been a recent one, we could not find a record of it. Bedbound patients especially need to have regular bowel movements, and laxatives can help keep the schedule regular.

Now Beverly was suffering unnecessarily. I felt awful. I promised Beverly to help her have a bowel movement that day and I told her (and myself) this would never happen to her or any of my patients again. She nodded at me, but there was no smile.

I began to prepare both of us for what would come next, the dreaded enema.

A Fleet enema is eight ounces of fluid in a soft plastic bottle with a lubricated tip. The tip is slowly inserted into the rectum, and the fluid is delivered by squeezing the bottle. Given her condition, Beverly's doctor ordered that Fleet enemas be administered until clear, which means keep giving the enemas every 30 minutes until there is a bowel movement and no more stool is expelled with the solution. The process causes stomach cramping and spasms. It is not fun, and I needed to coach and coax Beverly through an ordeal that she did not want to experience. Me either.

The Spica cast did not allow Beverly to turn onto her left side, the usual position for an enema. I put lots of pads under my young patient to catch any and all fluids and leaned over her to insert the Fleet. The bar from the cast that was keeping her legs apart impeded my work. To insert the enema, I had to slide my right hand under the bar and between her legs while holding the Fleet bottle. The right sleeve of my white uniform rumpled up against the bar of the cast as my left hand helped to guide the bottle in place. With my arm right arm under the cast bar, my face was positioned over her tummy.

Most of the first two enemas ran in and right back out, as there was not much space in her colon for it to occupy. Her colon was packed tight with stool. Beverly moaned, and I reassured her about how much better she would feel when this was over. I said I was proud of how good she was doing and that I knew she felt bloated and crampy and assured her that from now on we would have a calendar on her wall to keep track of her bowel movements so this would never happen again. Her eyebrows furrowed.

Distraction of any kind helped. Other nurses came in to offer encouragement. Beverly remained stoic. She did not want to frighten her brother, who was intently listening to her from his bed on the other side of the curtain.

Every 30 minutes, another Fleet was slowly given. As the stool softened, the fluid stayed in a little longer. This process took so much time because the pain medicine Beverly needed, together with her immobility, made her intestines sluggish and sleepy, and they resisted the urge to move. On and off Beverly silently cried, and I wiped the tears away, both of us trying to hide the pain she was feeling from her brother.

At 12:30, I reassured Beverly everything was going as it should, which was a lie. I told her I was going to lunch and asked that she rest until I got back. I asked other nurses to check on her and gave her the call bell if she needed someone in a hurry. Twenty minutes later, I returned to her bedside. She was moaning, then wailing from cramps.

"One more," I told her. Another lie. I had no idea how many more enemas it would take. She was crying out loud now. I prayed it would just be one more. I had made a promise I was not certain I could keep, a bad practice with any patient, no matter their age. Beverly nodded and sobbed. I smiled and pushed back the feelings of guilt with determination that this Fleet would work. I softly crooned to her as I began the enema.

"Good girl, you are the best little girl in the entire world. You are very brave," I quietly chattered. She squeezed my left forearm tightly with both her hands, and her eyes were squeezed shut. She was breathing fast and shallow, with her little head pressed back against the pillow.

"You are going to have the world record poop of all times," I told her. I wanted her to believe this would soon be over. I wanted to believe it myself.

Suddenly, her sobs turned to shrieks. As I began to slowly remove the tip of the enema bottle, an explosion of Fleet fluid and stool shot out of Beverly's rectum. It squirted up over my gloved hand, hit the crook of my right elbow, and shot up my arm into my neck. I lurched to stand up, but my arm was trapped under the bar of the cast. Beverly was screaming as spasms sent more stool splashing up to my chin. I lost my footing, and my right elbow pressed in to the bed. My chin hit the cast bar, and I could not breathe.

The second the stool hit my face, I threw up all over Beverly, her cast, and my arm. My lunch unexpectedly reappeared with a vengence. It was a body fluid Armageddon -- hers *and* mine. I frantically freed my arm from under the cast and used a towel to wipe the mess from my arm and face. I flew to the window, opened it, and stuck my head out to gulp fresh air. Hearing her screams, her brother joined in. The commotion brought nurses running into the room.

From his bed, Robert was yowling, "Help! That nurse threw up all over my sister."

By the time I caught my breath and turned around, Miss Hebel had a basin of water at the bedside. Two more nurses lifted Beverly, while others rolled up the soiled bed sheets and layered clean towels under her. More and more stool emerged. While cheering her to push it out, Miss Hebel contained the mess with plenty of padding.

Finally, with a big sigh Beverly relaxed, her bright eyes sparkling. "Did you see that my Nurse Susan threw up all over me?" she asked Miss Hebel sweetly. Miss Hebel told Beverly it was the biggest mess she had ever seen in her entire nursing career. The nightmare of the constipation was replaced with the juicy news of her nurse losing her tuna salad hoagie lunch on top of her and all over everywhere.

Beverly stretched the exciting story into weeks of tattling it to all who entered her room, enhancing the details as it went along. Every doctor, nurse, respiratory therapist, physical therapist, medical student, cleaning lady, and visitor heard of my lack of stomach control. The detail of what precipitated my vomiting was not revealed in her telling of the story. For a long time, staff and visitors gave me wide berth in the hallways, and I endured endless taunting. The payback did not console me. I harbored the responsibility of causing my patient to suffer. I was happy Beverly had "dirt" on me. It was an awesome gloom chaser for her. She took to shouting, "Write it down!" whenever she or her brother pooped.

Some years later, a similar episode occurred, as totally unexpected as the first.

I was one of two nurses working in a pediatric outpatient oncology clinic. Sixteen-year-old Tom came to the clinic one afternoon for his lab work and chemo. He had been diagnosed with testicular cancer at age 15 and had already had the cancerous testicle removed. Weekly intravenous chemo was in its fifth or sixth round for him. He would leave school early and drive himself to the clinic for treatment, then drive home. The chemo side effects would emerge later in the evening. He would take a pill to suppress the nausea and mostly sleep through it.

Tom was the entertainer of the oncology waiting room. As one of the oldest of the patients, he chose to chat with the little ones, holding them on his lap like a big brother, a big brother who totally understood how awful it was to have cancer and endure the treatment. The kids loved him for his charm and the bawdy way he would talk about losing "a ball" or "a nut." Mothers and fathers would shoot him "a look" when their children would ask what losing "a nut" meant. Often he would say with pride "It's a man part," and that was good enough for his young entourage.

On his clinic visit day Tom would get weighed and his vital signs taken. He'd see his doctor, have blood work drawn, then wait for me in the exam room to receive chemo. He'd sit on the edge of the exam table facing out the door five feet away and rest his feet on the pull-out step. We kept all the exam room doors open except when brief patient exams were being done by the doctor. The kids loved the distraction of watching the clinic activity. It helped to see they were not the only ones getting stuck with IVs. They'd holler and wave to each other and sometimes stand at one another's door to visit.

As I usually did, I stood directly in front of Tom this day. A small rolling table next to me held the needles, syringes, tourniquet, emesis basin, alcohol swab, and Band-Aid I would need. I inserted the butterfly IV needle into the vein on the top of Tom's left hand, flushed it with saline, taped it in place, and began the chemo infusion.

One drug Tom received was called Cytoxan. The chemical name is cyclophosphamide. Tom liked to call it cyclofucksmeup. For him, as for most patients, intravenous Cytoxan creates a heavy, foul, metallic taste within seconds of entering the vein. Tom and others hated that taste. It made some of my patients vomit just hearing the name of the drug. Most patients would fast before they came to try to stave off the vomiting. Nothing much helped, they retched anyway.

Tom's chemo treatments had always gone smoothly. If he was uncomfortable, he never let on about it. He had large full veins, so starting his IV was easy. During the 20 minutes or so of the infusion, he would entertain me with stories from home, school, and work. After school and on weekends, Tom worked as a waiter at the Burger Barn. He had a lot of friends working there with him, and he loved it. When the boss found out Tom had cancer, he told his well-liked employee to eat or drink whatever he wanted, whenever he wanted.

"Yeah," Tom told me, "the other kids think losing a nut is not too bad if you can eat as much as you want."

We chatted away as usual, and after the first chemo drug finished, I flushed the line with saline, then connected the Cytoxan syringe to the butterfly tubing. I began the slow push of the chemo medicine into the vein. Still standing in front of him, I shifted my weight and put one foot up on the pull-out step where his feet were resting and relaxed. We continued our conversation. Tom could talk to anyone about anything; he was in his usual groove of school news.

His first deep retch startled me like a sudden and unexpected clap of thunder. My right hand stayed on the chemo-filled syringe, while my left hand dove for the emesis basin on the rolling table. Too late. Tom hit me full force in the chest with explosive, voluminous vomiting. Within a fraction of a second, my own recently consumed lunch reappeared and hit him in the lap. I stood there holding the IV steady with my right hand and the empty emesis basin in my left. I tried desperately to kick the floor trashcan close to Tom for his second round of vomiting. Instead, the emesis basin overflowed all over my left hand. In just a few seconds, the whole horrendous episode was over, as vomit rolled down our legs and into our shoes. Wide-eyed, we stared at each other in shock.

Tom roared, "What the hell did you just do to me?"

Astonished and not thinking clearly, I asked him the same question in the same tone. The open exam room door quickly filled with spectators. Mary Jo, who was the other nurse in the clinic, a doctor, our secretary, and a few children who had either just gotten their chemo or who were waiting for it, along with a few parents, all stood gaping at us.

Mary Jo swooped in. "What just happened in here?" she asked but she could clearly see and shook her head, holding in laughter. Tom and I told our versions at the same time and at full volume. Mary Jo found out Tom had stopped at the Burger Barn on his way to clinic and had seven burgers.

"They were small ones," Tom whined. He'd also had a large grape soda.

She turned to me, "Did you ask him if he ate before he came to the clinic?"

"Uh, no. But he never eats before he comes," was my weak reply.

I could tell she started to say this would be the last time I would forget to ask. But by then, I was finishing up the IV and ignored her. Miraculously, the IV somehow had been spared the nasty spray.

"If you ever, ever, *ever,* eat seven burgers and drink a grape soda before you come to clinic again, I will put your head in the trash can for the whole treatment," I scolded Tom with a smile, eyebrows up. He ignored me and expounded to the crowd how I had spontaneously spewed forth my lunch on him.

"He started it," I countered. The children were laughing and calling for others to come see this mess. Mary Jo disappeared and returned with operating room (OR) scrubs for me and Tom. She ordered me out while she helped Tom clean himself and get into the scrub pants and top. Once dressed, he strutted from the exam room and announced with a grin that he was the new cancer doctor, and I was fired.

"Fine with me," I laughed. "*You* take care of these pukey kids."

I readied another exam room for my next patient. I put the trash can on the floor next to the exam table and asked, "How many burgers did you eat at the Burger Barn?" My little patient asked if I was done throwing up for the day. This time I stood to the side of the patient. She faked a gag.

Word of the event soon spread on the hospital grapevine. Doctors began asking their patients if they had heard that Cytoxan made nurses vomit. The story went viral, excluding the part about Tom getting sick. The children and their families enjoyed the diversion, and, for some reason, I enjoyed my strange celebrity status. For a while, all my patients and I greeted each other with a gag.

As my shift ended that day, a few hours after the vomit fest, a hospital laundry worker arrived at the oncology clinic to return my cleaned and pressed white dress uniform to me. I did not know Mary Jo had taken it to the laundry for me.

"What happened to your uniform?" he asked.

"Oh, a large unexpected spill," I replied. He waited for me to say more, but I thanked him and walked away without another word.

That day it was Tom's story to tell.

4

THERESA

My first hospital job after graduating from nursing school was in a Philadelphia hospital pediatric ward. Leaving that hospital one evening after 3 to 11 pm shift, I found all four tires slashed and the radio antenna broken off my dear Ford Fairlane 500. *That's it,* I thought to myself. *Enough of this crime fest of a city.* I was estranged from my parents who lived here, my boyfriend had followed a job and left town, and I was ready for something new and adventurous. During high school I had visited my cousin in Colorado and now thought it would be a glorious place to live.

I called my cousin in Denver and asked if she would house me for a week or two while I searched for an apartment. "Come on," she said.

Before I moved, knowing I would need gainful employment as soon as possible, I sent a letter to Denver Children's Hospital Nursing Department telling them I was headed their way and needed a job. Their hiring secretary sent me a letter back saying there were no openings. Distressed, I called and spoke to her. She repeated the same unfortunate response. I told her I was so hoping to work in pediatrics and heard this hospital was highly regarded. Not ready to take no for an answer, I told her that I was arriving in about a month, I did not care what shift, what unit, or what the salary was, that I *needed a job, please*. I knew turnover in all hospitals created openings from time to time, so I persisted. Her slow response was, well, in a month there would be a full-time opening for night shift on the oncology unit. Yes, I'll take it, done, what a relief.

I put in my two weeks' notice at work and, out of common courtesy, called my parents to let them know I was moving out of state.

Their tepid reply did not surprise me. "Let us know when you get there," was their response. There were no ties to sever.

I still blamed them for my disconnected upbringing and failure to go to college. I did not make nice, and neither did they. I did not go so far as to read good riddance in their response. It was more, "Susan will do whatever she wants, what good is it to say anything?" So they didn't.

As I prepared to move, collecting my meager possessions from my apartment, I told my roommate, Eleanor, also a nurse, I was headed to Denver. I could tell she was happy; her boyfriend would move in. I left behind my second-hand mattress and orange crate book shelves and packed my dark green Fairlane with my clothes, stereo, and books. In the front seat I stowed a box of Tastycake Krimpets, a box of Ding Dongs, a jug of water, and my map. Living on a tight budget, I did not want to stay at hotels along the way. At sunrise, I turned my car west, cranked the radio up, and, with a few stops for gas and bathroom, drove straight through to Denver. The combination of sugar and excitement kept me awake for the cross country trip.

Through the local newspaper my cousin had saved for me, I found a roommate wanted ad and quickly moved in. I settled in with two roommates. One was a masseuse, the other doubled as both bartender and pool shark. We had two dogs, a small Schnauzer mix named Donna, and a sleek female black lab dubbed Fat City. In rare letters home, I mentioned Donna was pregnant. With no other details, Mom assumed Donna was another roommate and wrote back asking how Donna was doing with the pregnancy. When I called to say Donna had seven puppies, Mom laughed hysterically. She thought it curious when I wrote that Donna was so big and pregnant, we had to carry her up and down the stairs.

For several months, I worked night shift on the oncology ward. When an opening came to work day shift in the outpatient oncology clinic, I jumped at the chance. Working night-shift hours was messing with my mind and bowels, making me mentally unstable and chronically constipated. My brain and gut could not tell if I was coming or going.

It was then I became nurse and friend to a little girl named Theresa.

When I first met Theresa in the clinic, she was 11 years old and had already had leukemia for six years. She had seen remissions and relapses of her cancer and been down the bumpy chemo road a couple of times. Theresa had great humility and a biting sense of humor, she knew life could be a bitch and then you die; she did not dwell on that. Her life was love in every moment. Her big picture plan came through her upbringing in the Catholic Church; she felt comfort knowing at some point soon she would be with God. She accepted and embraced that this was just the way it had worked out for her.

On the clinic visit days when her blood and bone marrow tests showed her cancer was back, she could read the faces of her doctors and nurses like a book. Walk in the exam room to tell her and her mother, Joyce, the test results, Theresa already knew. She would say, "Back again, isn't it?" looking directly at her oncologist.

Dr. Z would nod. I would stand there next to him looking like a broom was stuck up my ass, pissed, full of frustration and dread. *Why Theresa? Why her?* And thinking, *No, no, no.* I had become very attached to Teresa and her mother. We all clicked in a way not typical for nurses and patients. Her family, life, and illness became entwined with mine.

It was the same with Theresa and her oncologist, Dr. Z. Lines of professional relationships blurred. Caring for very ill children can create a challenge for nurses to stay at arm's length. And Theresa absorbed everyone she met into her universe.

"Shit," Theresa would say and mean it. Then she added quickly, eyebrows up and eyes sparkling, that this was the only situation in which she had permission to say shit. Cheering us up, that was one of her gifts.

Forcing us back into this moment, we would all take an angry turn. "Shit." We meant it, too. No use telling Theresa everything would be just fine. She had an exquisitely tuned bullshit radar. Theresa would start the chemo again with unending optimism tempered by realism. None of us wanted to jinx it.

It is horrible to feel like you know something the patient does not know. It is horrible to think you can see the road ahead and know this is probably it, the end. To pretty much know the drugs won't work this time because it is simply one time too many. Or that no one can figure out how to make the drugs work without killing the patient first. But the doctors try; all of us must keep trying to banish the cancer.

Oncology treatments were horribly inconsistent at saving lives back in the '70s. I hated that we knew so little, and each child's positive or negative response to the therapy led to protocol changes. But all that lack of success did not scare me away. I survived knowing we were doing the best we could, and when the treatments eventually failed, we gave our guts and hearts to help relieve pain and hold onto the families. With newer treatments and protocols, the doctors and nurses are much better at it now.

This time, Theresa's relapse occurred just as Christmas approached, but she would not let the return of leukemia mute her holiday jubilance. She boldly and cheerfully asked family and friends for gifts of money. They obliged with alacrity. Her mother told us, "Theresa has a plan. She's a 12-year-old with a plan." As the weekly chemo sessions stole Theresa's hair and her physical vitality, she kept smiling but talked less. Her little body became even smaller and frailer. Theresa asked her mother to throw a Christmas dinner party at home with festive decorations all around. She wanted the guests to be Dr. Z, her oncologist; Dan, our young Catholic priest and hospital chaplain who visited her often; and me, her nurse. Being invited to Christmas dinner by a patient and their family rarely occurred. The three of us knew this was Teresa's last and did not refuse the invitation. We knew it would be an emotional night for the family, too, maybe that's why Joyce pleaded for us to come, to grant Teresa's wish for us to be there.

Joyce made a wonderful dinner. Theresa presided over the table. Seated there were Theresa's' parents, Joyce and Tom; Theresa's' two older brothers; her older sister; Dr. Z, Dan, and me.

She watched us eat. She glowed with joy. She did not eat; she could not eat. Chemo had wrecked her insides, and there was no pretend plate of food, no pleading for her to just try a bite. She drove that bus. Period. We all knew better than to bother her with fruitless pleas.

After dinner, Theresa made her evening plans known. There were gifts for three of us. Clearly, she'd been rehearsing this in her head while lying endless hours in bed. It seemed she was never too weak to think. She spoke with cheer and childhood joy, her bald head covered with a fat, multi-colored scarf. Her skin was thin and pale and bruised, her arms and legs wasted and looking for all the world like jointed twigs. But she was shining like the bright summer sun. Theresa was dying, and she knew it. She knew it and was thrilled in her anticipation of executing her party plan. She had definite ideas about her legacy. There was no drama here. She held her head high and chest puffed out like a beautiful small bird perched on a sturdy branch.

Savoring center stage, Theresa slowly presented her gifts.

To Dan she gave a sweater, an envelope, and a verbal prediction. The sweater she wanted him to have so he would remember her when he wore it. I don't know what was in the envelope. The prediction was that he would leave the priesthood, marry, and have wonderful children. She was quietly confident that this would happen, while we were caught off guard and speechless. There was nothing to say, so we all stayed quiet. Stunned by the revelation, Dan looked down into his hands.

Dr. Z got a sweater, same reason. He also got an envelope; I don't know what it contained, either.

Theresa looked at me and grinned, a kind of baiting grin. "I will miss you when I'm dead," she said with chin lifted and eyebrows up.

"I will miss you more," I said quietly, willing myself to return her gaze without weeping. I squeezed my jaws shut and pressed my tongue to the roof of my mouth.

Nurses cry. Sometimes, a lot. It would have been an insult to say, "Oh Teresa, you won't die." I knew her well enough to know my place. She hated a liar. She gave me a sweater, an envelope, and a poem. In the envelope was her eighth-grade photo. On the back she had written, "Class of ____, I hope", the year left blank. A glint of hope still sparkled in her heart. Her poem was handwritten in pencil. It had colored pencil decorations all around it.

"Read it," she commanded.

"Nope," I croaked as I looked at the words blurred by tears. "Can't".

"Why?" she prodded.

"Theresa, you know I cry easy, right?" I said, pleading for a pass.

"Oh, yeah," she said, tipping her head side to side and rolling her eyes. This was Theresa at her wise guy best.

She had seen me cry before at the clinic when some other child had died. One day she was arriving at the clinic and did not know we all had just received this news when she said critically, "Are you crying?" mocking my behavior.

I replied in a pretend harsh tone, "Yeah, shoot me, I care about you and other people around here. I am sad. Can I be sad?" I leaned into her face with my eyebrows up.

She petted my head like a dog, laughed, and said, "Yeah, you can be sad." Then Teresa and her mother wrapped me in a long hug, her arms around my waist and Joyce's around my shoulders.

Now, here at the holiday table, both her brothers begged her to not make anyone cry at the table. "Crying is so stupid," they said as they slapped at her.

"Alright!" she managed to holler. She loved the fact her family was not treating her like a corpse before she was dead. She was still very much a pain in the butt to her brothers. She goaded them on every chance she could. Theresa had hogged the spotlight for long enough, and her brothers were restless.

She slowly read the poem to all of us, pausing to catch her breath between lines.

The poem was written in pencil on art tablet paper with the lines put on by ruler. Her words spoke about how she will feel about me after her death.

"I will think of you on rainy days, sunny days, snowy days, foggy days, humid days, cloudy days, misty days, balmy days, icy days, windy days, hot days, stormy days, calm days, breezy days, blizzdy days and clear days, And I'll miss you."

From Theresa F.

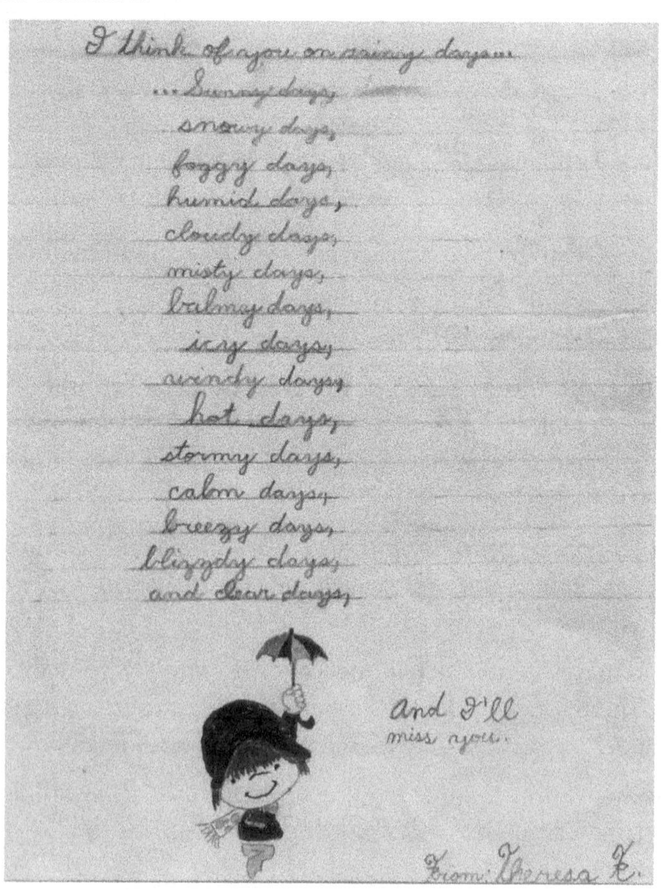

I think of you on rainy days...
...Sunny days,
snowy days,
foggy days,
humid days,
cloudy days,
misty days,
balmy days,
icy days,
windy days,
hot days,
stormy days,
calm days,
breezy days,
blizzdy days,
and clear days,

And I'll
miss you.

From: Theresa F.

When she finished, she asked me, "Do you like it?"

"Nope." I could barely squeak it out. Her eyes popped open . . . oh, I was wise guying her back. "I love it," I said.

"Ohhh," she protested, "stop that." We smiled and made faces at each other.

During the next few weeks, Theresa's bone marrow became packed with so many cells the pain grew unbearable. Medications could barely contain her excruciating agony. Morphine doses were increased to make her comfortable but also made her barely rousable. A final attempt to kill the packed-in marrow cells was tried by administering high-dose radiation to the bones. She shrieked in pain when she was moved from the bed to the car to go to the hospital for the daily radiation treatments. Theresa begged her parents and Dr. Z and me to let her go to be with God. She pleaded for more morphine to take away the pain. Dr. Z ordered her morphine to be given every hour as needed. The radiation treatments were abandoned. Teresa no longer ate, drank, peed, or pooped. Her body melted to skeletal, her skin went gray and waxy, her breath gurgled, irregular and loud.

I took off work to stay with Theresa during the day at her home. Joyce was with her at night. Friends came and visited, but nobody said much. Her brothers and sister came into Theresa's' room and sat, but all they could do was rub her arm.

About 7 pm on my third day with Theresa, I drove the 35 miles south back to Denver and home. Snow began falling in large, heavy flakes; the interstate roadbed wore a light blanket already. I got home at 8 and went straight to bed. At 11 pm, the phone rang.

Joyce whispered, "She's gone."

"I'm on my way," I exhaled into the phone.

When I got there, I found Theresa dressed in pretty pajamas and wrapped papoose style in a flowery quilt. Her eyes were closed, and the strain was gone from her angelic face. I laid my hand on her forehead and kissed her cheek goodbye.

This was the viewing. I looked up at the rest of the family. I could see exhaustion and relief. Theresa was finally with her God. Everyone else could breathe now that Theresa was pain free and at peace.

"Now what?" asked Tom, her father. I took a big breath and tried to get into my nurse mind. I sat on the bed with Theresa and closed my eyes to think. Joyce slumped in the chair next to the bed, where she had sat vigil so many nights for the last seven years. Theresa's brothers and sister clustered together, sitting on the floor at Joyce's feet. Tom leaned heavily against the door jamb.

"An ambulance?" I guessed out loud. I sighed again. I was not able to focus well. All the air was out of my balloon. No one was in much of a hurry; no one had air left in their balloons. It was OK if I was winging it. We all were. I looked at Joyce. She shook her head.

"Theresa hates ambulances," she said.

Slowly she continued, "I do not want a hearse, either. Not here, not in my street. I cannot bear to see Theresa leave here in a hearse."

We sat in stillness until I whispered the obvious, "That leaves my car, I'll take her in my car."

We settled on that resolution without moving. As the question of the legality of transporting a corpse briefly crossed my mind, I decided it was easier to say "oops" than try to get permission. Besides, there really was not another option for Theresa so screw whatever the rules or protocols were. I called Dr. Z to tell him Theresa was dead and that I would be bringing her to the hospital. He told me to drive to the hospital morgue door, he would meet me there.

At 2 AM, I made my way slowly down the interstate back to Denver, Theresa was tucked in the back seat of my car, cocooned in her pretty quilt. Heavy snowflakes gleamed in the headlights, flying up and over the windshield. Escorted by these scarves of white flowing around us, the snow reminded me of the murmuration of starlings on their fall migration. As if expecting our procession, the snowplows had recently prepared our way. I stayed gratefully in their plowed tracks. It was a peaceful and silent world with no pain. I told Theresa she better help me come up with a dandy reason for why there was a dead child in my back seat if the police should happen to pull me over. I could tell she thought that was funny.

Dan gave the eulogy at her subdued funeral. It was evident Theresa and Dan had discussed the ceremony. She did not want the usual "fought the good fight." To her, that was a crock. Theresa was gone, so that left nothing but sorrow for her suffering and our loss. Later at her house, though, stories of Theresa were studded with laughter and "remember when." The only part of Theresa not in the room that day was her cancer-wracked body. The universe was lit with the joy that was Theresa.

The journey of watching a vibrant, intelligent, exuberant child slowly die over seven years is unbearably awful. So many families make that journey with their terminally ill child. I never lost my admiration and awe of these families who let me share so intimately in their lives. Theresa had the gift of great strength through her faith. She showed us her anger and sadness at times but never any fear. She accepted every rotten turn, said she was pissed, and then put it behind her. She lived till she died, thinking of others and gracefully embracing her fate of a short, but well-lived, life.

There is the Nurse Susan side of me and the Regular Susan side of me. The nurse science side of me watched the clinical course of Theresa's illness and death with great interest. The chemo worked, and then it did not. Now she is not eating. Now she is not drinking. Now she is not making urine. Look at the blood pooling to the skin on her back. Feel her pulse so fast and thready. Listen to her gurgling breathing. Smell that stale, fetid breath.

It's ghoulish, really. I wonder why I am so compelled to witness this life process over and over again. I am drawn by the fear of it for one reason. What if this was me? How will I act, and how will I cope? I think of that every time I face a situation where I have no idea what to do next, what to say next. When the families flee or the families scream or the patients ask me to tell them what the hell is going on, I stay and help them think. I don't run, even though my Regular Susan side is hollering in my head, "Get away, this is too much."

What if this was me? I think this again and again. Will someone take care of me when every body fluid that is supposed to stay inside is coming out or when I can't talk or walk or see or when the pain is so bad, I am cursing everyone in sight?

But even as I ask it, I know the answer to that question. A lifetime of experience has taught me that a nurse will take care of me. It's what we do.

About three years after Theresa's death, I was talking with a nurse from another Denver hospital. She worked in the Newborn Intensive Care there and was sharing a story about a co-worker who had recently married and was having a child. We were talking about how nurses think every imaginable disease will afflict their newborn. We see too much to hope for a healthy child.

When I asked if the nurse had married someone who worked at the hospital, she said, "Yes, Dan, the priest who used to come visit the families. He left the church two years ago. They are so in love and wonderful for each other."

I envisioned Theresa at that moment, grinning and making a, "told you" face at me. I couldn't help but grin at the thought, knowing my little angel was watching over me, too.

5

SHIT STORM

The bright August morning was growing warmer by the minute when I pulled into the gravel driveway of a small brick rancher for the fifth of the day's planned ten home health visits. Standing in the doorway was a plump, pre-teen girl, noting my arrival with wide eyes. She looked anxious, ready to pounce. Before I could gather together my nursing bag and the patient's chart and head for the house, she hollered: "Hurry! Grandpa shit in the Barcalounger, and mommy is crying!"

Just moments before, driving through the rural Virginia country roads to get to this visit, I had been daydreaming about how close the beach was to this small rural community. If so inclined, I could wind my way from here and be at the Virginia Beach oceanfront in 90 minutes. The glorious periwinkle sky and soft breeze invited such a reverie. The mirage vanished as I let myself through the front yard gate, closing it behind me. I walked up the three brick steps, stood in the open front door and peered in past the little girl. I saw Mommy facing me, frozen in horror in the kitchen. In a single glance I saw the reason for her hysteria. The surreal scene of shit handprints on the wall and footprints leading from the kitchen down the hallway expressed the terrible tale of a laxative gone rogue.

Since 1993, I had been working weekends as a home health nurse; two 12-hour shifts. This Saturday-and-Sunday-only schedule allowed me to be a full-time Mama five days a week while still earning nearly a full-time salary with benefits. My two sons and I especially liked the summer breaks and having that stretch of time to enjoy one another's company.

As part of my work routine, I would call the agency office on Friday afternoons for an update on my weekend assignments. The day before this visit, Nurse Laura had informed me she had seen an elderly man that morning for evaluation of constipation. According to what his daughter had conveyed to Laura, he had not had a bowel movement for ten days. On Friday, Laura had given him two enemas without much result. The doctor also had called in a prescription for a liquid laxative. The daughter was to administer two tablespoons Friday night. I would visit Saturday to follow up with the care.

My patient, called Grandpa by everyone, was living with his daughter, Amanda, a single parent with a 12-year-old daughter. She had told Nurse Laura that her dad mostly smoked cigarettes and asked for candy and liquor. He ate very small meals and had done so all his life. Now he was nauseated and had abdominal discomfort and bloating. He was comforted some by a hot water bottle on his stomach to ease the pressure. He was quite hard of hearing and had some signs of forgetfulness and dementia. Unable to manage eating on his own, he needed daily help with meals and supervision. His daughters' biggest fear was that he would wander off, fall, or drive off down the nearby four-lane highway on his riding lawn mower. The concern was valid. He had already taken the lawn mower on the road once.

Amanda also told Laura that Grandpa had three children, two sons and her, who all took turns having him at their homes, usually a month at a time. Laura told me that Grandpa – like many thin, elderly men and women -- was always cold, and it had taken some convincing on her part get him to pull down his double pair of sweatpants to administer the enema.

Standing in the threshold of the front door, I saw Grandpa in the doorway to the kitchen glaring in my direction. His double pair of sweatpants bulged at the ankles with loose stool that flowed over the top of his shoes. Smeary poo handprints covered both refrigerator handles, and a butt print decorated one kitchen chair. The Barcalounger, sofa, coffee table, and walls leading down to the bathroom had evidence that Grandpa had recently been there. The Barcalounger had taken the biggest hit.

At the sight of me, the distraught daughter erupted in a screaming monologue. "I came in from working in the yard . . . sob . . . and saw shit everywhere . . . sob . . . There is even shit in the refrigerator . . . now wailing . . .and on the floor, and he won't let me give him a bath."

Amanda was shaking and frantic. Trying to calm her mother down, her little daughter said, "It's OK, Mama. This lady will help."

I set my bag and chart on the front porch, took a deep breath, and carefully stepped into the house.

As I approached them, Grandpa stood to his full five feet and defiantly shouted, "I don't know what she's a hollerin' and cryin' about. I can't see any mess."

I believed him. I knew his eyesight was poor. He probably couldn't see it. Sensation in his hands most likely was poor as well. He could not tell that when he scratched an itch, he got stool on his hands and under his fingernails. Nor could he smell the odor that was intensifying in the August heat.

Two things crossed my mind. One, I guess Grandpa won't need any more enemas. Two, good thing I got here when I did. It was evident to me that at some time during the prior evening, Grandpa had discovered the brown medicine bottle of liquid laxative, shaped temptingly like a small whiskey flask. He had drunk almost the full 16 ounces in one day. The suggested dose was one to two ounces per day. He had taken more than a week's worth of doses in less than 24 hours, and shit was everywhere.

Three people stood there in that house, all eyes looking at me to fix this mess. Right *now*. I tried to form a strategy, thinking I needed to be at least two nurses at once. Then, seemingly out of nowhere, an image formed in my mind. Maybe it was the fumes or, more likely, the desperate sense of urgency surrounding me. I was able to perceive this shit-stained scene as though it was a chaotic battlefield where three wounded people needed my help at the same time. I told myself I needed to channel a person capable of authority, fortitude, and confidence in times of crisis, a person unafraid of intestinal disaster. George S. Patton came to mind. I pictured him in his five-star army helmet, ribboned jacket, and saucy jodhpurs, heartily stomping his foot for attention, horse whip in hand. I actually thought this.

"OK, *men*!" I boomed, meaning all genders present; the poo fumes apparently were also affecting my choice of terminology.

All eyes snapped toward me. Mommy looked wide-eyed, probably thinking that on top of everything, this nurse is nuts but what the hell, how much worse can it get? At least, that is what I would have been thinking if I was her and she was me, both of us held captive in this particular ring of hell.

I pointed to the little girl and said in my calmest and most reassuring voice, "Honey, you go get me two big trash bags, some towels, clean clothes and shoes for Grandpa, and meet me at the bathroom door."

She grinned, shouted, "Ok!" and ran off to fulfill her task.

I pointed to the daughter. "You call your brother and get the Barcalounger and sofa out of here." She turned to the wall phone, made sure it was clean, and called her brother.

Still channeling Patton, I strode, carefully, up in front of 80-pound Grandpa, pointed toward the bathroom, and pronounced with gusto, "Get into the bathroom. You need a bath!"

His eyes widened. He shuffled a turn and made his way silently down the short hall to the bathroom without debate.

I cut in front of him while pulling on three sets of my disposable gloves and raised the toilet seat cover. "Pull your britches down and sit!" I directed loudly enough for him to hear and firmly enough to derail an argument. I got the towels and clothes from the little girl, who waited in the hall for me. Amanda was off the phone and told me her brother was on his way. He lived very close by and would be there in minutes. I asked Amanda what she wanted me to do with the stool-saturated clothes and shoes.

"Throw them out, he's got plenty" she told me as she headed for the front door. Just then I could hear her brother's truck crunching up the driveway.

Many old people hate to bathe because they get cold easily. I also learned later that Grandpa had bathed infrequently all his life, mostly when he swam in the river down the hill from his backyard, and usually once indoors for Christmas. I put warm water in a basin I found in the bathroom closet and set it on his lap. I asked Grandpa to wash his hands for me.

"Are you cold all the time?" I asked him.

He nodded. I could see he dreaded this bath. His sparse hair rested in oily clumps against his scalp, testifying to his infrequent hygiene. I put the pile of clean clothes on the deep windowsill where the sun was pouring in. They would warm up there. "I will try very hard not to let you get cold," I assured him as I put fresh, warm water in the basin. I asked his granddaughter to go find me cleaning supplies, a wash bucket, and paper towels. I told her I would be finished in here soon. She nodded solemnly. I added, "You are a fantastic helper. I am so glad you are here." Then I closed the bathroom door.

"I ain't never been sick my whole life," Grandpa growled at the floor. "Never been to a hospital, neither." Although grouchy, he seemed resigned to the situation at hand.

I think what he meant was that he did not want anyone, especially a strange woman, giving him a bath. "This will be very fast" I assured him, somewhat of a lie. I was telling myself it would be fast. With the heat and fumes rolling over me, I felt close to a swoon of nausea. I slipped his one arm gently out of the sleeve, washed that arm, half his chest and half his back. I folded the dirty shirt away and slid on the clean sleeve of long underwear and two flannel shirts that were warmed in the window. I pulled off the dirty shirts, washed the rest of his upper body, dried it, and rubbed his back briskly with some lotion from a bottle that I warmed in a sink of warm water. I pulled the long underwear shirt over his head, put the flannel shirts the rest of the way on, and buttoned them up. Grandpa was quiet but seemed relaxed. His eyes were downcast, and I hoped he was not humiliated.

I told him, "You are almost done." Not really, but I wanted him to focus on that idea. I helped Grandpa stand and had him hold onto the towel bar. I rolled his shirt tails up into a knot under his arms to keep them out of the way. He was able to step out of his shoes and pants one leg at a time. I rolled up the soiled shoes and oozing clothes, put them in the trash bag with my gloves, and tied it shut.

I tried to keep my gagging silent. The hot room and odor became overwhelming, but I did not want him to see my watering eyes and tight-lipped face. I stuck my nose into my T-shirt sleeve for a breath. Opening the door for air and to get rid of the trash, I called for the little girl. "Take this to Mommy. Tell her it's trash." She ran with the bag toward the living room. I could see the Barcalounger being heaved out the front door.

I finished his bath, tidied up the bathroom, and escorted Grandpa to the kitchen, where I helped him sit down in a clean chair. I gathered all the bath towels, put them in the washer and started it up.

"Where's my liquor?" asked Grandpa.

Yikes, where was that bottle of laxative? I wondered. I found it on the coffee table in the living room, poured the last drops of the laxative in the trash, and filled the bottle with water. I told him that the medicine was gone, and water was in there now, if he wanted it. He frowned but drank some of the water, then leaned to one side to tuck the bottle into his back pants pocket. His granddaughter made him toast. As he sat and pulled the toast into small bits to eat, my little helper and I got to cleaning. I gave her two pairs of nurse gloves and put two fresh pairs on myself.

"Let's clean up a little so when Mommy comes home from the dump she will have a surprise." My cheery assistant was happy to be fixing this awful problem for her mother. We used soapy water and Windex and 409 to clean the dirtied-up surfaces. We bagged up the rags and paper towels and put it all outside.

In the midst of our efforts, the little girl heard the pick-up truck pulling up outside and ran to the door. "Mommy, we have a big surprise," she announced. Jumping up and down and hugging her Mom, she proudly showed off the clean-up that was underway.

"I can't do this anymore," the daughter sighed to me as she and her brother sank heavily into the kitchen chairs next to Grandpa. "He can't be left alone for even a minute." She paused before adding, "I gave him the laxative last night. . . then look what he did." She said she had no idea that her Dad would mistake the shape and color of the 16-ounce brown, plastic, medicine bottle for a whiskey-filled flask.

Her brother told me how tired the whole family was getting of trying to manage their father. I offered some local resources for information about long-term or in-home care as I checked vital signs and finished my nursing visit. Situations such as theirs are painful and difficult, with no easy solution. They decide to call another family meeting, and I give them a phone number for the local Agency on Aging. Lucky for Grandpa, his children got along well. They were all trying to share the responsibility for his care.

I learned Grandpa had been a long-time alcoholic, living and working his whole life in the country. After his wife died and the kids married and moved away, his health and self-care had really declined. His son had recently taken over bathing Dad, but it was a fight every time. I made notes in the chart that no further enemas were necessary, as there had been good results from the liquid laxative.

Later I told Laura the whole story, especially the "flask" fiasco, just to make sure we never let another patient sip on medicine like an after-dinner toddy.

I got three big hugs as I left the house. None came from Grandpa.

Getting into my car, I checked my watch. An anticipated 30-minute visit had ballooned to more than an hour. My day was going to be a long one, but I could not have walked away from this family before they had received the care they needed. The more experience I have gained as a nurse, the more I have come to realize it is never just the individual patient under my care. It is the whole family. It is -- by extension – all of us.

We learn a lot about ourselves and our abilities when faced with the unexpected and the difficult. In caring for Grandpa that hot August morning, my mind had looked beyond my nurse's training to conjure up my Patton alter-ego and devise a plan that worked for everyone. In the process, it strengthened my conviction that if this patient was me, some other nurse would show up, muster the necessary resources, and get me through . . . no matter how shitty the situation happened to be.

6

BEHIND BARS

Throughout my career, the developing trend of buying, selling, and consolidating health care businesses has forced me to expand my nursing specialty horizons to stay employed. During my nine-year stint in home health care back in the 1990s, for example, the business I worked for, which had been started by a group of nurses, changed hands more times than I could count. Each transfer meant fewer benefits, lower wages, bigger caseloads, and a crazier schedule. It wasn't long before the weekend position I had relied on to meet the demands of hands-on mothering was eliminated to save the newest owner money.

I was not interested in the reconfigured schedule that required all nurses to work Monday through Friday, every other weekend, and rotating 24 hour on-call shifts. It was not a good fit for my young family and me. I decided it was time to explore other options.

The correctional facility nearby just happened to have posted a part-time position for an RN who would perform physical assessments on all newly booked inmates. That schedule would allow me time to be a Mama, volunteer at my sons' schools, and volunteer at the local library.

I had no correctional nursing experience but was hired over the phone by the out-of-town contractor that provided medical services to my local jail. I was surprised at the process of submitting my resume by email, receiving a phone call that day, and being hired sight unseen. "I'd like to see the facility and meet the Director of Nursing first," I replied to the woman who offered me the job. She convinced me all would be fine, to just take the job, which I did. *What the hell,* I thought to myself. *How different could it be from the patients I already have served?*

That question would be answered soon and often with the words, *totally* different.

On my first day in jail, I arrived at 8 am. The parking lot was full of cars parked around the perimeter. I assumed those were the employees and that the close-up spots were reserved for visitors, the magistrate, ministers, attorneys, and police. The front of the building looked like a school. This playground, though, had a 14-foot-high cyclone fence topped with interlocking spirals of razor wire. The double-door entrance led to a lobby very much like a doctor's office registration area. The disinterested receptionist at the desk pointed me down a long, downward-sloping, carpeted hallway. Lockers lined one side of the hall. The other side was a solid wall of painted concrete block.

At the end, I came to a glass-enclosed office in the center of the hallway, flanked on either side by large, half-glass, half-metal electronic sliding doors. The deputy stationed at the security desk there eyed me questionably and said he had no information that I was expected. He called the Medical Director of Nursing, who met me at the door and introduced herself to me with an apology for forgetting to notify Central Security that I was coming in.

I was told to return to the receptionist, who collected my ID info, performed some kind of online security check, and gave me a temporary badge to wear that day. I went back to Central and passed through the security door, jumping slightly at the slam and loud decisive pop of the lock behind me. I made my way down the hall to my next stop -- Booking. Another security door. I pushed the call button and waved to a deputy manning the booking desk through another half-glass door. He popped the lock for me to enter. As directed, I stood against the green cinderblock wall.

"Put your feet on the marks and take off your glasses," the deputy said with a bored sigh, as though it was the millionth time he had repeated those same words. I heard the camera snap. "You are not supposed to smile," he said flatly. "I have to take it again." I stepped back on the floor marks and put on my villainous look, with disappointing results. I thought I must look very much like Patty Hearst as the gun-toting Simbianese Liberation Army bank robbery bandit, and I couldn't help but imagine an assault rifle just out of the photo's range.

As I stood there waiting for permission to move, I saw two large holding cells across from the booking desk. They had half-glass walls and a half-glass door. About six inmates, some white, some black, most of them young, occupied each room. They all were looking my way. The holding cells were where the newly imprisoned waited a turn to, one by one, exchange street clothes for the requisite elastic waist blue jeans, white T-shirt, pale blue chambray long-sleeved shirt, jail undies and flip flops. Socks and shoes were available in the jail canteen for purchase. I would learn all of this in good time. I waved to them and smiled. They waved back. The deputy rolled his eyes and shook his head. Apparently, this is not what one does, wave at inmates in booking. I was trying to be friendly. Friendly, I learned, is off the table in booking. My return to scowling face drew imitations of it from the inmates.

I committed multiple security and protocol breaches in my first few months at the jail. To be fair to myself, however, I simply arrived there and seemingly was expected to know what to do, nursing-wise, security-wise, and otherwise. Thankfully, the other nurses and deputies embraced my willingness to learn and kept a close eye on me, keeping me out of harm's way when needed.

By noon on my first day there, the news of a new nurse in the jail flew through the 1,200-inmate facility by a grapevine I would come to know as second to none. Wagers were placed by inmates and deputies on how long I would last. Deputies said three weeks, inmates bet on three days. I stayed seven years until, once again, my contracted position was eliminated by a new medical services contractor who had undercut the bid by combining my job with that of the Director of Nursing. Ridiculous that one nurse could fulfill all the duties when combining both jobs, but that's how they got the bottom line lower and won the bid.

Finally, by noon on that first day, I completed my ID verification tasks and arrived on the Medical Unit. From Booking, I journeyed down a long hallway of pale green cinderblock and came to a matching green, solid metal door, camera above and to one side. I pushed the buzzer, looked up waving into the camera and the door lock popped. Down this hall I came to a door marked Medical. Central control was watching me. The lock popped before I pressed the call button.

I said "Hi" to the male inmates who were passing through medical. They all gawked at me. "New nurse" could have been stamped on my forehead.

Medical had an L-shaped Formica-topped nurse's station desk with a high counter around the outside and three places for nurses to sit to chart. A single computer sat in the bend of the "L." There was a black box the size of a rectangular laundry basket further down on the desk. It had a schematic of the medical unit floor plan on it with corresponding lights by each door.

"It's called the Black Creek," the Director of Nursing (DON) was telling me.

There were a pair of glass-front offices behind the nurses' desk, one for the DON and another for the Health Services Administrator (HSA). The HSA stood at the top of the pecking order of nursing administration, followed by the DON, then me, and then the two staff LPNs.

Three patient exam rooms lined the hall by the nurse's desk. They were reserved for the twice-daily sick-call screenings. One of these rooms is where I would do my assessments. Four partially glassed-in sick rooms for inmates who needed full-time medical observation and care were situated across from the nurses' station, the doors equipped with immense locks that needed a castle-sized key to open them. Each medical inpatient cell had a double-door configuration. The first door accessed a small anteroom with cabinets for supply storage. The inner door had a slot for passing through meds and mail to avoid the need to unlock it. White, linoleum-tiled floors and turquoise doors with white painted cinderblock walls made Medical look bright and clean.

"What's a Black Creek?" I asked but did not get an answer, as the DON had been called into an exam room. A female inmate had been brought in for an ultrasound of her baby's fetal heartbeat, and the staff nurse needed help to find the equipment. I stood there turning around in a circle to learn the layout of the unit. Door alarms beeped and lights flashed on the Black Creek. It obviously had something to do with the security system, but it was all alien to me. A long line of female inmates, dressed like the men in denim jeans and blue shirts, walked to the nurses' station area, where blue chairs made of molded fiberglass had been bolted to the floor to provide seating for the waiting area.

Suddenly I heard, "Hi, Susan. What are you doing here?" I turned to the voice, surprised anyone would know me in this environment. It was a woman I knew well from my sons' high school PTO.

"Working," I choked out, swallowing the rest of the sentence that had popped into my head, which was, "What are *you* doing here?"

"How are your boys?" she asked me. I was already breaking rules I had not yet learned. Do not share personal information with the inmates.

"Fine," I said awkwardly, then asked about her children. Before I could get further into the conversation, the desk phone rang. I looked around. The two nurses were still with the patient. The secretary was in the chart room down the hall, but I hadn't met her yet, and she was busy on the phone. On the third ring I picked up and said, "Medical, Nurse Susan."

A man's urgent voice said, "Hey, this is Fortune in the SHU. An inmate pulled the shower head off of the wall and stuck it up his ass, and he's bloody down there."

I looked at my watch. I had been on the medical unit a grand total of 20 minutes. Clearly, this was my self-directed orientation. It was a medically informed fly-by-the-seat-of-your-pants introduction to correctional nursing.

I was thinking, *Who is Fortune? And what and where is the SHU?* No time for that, some man needed assistance with an inmate. "How can I help you?" I asked.

"He's got blood down there," Fortune repeated. Deputy Sheriff Fortune would become a dear friend in the coming year. Right now he was just a voice who wanted help from a nurse.

I found out later that the SHU, or Secured Housing Unit, Fortune's duty station, is the area of the jail with single-bunk locked cells of six or seven to 12 cells per pod, a day room and exercise area in each pod where inmates could be out one at a time. Mostly the inmates in the SHU were locked down 23 hours out of 24 (called 23/1). There is a protective custody pod, a medical pod, a psychiatric unit, and cells that had cameras for inmates who needed constant observation. The work release inmates had a pod space there, too. This inmate with the problem was from the psychiatric pod.

"Describe the blood down there, Fortune. Is it gushing like a garden hose or dripping like a leaky faucet?"

"No," answered Fortune. "There are two dried spots on the back of his legs by the knees."

"Ok," I said. "How can I help?"

Fortune asked, "Don't you want to come get this shower head out of his ass?"

I'm thinking, *Uh, hell no. I don't want to do that.* Instead I asked, "Does this guy masturbate by putting stuff up his butt?"

"Oh yeah," sighed Fortune. "Yesterday he stuck two rolled-up magazines up there."

During my student emergency room (ER) experience, I saw a patient who slid a quart milk bottle up his butt and came to ER to get it out. Another patient did the same thing with some huge carrots. I was somewhat familiar with this practice for sexual stimulation.

"And who got the magazines out of him yesterday?" I asked. As I expected, it was the inmate who got them out. I asked if the inmate had done the shower head bit before and learned that despite close observation, this young man had been able to enact this and all other sorts of self-mutilating behaviors. I told Fortune to wait until the inmate removed the shower head, to call me if he sees active bleeding, then clean the shower head by soaking it in bleach solution when it became available for use again. I told him to call me back if he needed me.

He said, "Ok," and hung up.

I wrote down the inmate's name and discover during a follow up conversation with the nurses that he was being treated by the jail psychiatrist who knew well of his behaviors.

* * *

All of my previous jobs had had some sort of an orientation period that mapped out criteria to be met. In jail there simply was no one on staff who could allot time to spend the day with me. I read the policy and procedure manual and shadowed the staff and deputies to get up to speed. Deputies taught me security on the go, and what they missed I learned during reprimand sessions in the Watch Commander's office.

For instance, I gave an inmate staying in the medical unit a bar of soap when he asked me for one. *Big* mistake. First of all, I had entered an inmate's room without a deputy escort. Not that I didn't know I needed an escort. The deputy just happened to be at lunch. This inmate had AIDS, tertiary syphilis, and tuberculosis. It seemed to me that giving him soap would be a good idea. He was short, very thin, and moved slowly. He did not seem like a physical threat to me. This was a stupid move, I later learned, as inmates can fake feebleness to lure in a hostage.

Also, soap is a traded commodity in jail, and I needed to ask for a soap search before giving it out. A soap search? What? Is? That? First the deputy would search the cell for soap. If none is found, another bar can be given, unless it had been less than one month since the last bar. If so, no soap. The rules are the rules and not to be modified by the nurses. Plus, I was unknowingly fueling the black market of items that could be traded for sex and such. I got a deserved cussing out by the female deputy who returned from her lunch to find me alone in the inmate's room. I apologized to her, told her it was a dangerous and stupid move, and asked her to keep an eye on me for future security infractions. I was sincere, and she knew it. She went on to teach me many helpful things during our time together.

During my years working in jail, only one inmate attempted an attack in Medical on a nurse. Most inmates in my jail were awaiting trial or serving sentences of less than two years. Housed in large pods in which cells surrounded a day room, they typically were locked in the cell only at night. Inmates behaved because it was to their advantage. They could earn time for good behavior and, in this way, could substantially reduce time to serve if they kept out of trouble. They also could earn a trustee position, working off the pod certain hours of the day. Perhaps cleaning around the jail, working in the chow hall or outside on the roadside clean-up crew. They could participate in an inmate-managed substance abuse therapeutic treatment pod to learn skills to combat addiction.

Behave badly and lose these privileges or others, like visitation. Or behave consistently badly, and you were put in your own cell, locked in 23 hours and out one. Perhaps worst of all bad behavior consequences was being limited to meals of "the loaf," a pureed blend that days food and served loaf style. This was in the early 2000s, and I am not sure if this punitive meal approach is still an allowable option for punishment.

Inmates at this jail had the opportunity to request medical attention by way of a twice-daily sick call. The process was simple. They filled out a sick-call request, called a blue note because it was written on blue paper, explaining why they were requesting a visit to medical and gave it to the deputy in their housing unit. The sick call slip had their name, housing location, and a description of the medical problem. The slips were sent to Medical, and the nurses determined who needed to be seen in person or who could be managed with a written reply to their note.

Sick call requests ran the gamut from requests for pain pills and laxatives to asking for a frappuccino machine as a way to self-treat adult ADHD. That particular request was declined although the articulate query was well-supported with references to research studies and evidence-based data. The inmate was an attorney.

A sick call visit consisted of an evaluation by a nurse and either treatments pre-approved by a medical protocol written by the jail doctor or a referral to see the doc during his twice-weekly visits to handle appointments. Sick call visits cost $5. The inmates carried no cash, so the funds came from their jail account, which held the money they had on them when they entered jail and/or funds their families deposited for them to spend on weekly canteen visits. If a sick inmate had no available funds, the visit was charged and paid off if a friend or family member dropped money into their account. Otherwise, the costs were written off by the jail.

Medical emergency visits were free. We were not equipped to provide emergency services. After a quick assessment, any inmates in need of urgent treatments were sent by ambulance to the local hospital.

One afternoon, in the midst of my assessments and sick call visits, a phone call came to Medical informing us that two deputies from the SHU were escorting a male inmate to us. The inmate had told the deputies he had a medical emergency. I sent my group of six inmates, who were there for screening physicals, back to their housing pods so I would be available to help. I did so reluctantly, as the time for head count was approaching, and there would be no getting them back for the rest of the afternoon. Head count was followed by a deputy shift change. Afterward, the chow hall opened for dinner. This effectively ended any chance to get an inmate to Medical to complete my list for the day.

Our routine interrupted, the sick call nurse, the med nurse, the secretary, the HSA, and I stared at the SHU door, awaiting the arrival of the emergency. In our minds, we all were going over the possible scenarios: severe chest pain, stroke symptoms, blood sugar irregularity, stabbing, etc. The SHU door alarm announced our sick inmate's arrival.

Two deputies escorted a short, heavy-set black man through the hallway door into Medical. The inmate wore the suit specific to the SHU, blaze orange scrub top, drawstring orange bottoms, and flip-flops. His hands were cuffed in front. Usually inmates had their hands cuffed behind the back when they came to us. We could request the cuffs be removed, and most often we did. This inmate's rotund shape may be the reason his hands were in front, I thought, although I didn't know for sure. As nurses do, we all silently began the mental assessment as the inmate walked toward us. No shortness of breath, his color was good, gait fine, talking fine, not sweaty, no one-sided weakness, no visible bleeding or wound dressings. He seemed alert and oriented. Whatever was wrong, it was not adding up to an emergency.

The deputies escorted the inmate into the exam room nearest the nurses' desk. They backed him up to the exam table end and had him step backward and up onto the exam table step. As he sat, he scooted back on the table and the deputies removed his cuffs and waited for three of us to enter the room. They positioned themselves in the doorway. Our secretary and HSA stayed at the nurses' desk to answer calls or summon an ambulance if we needed one.

And then, it happened like this.

The inmate is shaking his head back and forth saying, "Oh man, oh man."

One nurse applies a blood pressure cuff. The other asks the inmate, "What's wrong?"

I stand back, available to assist.

"My balls are stuck to my leg," he says with great gravity. The blood pressure cuff is snatched back off with a jerk. "I have a medical emergency," he adds quickly to ensure he won't be charged $5 for the visit.

The deputies and I look at each other.

"What?" the desk nurse barks.

"I have a medical emergency," the inmate shouts. "My balls are stuck to my leg."

The deputies standing in the doorway throw up their hands. "Oh, hell no," I hear them say, among other frustrated remarks. Escorting an inmate to medical takes staff away from the required inmate rounds, head count, and other duties, as well as reports the deputies need to complete, throwing them off schedule. To have left their duty station for this absurd reason clearly pisses them off.

I go back into the hall and walk to the nurses' desk. I will not be needed to assist with this patient. The exam nurse is explaining that she will not do an exam, she will send him back to the SHU to fill out a sick call slip, and he will need to come back when it is his turn for a sick call visit.

The deputies reapply the hand cuffs and walk the inmate from the room. The deputies are shaking their heads and muttering that they do not go to the ER for stuck balls, they take a shower on a regular basis.

We are snickering at the comments. The inmate is not laughing. He looks furious. As he reaches the nurses' desk, he complains to the HSA that he is not being seen for his emergency. The HSA explains that a medical emergency is when you are not breathing, you are bleeding profusely, or you are unconscious. She tells him politely, "Having your balls stuck to your leg is not an emergency."

"The hell it ain't," he hollers. "How would you know, you don't have balls." He screams, lunging at the desk. He throws his hands over his head, squats, and jumps, landing on his stomach on the top of the desk counter top, beaching himself there. He flails his arms and legs while trying to move closer to her, spitting into her face. The deputies immediately remove him from the desk and put him face-down on the floor where he kicks and screams and spits. They uncuff him and hold him face down, his arms spread out in a T position.

"Hit the emergency button," we all chorus at the same time. We fight to get the chance to push the emergency buttons at the nurses' desk. None of us has ever used the button before. We all run to other rooms and hit all the help buttons. The deputies have the inmate under control. Why we think we need back up makes no sense, but when an inmate spits and screams, reflexes take over. In two seconds, the five doors that open into Medical are thrown wide. Swarms of uniformed deputies pour through. In under a minute there seems to be 25 to 30 responders, some wearing gas masks and holding pepper spray canisters ready to deploy. I back up to a wall and stand stone still, mouth open. Security staff members surround the inmate and all the nurses. I hear leg chains being clamped on the inmate, who still lies on the ground. It is oddly quiet except for the heavily breathing deputies who ran from all areas of the jail and are catching their breath. The air smells sweaty, like fear and power and a palpable readiness to rumble, the sense that somebody is going down.

The watch commander, the captain, the lieutenant, and sergeant are all there. One of them is writing down what happened. Another is dismissing unneeded personnel, one by one, back to their duty stations.

Before each of the dismissed deputies leaves Medical, they comes to the nurses and ask each one of us, "Are you OK?"

"Yes," we all solemnly reply.

I'm not sure if this is protocol or if it's just that we are like a family. When the deputies had heard the alarm was in Medical, they knew exactly which nurses were there. They did not know what prompted the emergency call, but they did know it could have been very bad. Could have been several inmates causing trouble, not just one. Could have been an attack with a jail-made weapon. Their minds had prepared them the worst. Maybe they asked how we were doing as a way to decompress.

For a while we stay flabbergasted by this show of force. It was so quickly executed and so organized. I realize that for as long as I had been working at the jail, I had never seen what these deputies practice and plan for, how they train for all the shit to hit the fan, any day, any time.

Soon Medical is just about emptied out. A few deputies stand over the inmate. I see one deputy on his knees next to the inmate's shoulder, his back facing me, his posture tense. He is speaking softly, slowly, and deliberately, delivering a final bit of advice, I assume. The deputy stands, sternly nods our way, and stomps out of Medical. The inmate is helped to standing without resistance and walked back by his two deputies to the SHU in silence.

The five of us stand in the quiet of Medical and talk about what just happened. We redefine our need to hit the emergency button and discuss a better way to respond if something similar happens again. A few minutes later, we look up sharply as the SHU door alarm beeps and swings open. The inmate with the adhering scrotal issue stands between the same two deputies. They enter Medical, approach the desk and face us, standing there quietly for a moment.

The inmate softly begins his apology with an "I am very sorry."

One deputy slowly turns his head to stare at the inmate.

The inmate looks at the deputy then back to us and adds, "And I will never, never make any trouble in medical again."

After a gentle "Ok, thank you" from the exam nurse, they all turn as a unit and quietly leave.

The inmate never did request a sick call visit to address his medical concern, but we did hear from the deputy that after the apology, his very next stop was the shower stall.

7

Yearly Evaluation

When I first met Mary, she had been living alone for six years. Her husband, John, had passed away. They had no children.

In her mid-80s, her weight and strength declining from diabetes, arthritis, peripheral vascular disease, and as she put it, "I don't know what all else," Mary was visited daily by a home health nurse. Nurses cared for her persistent leg sores, which had not healed because of chronic leg swelling. They removed old dressings sodden with drainage, gently cleanse the wounds, reapply bandages, and cover them with an Ace wrap. Add loneliness, poor and irregular eating, and forgetting to take her pills to the mix of problems, and you have a more complete picture of Mary's health – and life – challenges.

Ever so slowly during the last half dozen years, Mary's world had shrunk to the three rooms of her small, cement-floor cottage. The living room and kitchen, a combined open space, gave her a little area in which to navigate her wheelchair across the bare concrete floor. Her gnarled hands awkwardly gripped the wheels but are too weak to make much forward progress. To propel her wheelchair even the smallest distance, she must shove her swollen, slippered feet beneath her and push. This exertion typically taxes her energy and leaves her unable to stand and shift to the sofa. As a result, she often spends her whole day in her wheelchair.

The rest of the house is pretty much inaccessible. The narrow hallway to the bathroom and bedroom eliminates the possibility of a wheelchair approach. To get to those rooms, Mary needs to apply the wheelchair brakes, stand, and shuffle, breathing heavily, while bracing herself against the walls. Even with a rolling walker, it is too much. She is physically frail and fears a fall. A portable commode, parked next to the sofa, has become her bathroom. Piles of papers, medicine bottles, soda bottles, snack foods, grooming supplies, dirty and clean clothing, a landline telephone (cell phones are not in general use yet), and assorted necessities surround her sofa area.

Several days a week, food is brought to her by two kindly neighbors. One, a young volunteer firefighter who works as a mechanic, brings Mary biscuits from McDonald's and little pies and cakes from the gas station shop and go. During his visit, he empties the commode, feeds Mary's dog, Pup, and chats for a few minutes. The other neighbor, a middle-aged man, brings her yogurt and canned foods and volunteers as the caretaker of her small backyard during the warmer months.

Factor in her nurses and we all have become part of her patchwork quilt of living, whether we are starting a load of laundry, taking a bag of trash away, or rinsing a few dishes. A few minutes here and there of assorted chores done by many hands, not requested or orchestrated by Mary, yet just enough to keep everything functioning. It may not be an ideal situation, but this network of helpers performing basic tasks is just enough to grant Mary's wish to stay in her own home.

Of course, she is not totally alone. Pup, a goofy black lab who is Mary's devoted companion, helps keep her mind busy and cleans the cottage floor of crumbs. No one knows when or how Pup arrived on the scene, not even Mary, but he seems right at home in the cottage. His crate in the living room has a wonderfully thick cushion, and he likes watching me from his comfy cave, door open, on rainy days while I care for his dear lady friend. We, her home health nurses, assume a concerned neighbor brought Pup for Mary's protection at night, as she keeps her back door unlocked so both her neighbors and nurses can get in as needed.

That may have been the intent, but Pup clearly does not grasp his planned guardian role in Mary's life. During my first visit to the home, the happy dog spins in fierce circles around my legs with furious tail wagging and licks galore. I suspect that burglars would get the same enthusiastic reception. Mary is concerned, though, about the extra work Pup makes for nurses and neighbors. Often our first task when we come to check on her is to clean up the mess on the floor he has created when he is unable to get outside for relief. Sometimes Mary crates Pup at night to prevent the mess from occurring, but that does not let him free to defend her, if needed. Personally, I am OK with this added chore, as I see the value Pup adds to Mary's life. But some of the other nurses feel otherwise.

During my first home health nursing visit with her, Mary tells me her husband is dead. "He lives five miles down the road now, six feet deep," is how she puts it. I rarely hear more about him beyond this simple statement of status and location. According to my co-workers, that's all they have heard, too.

Every night, Mary sleeps either on her well-worn, over-sized sofa or in her wheelchair. She finds it too exhausting to walk down the 10-foot hallway to her bedroom. Her immensely swollen lower legs make it a slow and painful journey. Plus, that old bed is where she once slept with John, who is now five miles down the road, six feet deep, she tells me -- every visit. Sleeping on the sofa, she says, reminds her of nothing at all. Her sofa and wheelchair are much more comfortable than that old bed anyway, she insists.

The times Mary doesn't lie down to sleep but sits up both day and night are brutal on her circulation. Her lower legs balloon with fluid. In those instances, draining leg sores saturate the toe-to-knee dressings we come to change and reapply daily. All her nurses beg her to lie down and put her feet up at night and periodically during the day. We often get her onto the sofa ourselves and prop her feet up at the end of our visits there. She probably works her way back into her wheelchair as soon as we leave. She does this even though her chart contains pages of patient teaching about diabetes, nutrition, wheelchair safety, and the huge importance of elevating her feet to keep the swelling down so the wounds can heal. She sweetly and demurely tells us how hard it is to remember all that. We make several huge poster board wall signs for all the rooms: "Put Feet Up." No luck.

On the days of my weekend nursing visits, I try to arrive early to care for Mary's leg sores. If she wakes up before my arrival and releases Pup from his crate, I am greeted by a mess on the floor, as Mary can't fit her wheelchair through the doorway of the enclosed porch where the back door is located to let Pup out. When I arrive and let myself into the unlocked back door, I can tell what to expect based on the greeting I receive from Pup. If he is still in his crate, I free him to run past me to the far end of the fenced yard where he relieves his bladder. If he is there at the door, whirling and twirling in a cyclonic display of personality, I know a big clean-up will be in order.

When this happens, Mary is very apologetic. "Leave it," she insists. "My neighbor will clean it up." But I know that sometimes days pass between neighbor visits.

"This is no big deal," I chirp, while quickly sopping up and discarding the mess in the plastic grocery bags I stash in my pocket before every visit to Mary's home. I often need to clean the wheels of Mary's wheelchair if she has rolled through the soiled floors. I think of it simply as part of infection control management. I open the small wood-framed windows on the enclosed porch to flush out the odor. Then I wash my hands, fix Mary her tea, and scope out her refrigerator for something she can eat while I am there with her. Next, I refill Pup's food and water bowls.

Then, 15 minutes after my arrival, I begin what the physician's orders have sent me there to do. I check Mary's blood pressure and pulse, listen to her heart and lungs, and ask a few questions about bowel, bladder, and appetite. Then I do wound care on both feet. Once the dirty dressings are double-bagged and in the outside trash can, I check her pill box to be sure she had taken all her medicine. Mary makes it apparent she enjoys my company as I jot notes in her chart. When offered some patient teaching about the importance of hydration for someone afflicted with draining wounds (or whatever the topic of the day happens to be), she pays close attention and agrees to implement the recommendations ASAP. It is street theater on both our parts. I know she will do whatever she is used to doing, while she respects my need to teach her. Then there is the hug goodbye. I let Pup back in the house and leave. The routine rarely varies.

Of course, there are always exceptions. Arriving at Mary's cottage one spring morning, I holler a quick hello into the house as Pup circles my legs before bounding out to the back of the yard. I stop short as I enter the living room. There is no dog mess but Mary's soiled lower leg dressings, gauzes, and Ace wraps snake around the floor in long, twisted ribbons like the aftermath of some wild party. Mouth wide open in astonishment, my eyes scan the room. Mary sits in her wheelchair smiling, hands in lap, her lower leg wounds open to the air and saturating her slippers with watery drainage.

"Mary, what *happened* here?" I ask, sweeping my arm across the room, now scattered with bio-hazardous material.

"It took Pup hours to get them all off my feet," she chuckles, adding, "He sure had fun!"

"What a naughty boy," I admonish, much to her delight, as I pick up the soiled dressings with gloved hands. I wash the Ace wraps with dish detergent in the bathroom sink and put them out in the sun to dry. I speak to Mary about wound contamination and how it is not optimal to have Pup do the dressing removal. Also, far from ideal is the dog hair now sticking to her draining wounds.

"Where'd ya get them skinny legs from?" is her response.

"Huh?"

"Them's the skinniest legs I've ever seen," she persists.

I look down past my blue-and-white checked culottes at said appendages, trying to figure out what my legs have to do with wound dressings being contaminated by dog drool.

"Well?" she continues.

"From my Dad. I got these legs from my Dad," I reply with a resigned sigh.

"You mean your Dad had skinny legs like *that*?" She shakes her head and laughs.

"Yep," I laugh back. Her tactic works. I am distracted. We never get back to the topic of the dog removing the dressings. I reinforce her new dressings with extra tape to discourage Pup from a repeat performance and make a note in the chart for her other visiting nurses to beef up the outer dressings. On my next visit, I bring Pup a can of tennis balls to play with.

I continue to visit Mary as part of my regular schedule without anything eventful happening --until one memorable weekend during the heat of August. On that Saturday, I come and go normally, tasked with the usual. I let Pup out, clean up dog mess, fix breakfast, take out smelly trash that is stinking up the house in the summer heat, do wound care, wash the Ace wraps, and get Pup in from the yard.

"See you tomorrow morning," I tell her as we hug goodbye.

"Thanks, Nursie Susan. See you tomorrow," she answers, smiling back at me.

Sunday morning, I arrive at Mary's around 10:30, a little later than I hoped. The heat is already unbearable. I know the cottage probably has not cooled down much overnight in this sultry weather. I open the back door. No Pup. *This is not good,* I think. By this time of the morning, Mary usually has let him out of the crate. I walk through the kitchen and into the living area.

Mary lies sprawled out on the bare concrete floor. My first thought is that she is dead. She turns her head to face me. I see a saucer-sized puddle of dried blood behind her head. Pup whines in his crate.

"Hi, Mary," I say softly as I kneel next to her. "Are you hurt?"

"No, I'm just stuck is all," she says calmly, then smiles brightly.

"Can you move your hands and feet?" I ask.

"Sure," she replies as she demonstrates small hand and foot twirls.

After several more questions, I place a thin towel under her head to get her wound off the dirty floor. I open the dog crate and quickly escort Pup to the back door.

"How long have you been stuck?" I ask when I return, examining her arms and legs. She feels cool from being on the concrete. The swelling in her feet and lower legs has vanished. Her unlocked wheelchair is across the room from the sofa.

She ponders before answering. "I don't know." But she does know who I am, what day it is, and why I am there. Then it comes back to her. She remembers she had tried to get onto the sofa, the wheelchair had rolled out from behind her, and she had slid to the floor.

"Was it light or dark when you slid to the floor?" I ask.

"Light," she says. "Then it got dark then light again."

She has been on the cool floor all night. I am afraid to move her. I cannot safely pick her up, anyway. She could have fractured her hips or spine. Her scalp wound is caked with crusty dried blood; the wound looks to be two inches long. Why more blood has not poured forth from it is a surprise. She must have laid directly on the wound and the pressure clotted the blood vessels.

"Mary, you have a cut on the back of your head. It needs stitches," I tell her. "I can't do that here."

"No," she pleads. "They won't let me come home. No, I won't go to the hospital."

For 30 minutes I explain to her why a hospital visit is the best choice. Her firefighter neighbor stops by and helps me convince Mary. He tells her he will go with her to the hospital and make sure she returns to her cottage. We both keep vague about the timeline for coming home. He assures her he will also watch Pup until she gets back.

Mary ends up spending three days in the hospital. X-rays of everything reveal no fractures. Her stitched head wound heals nicely.

By the next weekend, I am able to visit her again. While I remove the stitches from the back of her head she tells me, "When I was on the floor, I called for John to help me. Then I remembered he was five miles down the road and six feet deep and could not come."

I laugh because she laughs.

Despite her ordeal, Mary shows no trace of humiliation or anger at having spent the night on the floor. I have learned she has no unrealistic expectations about this body that keeps finding new ways to let her down. She does not let incapacity torture her. She lives an "it could be worse" existence without saying it in so many words. She treasures her little home and what independence she does have, and this attitude makes it easy to treasure her.

About the time of this incident, my yearly performance evaluation comes due. It typically works this way. My home health nursing supervisor will join me on a visit, observe my adherence to policy and procedures, evaluate my documentation, and tell me the company has no money to give raises again this year.

Debbie, my supervisor, has worked as a visiting nurse from this office, and we know each other and our individual work ethic well. The evaluation form contains a section for improvements. The year before in that section's comment, she had advised me to be more time efficient, and that had annoyed me. Some things are outside the scope of nursing care but, I feel, need to be addressed to maintain the safety or health of the patient. When Debbie asks me to choose a patient for my evaluation, I choose Mary. If my boss has suggestions on how to squeeze Mary's physical and environmental care into 30 minutes, I am more than ready to hear and implement them.

On the drive there, Debbie asks the usual questions about office and procedural policies and thumbs through Mary's chart. I take her lack of comments at my notes to mean they meet standards. This activity is a formal matter. We do not chitchat.

We arrive about 10 am. Pup bounds out the back door and jumps on Debbie with wet paws. "Quick, get inside," I shout to my supervisor over Pup's yelps as I hold him at arm's length. She waits for me just inside the door. Ahead of her, the floors are soiled, as usual. I pull a plastic grocery bag from my pocket, grab paper towels from the kitchen counter, and clean up the mess.

"Hey, Mary," I call to my patient. "It's Susan. Say some nice things about me, my boss is here, too. Her name is Debbie." I have already warned Mary of the supervisory visit but also know it is unlikely she will remember a conversation from the previous weekend.

"Hi, Nursie." Mary waves, welcoming her guest from her wheelchair. "I love all my nurses," she continues, her hands clasped beneath her chin, elbows resting on the arms of her wheelchair.

Debbie watches as I ask Mary about her eating, bowels and bladder, pain level, and medicine compliance. I check Mary's blood pressure and pulse and listen to her lungs. I see Debbie surveying the cluttered room and stained floors, subtlety pinching her nose closed. Through the dim living room lighting, I occasionally glance to see her expression as she registers the enormous challenges of Mary's living situation.

I complete the wound care as Mary eats some yogurt. She is telling Debbie about John being five miles down the road, etc., and how I make her eat while I am there and how I make sure she takes her pills. She is tooting my horn, winking at me as she speaks. While cleaning up from the wound care and checking the wound care supplies, I keep looking at Mary. Something is not right. I notice a wet stain on the right side of her shirt front. Food stains down the front of her are expected. This wet spot, however, is not in the spill zone.

"Mary, when did you change your shirt last?" I ask.

"Oh, when my nurse washed me this week." She cannot remember the specific day. A nurse's aide comes twice weekly to bathe Mary, but that schedule is not in my chart.

"Well, this shirt is wet," I say as I pull on clean disposable gloves. Debbie has already moved toward the door. She shoots me a glance and tips her head to the back-porch door. I shrug and tell her I just want to get a dry shirt on Mary. Debbie moves back, puts on gloves, and helps me remove the shirt. A pungent smell becomes more pronounced. I realize I had caught a whiff of it earlier but did not think it was coming from Mary. I roll up the shirt and place it in the clothes hamper. Mary is wearing a white bra. Her right breast sits oddly higher on her belly than the left breast.

"What's.....*this*?" I gasp as I lift the large, floppy, right side of Mary's bra. Debbie and I slowly bend forward to peek underneath. Nestled between her bra and abdominal skin is a soggy, moldy half of a blueberry muffin, still wrapped in its pastry paper. The funky odor now blooms into the room, rolling over us like a wave of foul fog.

"Oh, I was looking for that," Mary says, in a tone of great relief. "I have to hide my treats from Pup or he will eat them, and blueberry muffins are my favorite."

The underside of the bra is slimy green, and her abdominal skin is fiery red with fungal rash. "When did you put this here?" I ask between gritted teeth, looking around for another used grocery bag to wrap it in.

"Don't know." She shrugs.

I hear the back-door slam and picture Debbie gulping for air while being accosted by Pup at the same time. As I bathe Mary, I hear Pup chasing a tennis ball being thrown by Debbie. I wash out the bra, and Mary and I discuss alternate Pup-proof snack storage ideas. I note in the chart for her other nurses to care for the fungal rash and discourage beneath-the-bra treat stashing.

Debbie and I drive back to the office in silence while she completes my evaluation paperwork. This time, I am happy to note, she leaves the improvement line blank. Debbie and I share our blueberry muffin experience with the other nurses. Everyone agrees that Mary may be the first to have discovered a functional, if not practical, use for large and floppy breasts as they age.

Several months later, Mary moves five miles down the road to be with her beloved John. Her firefighter friend is the one who finds her. Pup goes to live with him.

8

TRANSLATIONS

Nurses learn to talk medicalese early in their training. Knowing the correct medical terminology translates to factual and concise clinical nursing notes, adding necessary detail to "the rag, the bone, and the hank of hair" while subtracting the angst.

Doctors read chart notes from nurses, also physical therapists, and respiratory therapists -- to name a few -- to learn results of procedures or tests they have ordered. The better the notes, the better the doctor understands the patient.

Nurses have no autonomy in patient care. In hospitals, doctors write medical and drug orders, and the nurses see to it that those orders are carried out. A scrupulously documented patient's chart is like an architectural drawing: The more complete, the better the outcome.

"If it's not written down, it wasn't done," was drilled into my head from the first to the last day of nurses' training and by every head nurse and shift supervisor I have had since.

Forget to document a treatment or procedure, and the consequences will punch you from all sides of the healthcare team. Efficient, thorough charting is a skill that a nurse develops after much practice and concentration, it's an evolution helped along by a few stops on the disciplinary carpet. Getting confronted by a surgeon at the nurses' station in front of your peers about why you did not chart the urine output yesterday teaches you to concentrate even when it is two hours after your shift was supposed to end, your kids are waiting to be picked up, and you still need to buy groceries for dinner.

Doctors sometimes shimmer in and out of a patient's presence behind a self-sewn veil of verbal grandiosity. This is especially evident in a teaching hospital when the attending physician arrives accompanied by, in descending order of the food chain, the residents, the medical students, the nurses, the nursing students, and the patient's family.

I have often been at a patient's bedside when the doctor struts in, trailing his medical entourage behind him. In this situation, the patient – garbed in a hospital gown, which is little more than a cloth tent usually missing a few snaps – feels vulnerable and just about invisible, particularly when it comes to the doctor. As a result, he or she is on guard and in a chronic state of stress.

Since the medical parade arrives on its own unannounced schedule, patients often find themselves alone amid this barrage of professionals. With no family members present, patients must process information and make decisions alone. Often with so much to take in, they remember nothing at all. This is just one more area in which the listening ears and the language skills of a good nurse are pure gold.

A typical scenario unfolds like this. The patient awakens to see the medical mavens amassing at the foot of the bed. The resident starts off by listing the patient's medical status, the newest lab information, and whatever else is of interest to the other members of the medical team. In an awkward attempt to participate, the patient may try to interject a question or give a response. Sometimes overwhelmed by the dialogue, he does not speak at all.

I have been a witness to the following – or very similar -- exchange.

"How do you feel?" asks the resident while looking at the chart, not at the face looking up at him.

"Fine," the patient blurts out like an automaton, not sure if the question was directed at him and not really meaning that to be the answer.

"Good," says the resident quickly. "Any nausea, vomiting, diarrhea, shortness of breath, gas pain, joint pain, rashes, coughing, blurred vision, numbness, tingling, wheezing, weakness, dizziness, calf pain, fever, headache, earache, open sores, closed sores, bed sores? Any trouble sleeping, swallowing, speaking, arguing, ambulating, urinating, defecating? Have you fallen? Did you take your meds?"

"Huh?"

"Good, we'll be in to see you tomorrow."

End of so-called conversation.

After the clump of white coats turns heel and glides off, setting their trajectory for the next bedside, it is the nurses who remain behind to translate.

"What the hell was that?" asks my dumbfounded patient.

"Your sodium and potassium blood levels still stink," may be the reply from me.

"Am I going home today?"

"Nope," adding emphasis with an index finger stabbed once toward the patient.

"Shit, give me the phone."

For a nursing student, medical terminology class requires hours of memorizing lists of Latin-based prefixes and suffixes and words with convoluted polysyllabic combinations. At first the words seem foreign and the process of learning them is overwhelming, then insidiously they become part of your nature. For me, the words temporarily took over my life. Everything began to look benign or malignant -- my ponytail, my clothing . . . my boyfriend.

Despite all this preparation to get nurses to a place where they can talk the talk, it did not prepare me to communicate effectively with all of my patients all the time. There was no textbook chapter called "The 500 words for penis and poop" that would have been a timesaver for me and my patients.

"Private Parts Parlance for Nurses." Publish that in a pocket size booklet that fits in scrub pants pocket, and you would make a million.

This is an example of a phone conversation I once had with a man calling into a doctor's office where I worked.

"Good morning, this is Nurse Susan. How can I help you?"

"I need to see the doctor."

"What is your medical problem?"

"Uh, I have a, a, a, rash."

"Where is the rash?"

"Down there."

"Down where?"

"Down *there*."

"Your feet?"

"No."

"Your scrotum?"

"Uh, no."

"Your penis."

"No, the other one."

"Your testicles?"

Silence. Then, "Is that your balls?"

"Yes."

"Uh huh."

After everything I have heard and witnessed, I recommend new nurses go with "Got a problem with your privates?" right from the beginning. That way, they avoid having to learn the multiple, mother- and street-taught terms for crotch parts and their excretions. Going off from time to time – as I have been known to do -- on a "what is so wrong with the word penis?" tirade has proved pointless and non-productive. I've had patients stare open-mouthed at me. Some even laugh and say, "There's something wrong with you, man. Get over it."

Venting does help, though, and I always thank my patients for allowing me the floor for my soapbox speech. It gives them something to talk about when visitors wander in and ask what is new today. "My nurse went off her rocker about what people call their private parts," they say, grateful to avoid telling family or friends how bad they are really feeling.

The list of words I have heard over the years is endless. Pee pee, wee wee, whistle, ding dong, man thing, my boy, birdie, dick, prick, the chief, dada, rod, tool. Add your own penis synonyms in here. And women aren't exempt. They, too, take the same vague verbal approach to things gone wrong in the crotch region as their male counterparts.

Here's my most efficient approach to assessing female patients who seem awkward, embarrassed, or are struggling to tell me what the problem with their privates is. In years of self-directed clinical research, I have found giving women a selection of words to use that I find comfortable to say clears the path for accurate communication between us.

At times the conversation can be emotionally difficult.

This is a tough encounter I had with a 40-year-old woman during her visit to the doctor's office where I worked in the early 1980s.

"Why did you come to see the doctor today?" I ask, pen in hand, chart poised.

"I am in trouble," she says quietly, looking scared and humiliated.

I lower my tone and step a little closer to the exam table so she can keep her voice soft. "Got a crotch problem?" I ask quietly as I set the chart and pen on the rolling metal equipment tray nearby and wait.

"Yes." She nods and keeps her head down, twisting her wedding band around and around. Since she seems unsure of how to continue, I offer another question, hoping to provide her with another way to begin talking about the problem.

"Out hole or in hole?"

She looks up at me and tips her head, not sure what I mean.

"You have three holes in your crotch. One hole pee comes out, one hole poop comes out, one hole is for sex," I say as if I was talking elbows and noses.

Her shoulders droop, and she places her hands over face. She can't bring herself to talk. Again, I wait. A moment later she says, "Pee hole, I think."

"Does it hurt to pee?"

"No."

Now I sense she thinks I will be upset when she shares with me what has brought her to see the doctor. I read from her body language and lack of eye contact that she can't bear to say what caused her predicament. I can tell she is embarrassed and can't stomach the thought of sharing it, and I realize it must be quite serious for her to be here and face her issue. I reassure her that what she says is private and then I try to give her an out, seeing if not telling me will help spare her some embarrassment.

"I will only tell the doctor what you say. Or if you want, you can just tell the doctor. I will listen only if you want me to." I pause.

"My husband was masturbating me with an eyebrow pencil, and it disappeared. I can't get it out. I think it went up the hole where I pee."

She leans forward and rests her forehead on my shoulder and starts to cry.

I place a hand on her back and say quietly, "The doctor will help you. I am sure he can help."

Dr. Duffy, the physician I was working for back then, was one of the finest physicians I have ever known – smart, kind, sensitive, and compassionate. He never uttered a whisper of judgment toward any of his patients, no matter how difficult or compromised their health situations appeared to be.

My patient is sitting on the end of the exam table. I keep my hand on her back and wait until she can settle some before I go get the doctor. I give her a gown to change into and a sheet to cover her legs. She nods. She does not need instructions as to what to do with them. When the doctor and I return to the exam room, I repeat her information to him so she does not have to say it again but can add something to it if I missed anything.

Dr. Duffy quietly explains that he will need to examine her to determine the location of the pencil. In silence, he palpates her lower abdomen, and I stand by her side. I silently offer my hand, and she takes it. He tells her he can feel the pencil lying sideways in her bladder. After a brief attempt to turn it to see if he can coax it back down the urethra, he withdraws his hands from the exam, tells her why she will need surgery to remove it, and says he will refer her to the proper surgeon.

We leave the room to let the patient get dressed. She uses our office phone to call her husband while Dr. Duffy contacts the hospital urologist. Her husband tells her he will stay at home with their two little daughters until she can return home from surgery. My heart aches for her as she walks out of our office to face this ordeal all alone.

The challenge to quickly grasp my patients' concerns through the hodgepodge of terms and phrases they use has continued through my varied work environments. It is a challenge I have come to enjoy as I balance being respectful of their language and culture *and* making sure I understand exactly what they are trying to communicate.

During my time as a corrections nurse in jail, I encountered new words and areas for health education that engaged my depth of medical knowledge and teaching creativity. The principles of caring for the ill remain the same, no matter the environment, but it is empathy – the *art* of caring -- that enables a nurse to succeed in patient education.

In the jail system where I worked, certain procedures were standard. For instance, a mandatory physical screening was done on all inmates within 14 days of being booked. It had two main purposes: identify any chronic illnesses that need immediate medical attention or management and document the current state of oral and physical health of an inmate. It came in handy, for example, when an inmate claimed he broke his front tooth out biting on a hard baked bean in the chow hall and wanted to sue the jail to pay for new front teeth. If I had noted in his history and physical (H&P) that he had no front teeth when he was booked, then that is the end of that claim.

I wrote down what I observed and often encountered inmates who had never met a nurse or know what nurses do. When correcting an inmate when he or she addressed me as doctor, I would get a "same difference" shrug. Sometimes I would discover severely high blood pressure, undiagnosed diabetes, or badly infected needle tracks on IV drug users. Many of my inmates had never accessed the healthcare system and were wary of my questions. I was careful of my approach. I was not then, nor am I now, an overbearing, judgmental, or intimidating person, but I have always taken special care to make a positive encounters with all my patients.

The jail H&P took place in a small exam room. There was an exam table, but I didn't use it unless I needed to check the groin or upper legs for sores. The exam room door stayed open. A deputy always remained in my sightline. The inmate sat on a stool next to the counter top where I stood and wrote. There was a three-inch-square metal panic button on the wall behind me, although in six plus years there, I never needed to use it during my time with the inmates for their physical assessment. Precautions were always in place. If an inmate was considered a danger to me, the deputies did not let him come to medical in the first place. In those instances, I would chart that the physical cannot take place due to security issues. Dangerous or flight-risk inmates were sight checked daily by a nurse who made Secured Housing Unit (SHU) rounds accompanied by a deputy, asking those inmates if they have any medical concerns.

I started each assessment by taking blood pressure, temperature, and pulse, then listened to heart and lungs, checked for swollen legs, and asked about any sores, rashes, and other conditions. Then I asked questions about all body systems to identify problems or potential diseases.

Body piercings were not allowed to stay in. They were metal and of potential use to fabricate a weapon. For the most part, the booking deputy had taken care of these things. But if I discovered a tongue piercing, I would tell the inmate to remove it and hand it to me. If he refused or said that it did not come out, I informed the deputy, and the inmate was held in the SHU, in a single cell, not put in general population. If I saw a piece of wooden toothpick stuck through the piercing hole of an ear or eyebrow to keep the hole open, I taught the patient how to watch for the signs and symptoms of infection. Wood holds water, I explained, which can start an infection. Most inmates used a plastic comb tooth to keep the pierced hole open. Grills – ornamental silver or gold-colored tooth coverings -- needed to come out, too. The inmates did not want them off because their teeth had been filed so the grill could be cemented in place. It was their choice again, but usually when faced with the prospect of spending 23 hours a day alone in a cell, they opted for the piercing or appliance to be removed.

If an inmate had tattoos, I suspected they might be inclined to get another one while in jail. I advised them that a jail "tat" was a bad idea, as it carried the risk of exposure to blood-borne pathogens. Mostly tattoos were acquired in prisons, not in my jail.

This assessment time may be the only time with an inmate I would have. Once they were sentenced, they would move to a prison facility, so I would make the most of the opportunity. A tattoo from inside a corrections facility was a status symbol many younger inmates wanted to acquire. It was a badge of toughness, I suppose. The state health department saw several HIV cases coming from these tats. The ink used was from melted plastic or burned material, and typically each new jail tat did not get new ink. Because the inmates were terrified of catching "the virus, "I made clear the risk they took getting a tat in jail. "Make sure you get new ink and a new needle," I urged them if they were determined to get a tattoo, either in or out of jail.

I also learned how injectable breast implants were performed on the street from a transvestite who told me in a disgusted tone that he/she wasted money that way. Seems silicone caulk was injected via basting needle. This inmate showed me partially healed needle holes under the armpits that indicated where the needles were inserted. While the breasts looked great in the short term, soon the solution all leaked back out of the slow-to-heal puncture holes. I would think silicone would harden and must say I never saw this procedure done. For all I know, it could have been a fictional tale. Tell this nurse anything, she believes it. I asked other trans inmates about this and could get no one to refute it. The street cost for this breast augmentation told to me was 50 bucks. "Much cheaper than paying for actual surgeon-inserted implants," was the typical response.

Once I asked a trans inmate who was two weeks post-op breast implants from a plastic surgeon if there was any sign of infection or pain in the incision.

"Nope, they feel great," was the answer. "Girrrrrll, you should get you some."

"Uh, no thanks. I am too afraid of the infections I have seen in the implants gone wrong in some patients," I said. He then recommended that I get a water bra. At that, we both laughed out loud and got "keep it down" looks from the deputy.

At this time, inmates were placed in housing based on anatomical criteria as verified in booking by the deputy. I don't recall that any inmates in the process of gender reassignment ever protested, although that would not be an issue I would be likely to hear about.

This inmate had large new breasts, beautiful wavy hair, pretty eyes, and a big butt. He was very popular and in demand in his job as a street sex worker, as he self-identified, and on his jail pod. He sought the attention. I asked when his last screening for HIV had been done.

"Not for years," he shared, adding, "It didn't matter." Even if he tested positive, he said, he would not take the prescribed drugs.

In jail, medicines were brought to each building four times a day by the med nurse. Pill call took place at the dayroom pod door through a mail letter-sized slot. The nurse had her med cart parked at the door. A clear plastic cup holding an inmate's pills was filled with water and passed through the slot. The inmate swallowed it and showed the nurse his or her open mouth.

Pass a cup through the slot three or four times a day that is full of pills, and all the other inmates know what disease you have, this trans inmate said. He knew the revelation of HIV would end his run as the center of attention in his pod. I asked him to drop a note to medical to be scheduled for an HIV screen. He said he would think about it but never followed through. I informed the jail physician of this encounter, worried about the potential public health risk this inmate posed to the jail population. Dismissively, he told me he would take care of it. Unconvinced of his sincerity I adopted my own blunt strategy. I formulated a pop quiz for each inmate I encountered for a physical.

"Who do you think has HIV here in jail?" I would ask.

"How do I know?" or some variation on that theme was the usual reply.

"What about me, do you think I have HIV?" I would continue.

"Uh, no," would be the reply.

"Well, you should!" I proclaimed. "I am exposed to blood many times a day. You should think everybody you meet in here has the virus and protect yourself." I would then share a few facts about blood-borne pathogens and offer an HIV screening. Even with my cautionary words, I had very few takers over the years.

At the conclusion of every physical assessment, I offered the inmate a blood screening for syphilis. At that time, in the early 2000s, the state health department would pay for a syphilis screening for any inmate willing to take one. Once an inmate was convicted and sentenced to prison, a thorough physical including HIV screen was done when they are moved to the penitentiary. At jail, the history and physical or syphilis blood test is not mandatory. If an inmate wished, he could sign a refusal and skip it. However, if an inmate wanted to be a trustee worker within the jail, he had to have the H&P, and the syphilis screening had to turn up negative results. If they had syphilis, they could be treated, retested, and requalify for a trustee job.

* * *

One day an inmate urgently tells me during his assessment, "I got the girls jumpin' in the trees." He is looking up at me intensely from the stool next to my exam room desk top. I am standing off to his side and thoughtfully return his gaze. He waits while I think. He opens his mouth to speak, and I hold up a hand to stop him. I move around from his side to face him directly.

"Wait, let me figure it out," I say.

Hmm. Since he is a guy, I figure that "girls" is my first clue. If he were a woman, it would be "the boys jumpin' in the trees." Must be a crotch situation, I think. He watches me as I say slowly; "You got *girls. . .jumpin'. . .trees.*" He nods solemnly to each word.

My eyebrows pop up and I say, "I'll be right back." I go to the nurses' desk for a piece of scotch tape. I hand him the strip of tape, point to the hall bathroom, and say, "Go get me one. The bathroom is right there."

He grins and hoots, "You got it, Doc!"

Pubic lice.

* * *

Over the years, most problematic for my patients and I are encounters where I assume he or she knows what I am talking about. Terms I think are generally understood are not.

Close encounters of the worst kind with constipation during my childhood have made me intimately aware of the definition of "suppository." By the time I am a nurse, I think everyone knows the meaning of this word. Assuming this and other things, however, usually proves to be an ill-advised course of action for any nurse.

This first became apparent when I was a student nurse. During my six-week rotation through the OB-GYN outpatient clinic, I cared for a young woman with a raging vaginal yeast infection. The poor soul was in itchy crotch hell. I did great at the blood pressure and pulse and temperature and history of the problem etc. The doctor came in, did the pelvic exam, and made the diagnosis. I went to the drug cabinet and got the seven-pack of vaginal suppositories as I was told to do. I opened the pack, tore one foil pack off, and put everything on the rolling metal table next to the patient, along with the applicator plunger. I forgot gloves and the box in the exam room was empty, so I left the room to get some.

When I returned, my patient said, "That was the biggest pill I have ever seen. Man, it was hard to swallow."

I smothered a gasp and ran for my instructor, who returned with me. She calmly explained to the patient that these particular "pills" would work much better directly on the skin where the infection was located. Swallowing one pill was not going to hurt her, but now Nurse Susan would show her how to use the applicator to put the suppositories where they would do the most good. My instructor then left the room.

"Thank God," the patient told me. "I was dreading swallowing six more of those horse pills." She was relieved and not embarrassed. I was relieved but still felt as though I had been hit by a gong.

From this and other episodes of slightly misunderstood patient teaching, I became passionate about being thorough and clear, carefully choosing words that I felt were most accurate and least open to multiple interpretations.

Time can be tight if you have a huge patient load or a patient's condition deteriorates and requires more of your attention. Teaching is often the factor that gets dropped. Over my career, I came to consider it the most important aspect of all I do and sorely regret the times I was unable to complete the teaching task that I had wanted to do. Typed self-care guidelines are no substitute for verbal teaching. At best, they serve as a reminder of information a nurse has already carefully and thoroughly delivered.

During the years of doing jail health screenings, I began to see trends in the health consequences of confinement. There were common afflictions associated with sitting most of the day. At some point, I happened to have a conversation with an older female inmate, who told me many of the young girls in her pod came to her with health questions. As part of the substance abuse program in which this woman was participating, time was set aside daily for health instruction. The inmates would choose a topic, find information in the jail library, then do a poster presentation to the group. The woman told me a lot of the information was either old or not understood well and, therefore, was communicated incorrectly. Together, the two of us pondered if I might be able to help in some way.

When approached, both my Health Services Administrator and my Director of Nursing did not want me to have anything to do with teaching inmates about wellness promotion. They said I needed to focus all my time on health screenings. I thought about how many sick call slips could be avoided if all new inmates received information that could help them with common health problems related to being locked up. But I still needed to get around the fact that I did not have the time endorsement of my superiors to make it happen.

Then one day it occurred to me that I was the only non-smoking nurse on the unit. Two to eight times a shift, the other nurses would leave Medical, walk past Central Security, go up through the administration building, grab their smokes from a locker, and stroll out front to the smoking area. Every nurse smoked one or two cigarettes before coming back in the building, putting their smokes in the locker, retracing their steps through the administration building, going back through Security, and returning to Medical. I did the math. Five minutes each way, plus five to ten minutes smoking, two to eight times a shift. The Director of Nursing was the only nurse who went out eight times a shift. That looked like 20 minutes times eight to me. One hundred sixty minutes. I only needed 45.

At 3 pm each Monday, after all my assessments had been completed for that day, I'd tell my Director I was going on my smoke break and instead made a beeline for the women' s pod for a health seminar, topic determined by the group. My supervisor never said a word to me about the quality or quantity of the health screenings. I take pride in completing all my work to meet the state and nursing standard of care and beyond. I was not challenged regarding my sudden development of a smoking habit after years of uninterrupted nose-to-the-grindstone work at the jail.

During the time when inmates were back in their pods for headcount, it had been my habit to help the unit secretary file charts or papers into charts, fill the copy machine with paper, or empty trash. She gave me her blessing about the class and a few ideas of topics to cover that the inmates had talked to her about. The sick call and med nurses fed me the health concerns of the week to address while I was at the pod sharing with the ladies.

The day of my first group teaching session arrives. The inmate who came up with the idea of me joining the women's inmate group during their time of health education introduces me at the first meeting. She tells the women that I do not have permission to teach the class but that I am using my smoke break to come join the group. I hear har hars all around and feel welcomed by most of them.

We sit in a circle, in white plastic lawn chairs in their carpeted dayroom, two levels of cells around the perimeter. Every cell door is open. A female deputy, dressed in a brown uniform, sits at a desk near the pod door just outside our circle of chairs. The deputy carries no weapon, only handcuffs, keys, and a radio.

Gray carpet, turquoise doors and white-tiled floors in the cells give a clean look to the pod, even though it is spare of furniture or decoration. A few posters that have been drawn by inmates hang on the walls. Each cell sports single metal cots with worn two-inch mattresses draped with white sheets and Army-style blankets. There is one pillow per cot. Any inmate who wants an extra pillow simply folds up her clothes and tucks them into the case for added height.

The women inmates are dressed in jail-issued blue jeans, light blue cotton button shirts, and black cloth sneakers or flip flops. They are given two white cotton undershirts and two pairs of white cotton, waist high, "granny panties" to wear. They also are allotted two bras, but only if their size is available.

No make-up is allowed, nor hair extensions. No jewelry except for a wedding band and a small religious necklace. This is a substance abuse treatment program pod. Perhaps other pods do not allow the necklace; I do not know all the security details.

Some women buy Skittles candy during weekly canteen visits and use the dye from the candy to make lipstick or eye shadow. They are reprimanded when caught and made to wash it off. It doesn't happen much on this pod.

Because the substance abuse rehab program is inmate run, rules are strictly enforced. The three group leaders are voted into place and hold office until voted out, moved to another facility, or released. Inmates apply to get in to the program and either participate by the rules or are kicked out by the inmate leaders. No negotiations. They get two warnings per infraction. The third time the rules are broken, out they go. Since participating and graduating from a program like this is looked upon with favor by the local judges, who may adjust the sentence length, there is plenty of incentive for compliance, even if it is done reluctantly.

On this day, I sit between two inmates who smile warmly at me. I wear pink scrub pants, white shoes, pink socks, and a flowered pink scrub top. My straight brown hair is pulled back in a ponytail with a bright pink scrunchie. I slowly scan the circle and smile at those who look my way. Some women keep their eyes downcast. They are young and old, late teens to mid-70s. Black and white. Thin and heavy. Well-groomed and tidy.

Sitting together are six young white women, perhaps late teens or early 20s, who had been arrested at a recent college party for heroin possession. They are awaiting trial. Two years from now, after three tries at rehab, one of them will be dead from an accidental heroin overdose. Now she looks vigorous and full of life, her thick red hair curling around her small freckled face.

I also see three visibly pregnant women.

The group meeting starts with the leaders asking for comments. The rehab program runs from 5 am to 7 pm with classes, group sessions, and exercising -- all mandatory. A note from medical for very short-term absence is allowed on a case-by-case basis. The standards for participation are rigorous.

A few inmates raise their hands, and one is acknowledged. "I want to give a push up to Mandy for not getting mad when I told her that her breath was bad and she had to brush her teeth. She just went and brushed her teeth." Members of the group raise their hands, palms up, and chorus "Push up, Mandy." More push-ups are offered, as well as a pull-down. The pull-down concerns haughty behavior over a cup of tea. A solution is discussed, and an apology is given.

The group leaders nod my way. My inmate friend introduces me, "This is Nurse B." B is the first initial of my former last name. She says it in a way that makes me realize they knew I was coming.

"Hi, Nurse B," I hear 25 voices say all at once for the first time. It startles me, and I let out a giggle. Some of them giggle back. I stand and begin to walk toward the group leaders across the circle to give them handouts on the health and wellness seminars I am proposing.

"Stop," one leader barks harshly. "You are breaking the circle."

I return to my seat. I apologize and say that I do not know the rules. I ask that they teach me the rules so I will not unintentionally disrespect the group. I am serious and sincere. There is dead quiet. My inmate friend tells me to walk around the inside of the circle. I get up and step tightly around the inside curve of the circle, give the leaders their copies of the two-page handout, and ask them if I can hand the rest out. They answer, "OK."

As I finish, my inmate friend addresses me, "Nurse B, we are not allowed to have anything with a staple in it. These are stapled."

"Thanks for telling me. I will come back around. Everyone remove the staple and hand it back to me," I say as I once again make my way around the inside of the circle. This time, more of the women look right at me. Some seem to be looking to see if I am pissed at being reprimanded. Others smile encouragingly. They all have been through learning the rules. Now it's my turn.

I return to my seat and tell them this handout is a draft of an idea and that I want to offer ideas on how to stay well in jail to all the new female inmates. I ask them to read it, tell me what they think, and give me more suggestions to add to it. Under the constipation section, several inmates recommend I include "Eat the jalapeno cheese crackers from canteen," as they give everyone the squirts. Also, that I add that using toothpaste helps with an acne breakout. Save your shampoo bottles, fill with warm water, and use as a warm compress on your stomach when you have menstrual cramps is another suggested addition.

Over the next few weeks, we review the document, and they are very proud when they receive the result. It is jail health and wellness management written by these incarcerated women to help other women during their time in jail. The group leaders take the task of giving it to newly committed inmates.

On another one of our Monday sessions, I arrive to obvious turmoil in the group. A debate had started earlier that day and would be the topic of today's health meeting. I was told I was to announce the solution, and it would be respected as the final decision. The tension in the room washed over me, and harsh glances flew my way. Whatever this was, it had created strong opinions on either side.

The meeting began, and I waited for the nod. There were no raised hands. No push-ups today. "OK, Nurse B," I hear. "You're up."

"Hi, I'm Nurse B."

"Hi, Nurse B."

The room feels edgy. I have no idea what is causing such friction. I wait. Hands fly up. I point to what I thought was the first hand to go up.

"You believe in underwear. Don't you, Nurse B?" the inmate asks pointedly, leaving no question as to her stand on the matter.

While still processing her question, I point to another hand. As high as this woman is reaching into the air, I could tell she is a member of the opposing team. "I never wore underwear, and I am never gonna wear underwear," she states. "My Momma did not wear underwear, and my baby don't wear underwear."

I keep pointing until I have heard from every raised hand. The votes seem somewhat in favor of underwear vs. no underwear. The deputy leans forward on her elbows at her desk watching the scene with interest. Her chin is tipped up, and she is smiling. I briefly wonder if there are side bets on this performance of mine. By now, the deputies have seen me maneuver my way out of many a verbal duel over topics such as this. The deputy probably just wants to see how I will pull it off. For me, this is the fun part of nursing. Underwear is not a chapter topic in any nursing curriculum, but I can clearly see it as a health-related issue.

After everyone speaks, I pause a few seconds to gather my thoughts and allow the silence to pull their attention toward me. My first approach is to discuss the brief history of underwear as I know it, along with its purpose. We all agree that underwear protects the outer clothing from crotch fluids. Except, of course, for thongs, which I note are just a highway for bacteria to stroll straight from the anus right to the vagina and bladder where they do not belong and can cause infection.

"And while we are on the topic of thongs," I say. "I cannot recommend wearing the black plastic thongs some of you are making from the Hefty trash bags."

"Ooh, Nurse B, how did you know about that?" someone asks. I see hands over mouths and hear giggling. I ignore the question and proceed.

"Yes, and another thing while we are having this crotch discussion. I do not recommend sharing your homemade, washcloth dildos, as they cannot be thoroughly cleaned, and you know that HIV can spread that way, make your own and use it on your own self. Actually, just use your fingers. They can be washed well." I say all this as if I am teaching a patient to use an inhaler. I sit back and let it all sink in.

I look over to see the deputy, who is now on the phone. I can't read lips, but she is talking furiously, then laughing out loud. She cannot be heard over the mayhem in the circle.

"This is information you need to prevent exposure to infections that can kill you." That's what I tell the group when the leaders finally restore silence.

The laughing break had given me time to think back to the controversial underwear dilemma. I tell them that as long as I can remember, I had never gone without underwear. I put it on right after a shower, wear it to bed and under my clothes, and change it every day. I would not be able or willing to go without underwear. I do not want anyone to tell me to not wear underwear; it is what I am used to. I would not tell anyone to wear it or not wear it. Cleanliness is the issue, I tell them. But keep in mind, I add, clothes that get wet in the crotch area are a breeding ground for bacteria and yeast and fungus.

"Ever see a diaper rash?" I ask. Oh yeahs, all around. "Ever see athlete's foot?" Oh ,yeahs again. "They develop because organisms that cause infection have a warm, dark, moist environment in which to breed. Bugs love warm, dark, moist places. As long as you keep yourself clean and dry," I note, "whether with underwear or without, the bugs won't grow." I conclude with, "Nothing else counts, only cleanliness. So, keep yourself clean and dry and mind your own beeswax about what everybody else is wearing or not wearing."

Everyone seems to think her side won. I hear, "Thanks, Nurse B," from numerous voices as I leave the pod.

The next week during my shift on Medical, I hear from some deputies, who thought I would deny it, that I was anti-thong and pro individual dildos.

"That's true," I reply.

"Oh … uh, yeah," the deputy stammers, surprised by my response.

"It's about infection control," I say.

From then on, the deputies call my weekly health meetings "coochie class" instead of my cigarette break. As the months pass, the ever-changing ebb and flow of inmates spurs discussions on a huge variety of topics, including cancer, diabetes, obesity, eating disorders, even meth mouth.

IV drug users ask if the burns they got from cutting drugs with vinegar before injecting them would ever heal. "Heal, yes. Scar, yes," I tell them. "Bad idea. And use your own works, clean it with bleach, and don't share," I would add.

We keep a three-ring binder for the handouts I bring with information I had researched on the Internet about all these topics.

Our weekly visits continue for about two years. I learn a lot of rules. On the occasion when I speak out of turn, I am told to wait. I soon feel very much a part of this group of women. On Valentine's Day, I am presented with a fancy handmade card, signed by all the inmates, each offering a few words of thanks. It has been colored using Skittles water.

Opening the card, I cry. The women are upset by my tears, but I am touched beyond words. I want to hug the young woman who presented me with the card but that is not allowed, and I can't break the rules – inmate or not. I respect their standard and live by it.

At some point near the two-year mark, a schedule change in the inmates' drug rehab program bumps coochie class out for another activity. The inmates and I protest, but the decision has come from the higher ups and is final.

Not long after that, a new medical contractor change at the jail bumps me out of a job. Their human resource director, a twenty-something female, tells me my position does not fit their financial matrix. She assigns my job duties to the Director of Nursing.

I had served almost seven years in jail as a nurse and was sorely disappointed to be leaving. The men and women I had met and taught any variety of health care and self-care instruction enriched my understanding of myself and humanity and the life of those in the vast world of correctional systems who cope in ways that are sometimes against the law but often needed for self-preservation.

Through my work at the jail, I learned that being incarcerated is sometimes a safety choice made by pregnant young women so they can receive regular prenatal care, have a clean bed, and not be assaulted by siblings or other family members. Twice during my time at the jail, I saw two young girls choose this strategy to keep themselves and their unborn babies safe.

Others committed non-violent crimes just so they could come in for chemo, dental care, dialysis, or protection. In jail, the state pays for your medical care. Psychiatric care there provided access to a psychiatrist and meds, and inmates recovered and became functional. They felt so good that when they left and had no money for their psych medications, they did not think they would need them. Off meds, however, they became violent again. It was a revolving door.

I came to know a young black man who spent time in medical after being blinded in a gang gunfight. He was in jail for selling drugs out of his grandmother's home, but his sentence was commuted due to his visual disability. This inmate begged not to be released. He was now considered a rat and knew his testimony in court had convicted several opposing gang members to long sentences for his wounding and other homicides. His family convinced him he was safe to come home. No one would shoot a blind man, they reassured him. They would be there for him, to guard him, to protect him, and to be his eyes.

He was shot dead in his home, while sitting in his wheelchair, the day after his release from jail.

9

JOSEY

Determined to become a nurse but too young to qualify for a job with pay, I looked for ways to get health care experience before I turned 16. For two summers, beginning in 1966, I volunteered as a candy striper on the pediatric ward of Philadelphia General Hospital, bathing children and babies and changing diapers. The work, as basic as it was, not only touched my young heart, it underscored a growing certainty that nursing was my life's path.

When I finally became old enough to apply for a job with compensation, I looked for a nurse's aide position at a nursing home within reach from my home by bus.

For economic reasons, I assume, the director of Blessed John Neumann Nursing Home hired a dozen or so teenage girls and a few boys every summer as nurse aides to augment her staff and provide backup while regular employees took vacation time. During my interview, I told Sister Beatta, the director, that I planned to attend nursing school and wanted to gain patient care experience. I was hired on the spot and started the very next day.

Commuting to the nursing home took at least an hour – a two-block walk to the Bridge Street bus stop, a ride from there to the bus depot, and then a transfer to the Roosevelt Boulevard bus that dropped me off at my new place of employment. To be at work by 7 am, I left home at 5:30. I never minded the early start. With everyone still asleep, the house was quiet and peaceful for my bowl of cereal and cup of tea. The fully loaded buses carried men and women to their jobs all over the city, and I found the rocking side-to-side motion of the oversized vehicle soothing. My Dad's interest in people watching spilled directly into my bones, and every bus ride provided endless entertainment.

My first day at the nursing home was pretty much sink or swim. There was no formal orientation for new employees nor instruction on basic patient care. I shadowed the nurses and nurse's aides for my first few days, then was given assignments on my own. Being surrounded by co-workers my age made for a festive and supportive work environment. From day one, I was in my element. And Mrs. O (as she was called because of her hard-to-pronounce last name), our extraordinarily kind and compassionate head nurse, allowed our playful behavior to blossom once our assignments for the day were complete.

Seven of us teenagers -- six girls and one boy -- worked day shift on Mrs. O's wing my first summer there. Like the rest of the girls, I wore a white dress uniform, white hose, and white cork-bottomed clogs. The ends of the white ribbon holding back my hair in a long ponytail trailed down the middle of my back. I thought I looked very cool and professional.

We were permitted small earrings and a small chain necklace, our fingernails had to be trimmed short, and eye shadow was not allowed. Mrs. O only enforced the eye shadow ban if bright blue appeared. Although it still felt naughty, we would wear silver shimmer shadow, eyeliner, and mascara when we thought we could get away with it. Yes, we told ourselves and each another, we were *bad*.

The nursing home, a one-story brick structure, was built on a rise of land overlooking the 12-lane thoroughfare of Roosevelt Boulevard, a main access road to downtown Philly. The building was divided into four wings. I worked on the wing that housed about 30 bed-bound men and women. Some had been there for years. Most left only to be buried.

Our wing was V-shaped. The nurses' station desk sat at the point of the V. The white tiled floors echoed our hurried footfalls as we carried out our daily assignments caring for the fading, infirm population. Rooms were sparsely appointed. Each resident was assigned a hospital bed, a bedside table, and a rolling table that could be positioned over the bed as needed. Each room contained a single long closet with sliding doors that held the clothing for all a room's occupants.

The men residents lived two in a room. A few women residents had a private room, but most lived four beds to a room. Other than their wheelchair, clothes, eyeglasses, a couple of books, a photo or two, and – more often than not -- dentures, these elders had none of their personal belongings to reveal anything about who they were or where they had come from. Visitors were scant, with most arriving on weekends, especially on Sunday mornings for Mass in our small, tranquil chapel.

Each morning, Mrs. O would hand out the bath assignments and provide any updates on needed care. Usually, nothing was new. She designed the assignments so that if four patients were in a room, I got two, and Denise got two. If two patients were in a room, I got one, and Denise got one. How the work was done and in what order was up to us. Mrs. O was training us to collaborate on patient care, a skill I would treasure for the rest of my career. Due to this clever assignment strategy, Denise and I – not only co-workers but also friends -- often teamed up to bathe and groom our patients.

After breakfast finished and all trays collected, we would begin giving shower baths. We used a rolling aluminum chair fitted with a toilet seat perch to move a patient from the bed, down the hall to the shower room. It was an easy and safe transport, and with two of us working together we could lessen the length of time our blanket wrapped but easily chilled patients were naked. Most of our ladies delighted in the commotion we created as we hastily undressed them, wrapped them in a white flannel bath sheet, and transferred them to the shower chair. The process could mean a stand and pivot or a simple lift from the bed to the shower chair, one of us holding the patient under the arms and the other under the legs. Most of our ladies were on the small side and were easily moved without risk of us injuring ourselves. Then we rolled them down the hall in their flannel blanket cocoon to the steamy shower room. For some -- our patients who liked it -- we pushed the chair at a brisk clip hollering, "Don't get cold. Don't get cold." It was easy to see that the summer's upbeat pace of care and activity delivered by youthful aides lifted spirits after the long, quiet months when there were few, if any, teens on duty.

Mrs. O allowed us to bring a record player to the unit. We would play Motown songs while we worked. Because so many residents had age related hearing impairments, we played Smokey Robinson, The Four Tops, and The Temptations at full volume. Occasionally one of the male aides would dance and twirl to the music at the resident's room doorway. Despite dreadful imitations of some of the more popular musical groups' moves, the staff and residents laughed and applauded generously.

Among the residents, Josephina, or Josey to us, became an immediate favorite with all the teens. We often would start the shower rotation with Josey, who loved to be squeaky clean.

"OK, Josey. Time for your bath!" We'd hoot this while getting together her bathing supplies and outfit for the day.

"Oh, nichts, nichts, nichts," she would tease in her deep German voice, mocking the three other women in the room, who disliked their shower and complained loudly when it was their twice-weekly turn. Josey did not speak English, and we did not speak German. But together we developed a collection of signs and phrases we mutually understood, and Josey would fill in the blanks with her goodhearted and cheerful boops and whoops, finger pointing, and infinite patience. She was a magnificent woman, tall and big-boned. At some point in her not-too-distant past, a poorly mended broken hip had rendered her unable to walk. But she could hold onto the bed rail and stand on her strong leg, turn, and, with our help, guide herself into the wheelchair. We could tell getting from here to there was painful. We could see her silent grimaces.

Most mornings when I greeted Josey, she would be sitting up in bed, legs stretched out in front of her, knees gently bent. She would be clutching her worn flannel nightgown to her chest and grinning, while her thick, shoulder-length hair looked for all the world like a tousled crown of silver, still tangled from sleep.

I'd rub my chest to pantomime. "Josey, your bath will be fast. Schnell, schnell, schnell," I would say with a grin back at her, adding to the show.

"Goot, goot, goot," Josey would answer with many nods.

Denise and I had worked out a routine. She stood behind the shower chair, locking it next to the bed and steadying it while I helped Josey scoot her legs over the side of the bed and stand slowly on her strong foot, turn her back to the shower chair, then lower her into it, my arms wrapped around her waist, her arms wrapped around me. Denise would pull up the often sweaty and sometimes urine-soaked nightgown so Josey would not sit on it. Gathering up the nightgown from the back, I would quickly ease it over Josey's head while Denise wrapped the flannel sheet around Josey, being certain to cover her completely for the trip to the bathroom and then the shower room. Denise always added a hug as she draped the sheet around Josey's shoulders. In return, Josey would grab Denise's hands and press them to her sheet-covered chest. This was our bath-time ritual.

We would roll the shower chair over the toilet bowl, and Josey would pee with a vengeance, the urine stream splashing loudly, a sound that obviously tickled her. Her eyes would widen, and she would round her lips into a big O, let out a deep-throated whoop of relief, and laugh. While she finished in the bathroom, I would remove the bed sheets, wipe down the mattress, and allow the bed to air out.

"Gosh Josey, you really had to pee," one of us would say, pointing to the toilet bowl in wonder.

"Oh, ya, ya, ya." She would nod furiously, her blue eyes twinkling. Josey's daily schedule was not under her control. She went to bed when the staff could transfer her there, ate when the dining hall served food, and sat in her wheelchair all day. She knew that activities, diversions, and entertainment would have to be of her own making – with a little help from a couple of youthful accomplices.

With great care, we would maneuver the shower chair from her bathroom out into the hallway. Denise would tap Josey's outstretched legs, prompting her to hold them up. Josey would lean back and grip the chair arms. Denise loved to rocket Josey down the hall with accompanying engine noises and screeching brake sounds, but only if Mrs. O was out of sight. Josey and Denise got caught in this routine one day. Mrs. O shook her finger at Denise and gave her "the look." Josey responded with a deep "Uh-oh, uh-oh," covering her face with gnarled, arthritic hands. Once they had reached the shower room, though, they both laughed loud and long, the sound echoing all over the wing. Mrs. O just shook her head and smiled at me as I hurried down the hall toward the shower room to help.

The communal bathing room, with its white-tiled walls and floor, held twin shower stalls, a single tub with a lifting sling, and wooden benches for supplies. A drain in the center of each three-walled shower stall kept the floor safe for the staff. Once we were all inside, the windowless door would close behind us with a thud, signaling that it was time to get to work. I never entered the room when it was occupied by another patient and nurse. Even though there were two shower stalls, there was no curtain between them. Privacy, I understood, was too important to sacrifice for expedience. Not all the staff felt the same way.

To begin the bathing process, Denise would start the water flowing from the hose nozzle and regulate the temperature, holding it over Josey's outstretched hand for approval. When Josey gave the nod, Denise would hand the nozzle to Josey, who would wet her own hair and body. Always careful to avoid wetting us, Josey would let the water run over her legs as we soaped her upper body. Then she put the water stream over her chest as we washed her legs. I would take the nozzle to rinse Josey's hair, waiting to see that her eyes were squeezed shut and that her fingers covered her face as well as they possibly could. Josey loved this part and rumbled a deep and long "Hm, hm, hmmmm."

As I worked, I would study those big hands, wondering what loving labor they had performed during her long life. Had she been a banker, a scientist, a seamstress? A farmer or a musician? A mother or aunt? All of these . . . or none. Josey was 94. The entire time I worked there, no one ever visited her. And because she and I didn't speak the same language – at least in words – I never was able to ask her my many questions. But even at my young age, I recognized that our bathing ritual was an ongoing and dependable form of communication. In a very real sense, we let our hands do the talking.

By the time I finished rinsing Josey's hair, Denise would have three towels at the ready. We all got a towel. Josey dried her arms, chest, and thighs. I would gently dry her hair, and Denise would dry whatever Josey could not reach. The shower room would get steamy and very warm as we proceeded, and Denise and I would work up a sweat. One of us would squeeze lotion into all three pairs of hands, and together we would gently and firmly rub Josey's papery skin. She would lean forward, hands tucked over her tummy so her back could be rubbed and massaged. She was quiet for this. With closed eyes, she would relax into our gentle, rubbing motions.

In a precision-type drill, we then pulled an undershirt and dress over Josey's head. Always as I reached her hand through the dress sleeve, Josey would squeeze my hand to her chest and smile at me. I smiled back. White cotton socks and black, chunky-heeled shoes went over Josey's feet. Sometimes I would take off my corked clogs and slip into Josey's immense black shoes, size 12 or bigger, and slap around the shower room announcing with each step, "I am Josey."

"Oh, nichts, nichts, nichts," she would say, grinning and shaking her head in delight. She would point to herself and tap her chest.

We would maneuver the shower chair until it sat next to the grab bar on the wall. Josey would hold the bar with both hands, and with my hands under one armpit I'd help her stand. In that position, I would hold up the back of her dress while Denise dried and rubbed on more lotion. Denise would pull up the underpants, pull down and straighten the dress, and remove the shower chair. The wheelchair that had been waiting was rolled into place, tapping Josey lightly behind the knees. On that cue, Josey would lower herself into the chair, holding the armrests for balance.

Out into the hallway we'd go. Six more ladies still needed their showers. Josey would grab the wheelchair grab bar that ran the length of the hallway parallel to the floor about three and a half feet up. This is how she would navigate her chair down the hallway, pushing with her feet and pulling with her hands as she began her slow, daily excursion around all four wings of the home via the connecting back hallways.

Josey had assigned herself the job of floor inspector. For hours she patrolled the building, thoroughly engrossed in picking up the slightest speck of dust, thread of clothing or particle of food she found on the hallway floors. When she appeared in front of her room at lunchtime, I would hold both my hands out, and she would deposit her morning findings.

"Ooooo, boop, boop, boop," she would murmur to me quietly.

"Man, Josey. Good job." I would nod approvingly and take the collection of threads, paper, and dust to the trash can. Josey would wheel herself into her bathroom. I would get the sink water warmed and soap up my hands. She would reach her hands over the sink and put them under the water. Once they were wet, I ran my soapy hands over hers, my right hand into her left hand, my left hand into her right hand. Once our hands were rinsed, Josey would often squeeze mine with her own, letting out a hearty, "heeheehee."

After lunch, Josey would head to the connecting back hallway at the end of our wing. Every day she sought solitude and privacy in those unused corridors. At intervals I would peek around the corner to be sure she was OK. She would be looking out the floor-to-ceiling windows at the courtyards' grass and trees. She loved birds. Sometimes if she caught me looking, she would point toward the birds and hold her finger to her lips, signaling me to be quiet. I would nod and step back. This was her time. Sometimes she would doze in her chair, and sometimes she would sing. "Ave Maria" was the only song I ever heard her sing. Her deep melodic voice boomed from the back hall, causing the rest of the ward to fall silent. Residents and staff would slow to a stop, standing in place or maybe leaning on a wall. The sound of her voice was haunting and emotional, reverent and poignant. Once when I tried to sneak a glimpse of her singing, she caught me looking, immediately stopped, and shook her head. No one would ever see her sing, not even me. *No one.* This was her sacred time and space. But many of us chose to remain silently out of sight and just listen.

Early one warm summer morning, I entered Josey's room to greet her. Usually I would hop onto the mattress at the bottom of the bed, and Josey would sit up, hold her gown to her chest with one hand, and point to the window at whatever was unfolding outside in nature. Softly she cooed, "Ooo, boop boop boop." I would nod and watch for a few moments in silence with her.

On this morning, however, as soon as she spied me, she jerked to a sitting position and frantically beckoned. She pointed to the bathroom and whooped urgently. *Uh oh*, I thought. I needed help fast to get her to the bathroom, and everyone nearby was busy. My inexperience then led me into big trouble.

"OK, Josey. I will help you." I said as I quickly lowered the bed's side rails and locked her wheelchair next to the bed. Josey painfully shoved her legs over the side of the mattress and wiggled until she was sitting on the edge of the bed. I straddled her legs, squeezed her feet together, blocked her knees with mine, and shoved her arms around my back. She squeezed my shoulders. I wrapped my arms around her waist and moved my feet in front of hers to support her while she stood.

Softly but urgently, she continued to moan, "Booop, booop, boooop." Without a cue from me, Josey tried to stand, and I tried to pull. Somewhere between the standing and pulling, Josey's cotton-stockinged feet began to slide away from the bed. My feet shifted to try to stand her. But once her feet broke traction, there was no stopping her.

"Oh no," I groaned.

I knew Josey was twice my weight. I knew I could not lift her. I knew I could not get her back sitting on the bed. I tipped her back toward the mattress and tried to rest her back and shoulders on the bed, thinking I could pivot her legs back onto the bed. Instead, I became tangled in her feet. I held onto her waist with all my might. She managed to get her back onto the mattress but not far enough. I was now lying on top of her. She was in a slow slide toward the floor. Gravity was finishing us both off. I was now on my knees holding her under the arms so she would not hit the floor hard. Thankfully, the bed was in the low position, so it was not a long journey. When her butt touched the floor, I breathlessly asked, "Are you OK?"

Josey released a deep-chested, rumbling laugh, nodding yes in reply, then threw her head back and let out a loud belly laugh. Kneeling between her feet, I laughed, too, tears of relief welling up as I realized she was unhurt. The next moment I saw that her laughter wasn't just because she was unhurt. It was obvious she no longer had an urgent need to get to the bathroom. A pee puddle had begun to emerge from under her read end. We both looked wide-eyed at the growing stream, then at each other and laughed harder, making the pee come even faster. I pushed myself back away from the river that was headed my way and stumbled to stand, weak from both relief and laughter.

Mrs. O heard our commotion, which had prompted the three other women in the room to scream for help. Entering the room hurriedly, she stopped at my feet to survey the spectacle. She could see we did not seem to be hurt. There we were, Josey, me, the pee puddle, and the bed sheets and blankets that had slid with us to the floor. Josey held her sides and laughed harder. Mrs. O joined in.

Before it was all over, the entire ward staff stood over us. Each new staff member who entered the room got a bug-eyed funny face from Josey, who would then point to the pee, offer up a few "boop boops," and start laughing again.

I learned my lesson. Never again did I escort a patient to the floor because of a poorly planned bed-to-chair transfer. I waited for help, no matter what. For her part, Josey developed a pointing-and-booping retelling of the story of that day that never ceased to delight me. With beautiful comic twists of her mouth, nose, and eyes, we would relive our misadventure. I egged her on, miming parts of the scene. Josey forgave me through this retelling. She replaced her own embarrassment with joyful glee. She replaced my catastrophizing with knowledge.

I left Blessed John Neumann Nursing Home at the end of the following summer. I was beginning nursing school and needed a job closer to my dorm downtown. My last day with Josey was pure agony for me. I told her I was leaving for school to become an actual nurse. I don't know if she knew I would never see her again. My heart ached, but even in my sorrow, I understood I carried part of her undying presence with me.

After all, Josey taught me about spirit, dignity, humility, and laughter. She taught me her own unique boop boop and whoop whoop language. She taught me how to live well and on my own terms, no matter the situation.

Josey and the other nursing home residents made a lasting impression in another, more personal way, one I have carried with me throughout my adult life. As a result of my interactions with these men and women, I have begun to prepare myself for – if not the inevitable – at least the possible.

Because -- as you probably know by now --I always have been someone who likes having her ducks in a row.

Two years ago, for instance, I purchased some provocative pumps -- stiletto-heeled, leopard print slip-ons -- to wear when I decant myself into the Groovy Ladies Nursing Home, the possible residence I foresee for my golden years. As there is no way I can walk in them now, I consider these heels the perfect non-ambulatory, wheelchair accessory. Just in case I can no longer talk, these shoes will speak for me. "I like prints and colors," they will say to everyone around me. With a flick of my ankle they can be used in self-defense should an interloper attempt to steal the taco I plan to stash from my lunch tray under my wheelchair seat cushion. Easy on and easy off, too. I can cross my legs at the knee and shake my foot to show how pretty they are. If I have Parkinson's disease, they will shake a lot. Maybe I should sew a little strip of elastic on the back. Not enough to be noticeable or prevent a self-defense move. Just enough to keep them from unexpectedly rocketing across the room into someone's denture cup, should I have a sudden and violent calf spasm.

So far, my wheelchair couture collection includes the leopard print heels and a black t-shirt that says, "Don't make me violate my probation." If I ever wind up in a nursing home, I plan to be a fierce invalid. No matter the age, fun clothes make a fun lady. Teenagers know this best.

Preparing for the unknown may be helpful, but the most poignant lesson my nursing home patients taught me is that we can choose to live until we die. With this thought in mind, I plan to get out of my bed each morning and, in my trusty wheelchair, prowl the halls of Groovy Ladies, gathering together whatever I find, talking to whomever passes my way, and pausing to watch the birds outside the window.

And with a thank-you nod to Josey, I will appoint myself floor inspector. I will "boop boop," I will "whoop whoop," and I will keep a watchful eye out for any teenage nursing aide who tries to transfer me from my bed to my wheelchair in my stocking feet without a helper.

10

SMALL TOWN PRACTICE

In 1978, my first husband, M, and I moved to the small university town of Pullman, Washington. We had been married less than a year, and upon completing his internship in veterinary medicine in Colorado, he had accepted a job as a canine oncology resident three states away.

I was 26, delighted to be married, and looking forward to starting a family. Despite my enthusiasm, my husband insisted it was not time for children, even going so far as to track my daily use of birth control pills.

When I first met M, his mother was undergoing treatment for cancer. I did not know it at the time, but it was her dying wish for M to marry and have children. She joyously attended our wedding, hinting at her hopes for a grandchild in the not-too-distant future. But it was not to be.

During the year and a half we lived in Pullman, M became increasingly withdrawn and spent many hours at work. I began to realize there was another woman in his life. When confronted, M said he wished to stay married, have me keep house, and be allowed to continue his relationship with the other woman. Burned into memory are his words, "You don't have the guts to leave me."

We stayed married a few months longer while I worked through my situation. Most days I was unhappy in my personal life, but I cannot discount the valuable lessons I learned. Namely, once you survive being duped and having your heart broken, you find that driving a U-haul truck over the mountains while towing your car behind you is a piece of cake.

But I have raced ahead of myself and my story.

Pullman was a warm and welcoming town, and I made many new friends. There were no nursing jobs available at its only hospital, which was very small. With one operating room, a single delivery room, 40 beds, and no ER, nursing job opportunities only opened when a nurse retired or died. There were a few doctor's offices in town, but all of them pretty much offered the same employment opportunity scenario as the hospital.

Out of necessity, I took whatever job I could get.

My first stint was as circulation department manager for the town newspaper. Most of it was nightshift work. I found the hours deadly and, though I tried to persevere, the job was not for me.

When a clerk position opened at the hardware store, I jumped at the chance to work full-time there. I had enjoyed shopping in hardware stores since I was a little girl. Dad would take me with him, patiently explaining the purpose of tools and hardware, teaching me the language of laborers. I remember thinking a "snake" was a great name for a plumbing tool used to clear drains. As in other areas of my life, I liked learning how things worked, came apart, and were put back together again, whether mechanical, like a lawnmower engine, or physical, like the human body.

M did not share my enthusiasm at being a hardware store clerk. He considered it a lowly position and worried out loud that his co-workers would think less of him due to my employment. Despite M's twisted attitude about a store clerk being too humble an occupation for his wife, I thrived in my new working environment. I dressed display windows, mixed paint, and rearranged shelved merchandise. I got to know my customers by name. And my employers were gems. In the late afternoons, when business was slow, I watched the small engine mechanic do repairs and, before long, was able to assist him. I found it like nursing. A part either is not functioning, or it is wounded in some way. Patch it, replace it, or make the sign of the cross over it and say goodbye.

As much as I loved the work and the people at the hardware store, my heart knew it would have to follow its calling whenever the opportunity arose.

One day – after I had been living in Pullman about nine months – I spied an ad in the local paper that read, "Office Nurse Wanted," with an accompanying phone number. I called. Interviews were concluding the next day, but I was lucky enough to get the last open interview slot on the calendar, scheduled for the end of the work day.

"How many nurses have interviewed so far?" I nervously asked the secretary while I had her on the phone.

"Forty-four," she replied in a "why are you even bothering" sort of voice. *Oh well,* I thought. *Surely a friend or relative had the edge, but what did I have to lose?* I decided to go to the interview despite my misgivings.

Late in the afternoon the next day, the secretary ushered me into the office of Dr. Duffy, who was sitting behind his desk writing when I walked in. He waved me into the padded leather chair next to his desk and leaned back in his own chair.

He looked exhausted. This was a general family practice with one doctor, one nurse practitioner (NP), an employee who did medical billing, and a secretary. I later learned that Dr. Duffy had been up the night before my interview with a difficult baby delivery. Apparently, the town obstetrician already had a patient in labor, so Dr. Duffy delivered this baby himself. Then he made hospital rounds and saw a day's worth of patients before it was my turn to venture into his office.

I handed him my resume as I took a seat. He glanced down at it, dropped it on his desk, and sighed. For a young and fit physician of 40, he looked too tired to read or think.

Knowing how many other job applicants there were, I was thinking we both were wasting our time. I assumed he already had chosen a nurse to fill the vacancy. So, before he could speak, I went into my "what the hell zone" and said rather bluntly, "You look exhausted. I'll tell you why you should hire me. I rarely call in sick. I show up earlier than on time. I complete my work. I get along with everyone, and everyone gets along with me. I learn fast and can already do EKGs (saw the machine from the hallway). I am good at venipuncture and can do pregnancy tests, read blood counts, and do urine screens under the microscope (saw the lab equipment in the EKG room). I can assist you without getting in your way. I don't mind making the coffee, emptying trash, or vacuuming the office." I added gently as I stood up, "Go home to bed." I shook his hand and left him still leaning back in his chair, mouth open.

As I got home, the phone was ringing.

It was a man's voice. He said, "You're hired. Be here at 8 tomorrow." Click.

I was there at 7:30.

So was Dr. Duffy.

I knew in that moment we would get along just fine.

Dr. Duffy was a Vietnam war veteran and experienced Mobile Army Surgical Hospital (MASH) surgeon. He had a brilliant mind and could teach a doorknob how to analyze symptoms and come up with a plausible diagnosis.

The doctor liked to call the four of us 'his broads': the NP, the secretary, the woman who handled billing, and me. In the context of his vernacular, this was not in the least insulting. He meant that we ran the ship. He did the doctor stuff and left us to handle the rest. He was fond of all of us, as we were of him. He thanked us often. None of us ever doubted his demeanor was genuine.

The office saw 40-plus patients a day. Because the town hospital had no ER, whatever emergency that did not get flown out by police helicopter or sent to the big city by ambulance came to us or the other general practitioner in town.

Pullman was a university town, meaning the population doubled during the school year. If it wasn't summer, we were slammed with work every day. Dr. Duffy was efficient and had a biting sense of humor, keeping us both hopping and amused. Work hours flew by for all of us.

Even during this non-stop business, however, the good doctor wasn't beyond playing the occasional prank. He quickly discovered I was an easy mark.

In nurses' training I had learned to *always* label a specimen -- urine, blood, sputum, stool, whatever . . .*right away*! No exceptions. My observant boss soon took note that I was beyond meticulous and nearing maniacal about making sure this was done.

One morning he nonchalantly said, "Hey Susan,run the urine specimen that's in the bathroom for me," meaning check it for blood, protein, etc., with a dip stick. Following the dip stick, I would put a drop on a glass slide and examine it under a microscope for red or white blood cells or bacteria.

In the patient bathroom, to my horror, I discovered six urine specimens, none of them labeled. I gasped. I ran to the desk and asked the secretary, the billing agent, and finally, the NP in her office the same urgent questions. "Who left a urine sample? Why are six specimens in there? When did they get there?" None of them knew why.

Even though no patients were currently in the office, I knew that sometimes a patient would just come in and leave a specimen, then call back for the results. *How and why had this happened? And why hadn't I been told about it?* I groaned to myself over and over. I was coming unhinged and was putting everyone else in a tizzy.

Leslie, the NP, came back to the bathroom with me. Six specimens. All different colors. One very dark, one clear as water, four varying degrees of in between. Some cups brimming, others containing a mere splash. We stared at them, willing each sample to reveal its source.

Leslie pressed her hands onto her hips, thinking. Then she slowly turned her head toward me. She put her index finger to her lips. She nodded in the direction of Dr. Duffy's office, pointed to the urine, then stabbed her finger toward the Doc.

She left the bathroom with me right behind her.

"Very funny, *D*oc," she huffed. "Nice way to give Susan a *stroke*."

He blew up with laughter, clapping his hands. He'd been watching me panic and fly around the office, and Leslie acting annoyed pleased him to no end.

After cleaning up the anonymous specimen collection, I stood in his office doorway and slowly raised one eyebrow at him. "Payback. Is. Hell." I slowly whispered through the door, emphasizing each word. He just kept laughing. Eventually, though, I couldn't help but join in, acknowledging he had gotten me good.

Not long after the specimen circus, Leslie and I schemed our turnabout-is-fair-play plot. We knew Doc loved canned orange soda. Cans at that time had pop-top lids. We'd hear *pop* several times a day coming from his office. On the day in question, we decided we would wait until Dr. Duffy closed an exam room door behind him, and we would drink what was left in the can. It took four mostly empty cans before he bellowed, "Who's been drinking my orange soda?"

We all had a good laugh at that. Pee incident payback accomplished.

Even though I was steady and fearless in most medical scenarios, the good doctor had to tolerate my discomfort with trauma patients. Either Leslie or I would assist when some injured patient walked through the door. Most folks needed just a few stitches. But even so, I have always preferred my patients already stitched up, every body part facing in the correct direction.

As luck would have it, I happened to be Doc's right hand the afternoon a young university professor came in after a lunchtime misadventure on the racquetball court. While playing, he had stepped backward to hit the ball, lost his balance, and smacked the back of his head into the cinderblock wall framing the court. He never lost consciousness, but he did have a golf ball-sized lump on the back of his head, the bulge stretching the skin tight as a drum. The patient's neurological assessment seemed within normal limits to me, and Doc agreed after doing his own testing. Then he saw the bulging knot.

"Lie down on your stomach," he told the patient.

To me he said, "Get a suture kit," a sterile stainless steel tray with scalpel, sutures, gauze, hemostats, everything you need for stitching someone up. Doc scrubbed his hands, put on gloves, and cleaned the area with saline. Then he washed his hands again.

While he washed, I opened the cloth cover of the suture kit on a rolling table and placed it next to the patient's head. Doc was left-handed, so I placed it where he could reach the tray easily. Looking toward Doc, I silently held up extra packs of 4×4 gauze. He nodded. I opened them onto the tray. I held up another pack, he nodded, onto the tray.

That was how we rolled. No unnecessary talking. Silently I would hold up what I thought he needed. When necessary, he would point at the stuff I did not know to offer. I retrieved a small bottle of injectable lidocaine and held it up. I thought if he was going to slit the knot open to release the blood, he would numb it first. He shook his head no. He told me later there was no sensation in the skin, as it was stretched so tight. Plus, a puncture by needle would burst the whole thing, he added. He wanted a controlled incision. That was his plan, anyway.

With the patient lying face-down on the table, Doc stood to the patient's left with me opposite. I had placed sterile drapes around the bulging knot and on the patient's back, creating a clean workspace for

Doc. I scrubbed my hands, put on sterile gloves, and stood ready with my folded hands in front of me. We both wore disposable gowns.

Doc wanted to create a small incision at the base of the knot near the skull and express the blood from the hematoma. He cleaned the area with a swab dipped in betadine – an antiseptic -- and dried it. He took the scalpel handle and fitted it with a small, rounded-tip blade that I had opened and placed on the tray.

He went to work. His scalpel barely touched the skin. Under high pressure, a thin torrent of blood shot explosively from the wound, right past the front of my face and diagonally ten feet up to the top of the wall across the room. Doc meant to get a gauze over it more quickly, but just the slightest touch of the scalpel had been enough to burst the taut skin.

"Oh, *SHIT*!" I shouted in shock.

Mistake #1.

The patient tried to get up. He asked, "What the hell happened?" He had not felt the scalpel.

Doc commanded, "Lay back down," glared at me, and mouthed, "What the hell is wrong with you?" Then he told the patient I was clumsy with the instruments and had pinched myself.

Blood pooled on the gauze as Doc sopped it up. I got to work on the wall. Doc said sweetly, "I could still use help here."

Mistake #2.

He needed more gauze, a lot more. My first job was to help him and the patient. The blood dripping from the ceiling to the counter below had made me momentarily forget that.

Doc stitched the incision and applied a dressing. The patient left, never noticing the wall near the ceiling. I had already wiped up the blood from the counter before he was ready to stand up and go. I waited for the reprimand that I knew I clearly deserved. I was humiliated and embarrassed.

"Next time keep your mouth shut," Doc said in a business-like tone, not looking at me, and left the room.

"Yes, sir," I choked out softly. He never told the rest of the staff what I did. He let it go, and we moved past it. Further evidence – although by this time, I needed none – that Dr. Duffy was a class act.

Doc had many gifts, not the least of which was his expertise at patient teaching. He did not beat around the bush, though, and some patients did not care for his direct approach.

For example, following a series of blood tests, he told a female patient she had diabetes. She cried. He gave her the necessary prescriptions to treat her disease and told her if she lost 100 pounds, she would not need the meds because the diabetes would go away. He explained the complications of diabetes that happen over time and said if she lost the weight, they would not occur. She came back in a month, down 35 pounds. She never asked for a diet, never changed what she ate. She said she ate less and walked more and her husband – now on the same diet and exercise "program" -- had lost weight, too. In a year, this woman shed the prescribed 100 pounds and then some. She looked incredible. Doc heaped praise on her and her husband at every visit. At the end of that year, he told her the diabetes was gone. She cried, this time out of happiness. He beamed at the tenacity and determination that had led to her success at healing herself.

He talked about her to the other patients with diabetes. Through sharing her story, others were inspired and motivated to do the same. It was a small town, where most everyone knew each other. This was peer pressure at its best.

There were also a very few patients Doc asked not to come back to his office. They were those who would not take their meds or lose weight or stop smoking, even though their lives depended on it.

I was in the exam room checking a long-time patient's blood pressure one morning when Doc opened the door and asked her, "Are you still smoking?" No greeting, just the one question.

"Yes," she replied quietly, looking directly at him.

"Don't waste your money or my time. Leave," he said. Her lungs were deteriorating, and the cigarettes were just hastening the pace of the destruction.

He left the door open and walked back to his office. I pulled the blood pressure cuff off. She sighed and left. Not angry. Not ashamed. Just walked out in an "oh well, he's right" sort of way.

This time, Doc's straight-forward technique worked. The patient returned three months later, smoke-free. Doc had a heavy smoking habit himself during his time in Vietnam. He also had found it difficult to quit. Even all these years later, he still wanted a cigarette every minute of every day. That's what he told the woman when she came back. They both stayed smoke-free, and only they knew the struggle it was. One visit I overheard them reminiscing about their favorite cigarette of the day, the one they most missed. Hers was before breakfast; his was after dinner.

Doc may have had a uniquely positive bedside manner, but he had one enormous bad habit that drove us nuts. If he was first to arrive into the office in the morning, he would start the coffee pot. But instead of placing the carafe under the drip basket, he would put his mug there. Most days, he remembered to go back to the reception area to get his mug and put the carafe back in place. But on the days that he forgot to make the switch, the next person to come in was greeted by a huge mess. Coffee everywhere. Doc would hear one of us scream and come running and say, "Oh no! Oh no, oh no." Then "Sorry, sorry, sorry," while trying to mop it up.

"You are impossible! Stop *doing* this," whichever one of us it was would holler. He'd remember for a few weeks, and we would arrive to the smell of fresh-brewed coffee still in the pot. But there was always a next time.

Dr. Duffy's working life was tough with long days. Hospital rounds first, then the office, then back to the hospital, then home. Always on-call for his patients, he would sometimes be out all night. There were times when he would lean forward onto his desk in the middle of the day and fall fast asleep. If the patients that day were coming for a follow-up visit or some non-emergency issue, we would tell them he had a call to attend to and let him doze 20 or 30 minutes.

The patients never seemed to mind. We would shoot the breeze with them, maybe do some teaching, clean ear wax out, whatever we could think up. We respected this doctor for his devotion to his patients and community. He treated us like family, and we protected him from the minor details and the bullshit. On the rare occasion he needed a rest and it was doable, he got his nap.

Doc was a problem solver. He would ponder a patient's symptoms and posit a diagnosis. He was uncannily good at it. Obscure stuff, hardly ever heard of stuff. It seemed he remembered everything he had ever read or heard, and he read a lot. From medical school, the army, his mother, his fishing buddies . . . he apparently retained everything, and he used it all. He might not know the answer in that minute, but it usually came quickly.

However, sometimes it was not his knowledge but his patience that was tested.

There comes a day in every medical practice when the outrageous happens and can precipitate a wholesale loss of cool and common sense. All fingers lose grip of the rope, and the lifeboat drops to the sea with not a single survivor on board.

On this day, poor Doc was in the center of a gale that we never saw coming.

One of his older female patients had been complaining of lower abdominal pain for months. This was her third visit in three months with the same complaint. Dr. Duffy had ordered X-rays and blood tests and done a pap smear. All that could be tested was tested. None of the findings indicated any pathology.

But here she was, back at the office again with the same complaint.

This woman was obese, and her attention to hygiene lacked regularity. Her teeth were unbrushed, and her breath was strong. Her hair was oily and unkempt, and her clothes were stained. During every visit, whole families of fleas jumped off her and her husband. She acted and spoke as if sedated, though Doc had prescribed neither sedatives nor pain meds to her. The husband's demeanor mirrored his wife's. A cognitive deficit of some kind was evident.

For this kind of complaint, I would give the patient a gown and sheet, tell her to remove clothing from the waist down, and put on the gown with the opening down the back. "Sit on the exam table and wrap the sheet around you," I would explain, then leave while she changed, returning to the room with Doc when she was ready.

I was always in the room when Doc did a pelvic exam, both to assist and to be a witness.

Outside the room this day, I waited for Doc. I had set up the exam table for a pelvic exam. Stirrups were out and open, rolling metal table next to it outfitted with glass microscope slides, sterile Q-tips, gloves, wipes, and lubricant. Whatever possible piece of equipment I could anticipate he might need; I had positioned where it could be of use.

I shrugged when I saw Doc come toward me in the hallway and said, "Same complaint."

He shrugged back at me. "Let's go see."

Usually he would challenge me to come up with a diagnosis of my own, making me think harder if my guesses were way off. I learned a lot about the process of elimination and the keep it simple stupid (KISS) approach.

This day, we skipped it. Been there already -- twice.

After a few brief questions, Doc readied to do a pelvic exam, and I helped the patient slowly and carefully lie down on her back and scoot her bottom down to the edge of the table. The odor was strong from between her legs. I held my breath until she was settled and went to the other side of the room to take in a new breath of fresher air.

Doc had his shirt sleeves rolled up, his tie tucked in his dress shirt front, and disposable gloves on. He sat on his rolling stool and slid into position. First a vaginal palpation, then a rectal exam. He held out his gloved index and middle fingers toward me, I squeezed out a blob of lubricant onto them.

The patient was saying, "I eat like a bird but still gain weight."

He looked up at me with his brow knitted. It seemed to me he was wondering, 'what kind of bird' but he remained silent and began the exam.

He inserted his left two fingers into the vagina and palpated the abdomen above with his right hand, standing slightly to change angles. "Does this hurt here, here, here, here?"

"Nope, nope, nope, nope," was the response.

"Alright, then," he said. "Now I will examine your rectum." I squeezed more lubricant onto his fingers.

"OK," replied the patient calmly, lying there as if she was stretched out on a towel at the beach.

Doc stood from his small rolling stool, his eyes narrowing as he inserted a finger and felt around. I could tell by his face as he palpated with his right hand on her abdomen there was nothing new to discover.

As he was withdrawing his finger from the rectum, the lady expelled a loud, wet fart. Then, as Doc sat back down, she farted loudly again.

But this time, about a quart of liquid stool exploded right onto Doc's lap and legs before running down into his shoes.

Doc and I both gasped.

Looking right at me, the patient said in an unconcerned voice, "Did I tell you I've been having diarrhea lately?"

In shock, I ran for the door. I ran down the hall and into the supply closet and closed the door. I did not want the patient to hear me. I gulped for air and hands over my mouth, laughed until tears came down my face. The staff ran to the closet door and peered in at me.

"What happened?" they chorused.

"Call Doc's wife. Tell her we need an entire new set of clothes and shoes," was my answer.

In the exam room, ignoring the presence of the patient and her husband, Doc silently stepped out of his shoes and pants. He removed his tie and shirt and dropped them onto the floor, working his way down until only his boxer shorts were left. They were the only item of clothing spared the spray.

The exam room door opened, and we all saw the mostly naked, thin, and bandy-legged Doc walk across to his office and slam the door.

We all shook with laughter at that amusing sight.

To Doc, though, there was nothing funny about any of this. But for us, in that moment, it was hilarious. We couldn't help ourselves. We stood there, hands clapped over our mouths, tears flowing down our cheeks, our bellies shaking with laughter.

This woman had been the last patient of the day. Because of the fleas she tended to leave behind, we always scheduled her in that time slot. After every visit, we would thoroughly sanitize the exam room and waiting room as soon as she and her husband left. This day, the clean-up was more substantial. Shit covered the end of the exam table, the step, and the floor, and smears trailed out from the spots where Doc had stepped away.

Doc sat in his boxers at his desk completing the charts on his other patients. He wasn't going back into the room to get this patients' chart. He called for Leslie and had her refer the patient to a gynecologist in the next town over. He wanted the chart to say that after extensive testing and thorough examination, he was unable to come up with a diagnosis. No mention was made in the chart of the diarrhea episode.

Doc's wife soon arrived with fresh clothes. I took them into the office and found him writing in a chart. He made no comment to me. I left, gently closing the door behind me, realizing just then how hard this incident had hit our good doctor.

He emerged neatly dressed, thanked his wife, and left. Not a single word was said to the rest of us.

What every one of us had not appreciated was the terrible effect this had on Doc.

He got shit on. No apology from the patient, and worse, no compassion from us. No one by his side to help him out of the clothes and offer support. Abandoned physically, emotionally, and psychologically, we had neglected to care for our Doc. We were ashamed of our disappointing behavior.

The following morning, we went into his office together and delivered our heartfelt apologies.

He nodded and went back to charting.

A class act, indeed.

11

IT'S A LIVING

When my weekend home healthcare job ended in 2001, I found a university part-time teaching position in its school of pharmacy, training the doctoral students in physical assessment, how to give an injection and other medical skills. To boost my income, I also accepted a weekend job pro re nata (PRN, which is Latin for, "as needed"), working at an inpatient rehabilitation center. My assignments there consisted of caring for patients recovering from a stroke, a fall, surgery, or severe autoimmune diseases of many stripes.

It has been my experience that part-time nurses often are assigned the difficult patients, the ones from which the full-time staff nurses need a break. That seemed to be the case at this facility. I came to expect at least one of my patients would be extremely time-consuming due to weight, meds, feedings, temperament, or they were just peculiar in some way. Call it a nurse's sixth sense.

One evening shift I was assigned to care for Mr. Jones. It was then my suspicions were confirmed.

Mr. Jones, one of my six assigned patients for the evening, was a pleasant-looking, older, black gentleman, thin and alert. Recovering from a stroke that had left him with mild left-side weakness, he was able to feed himself a soft diet and, with supervision, walk slowly with a rolling walker.

The evening we first met as nurse and patient, he was scheduled for his bowel program. I was to give him a suppository to generate a bowel movement, which is routine therapy for anyone recovering from a stroke. Mr. Jones occupied half of a two-bed patient room. Of the two, his bed was farther from the hallway, next to the large, single window. His second-floor view overlooked the woods. His room was across from the nurses' station, always buzzing with many nurses, visitors, patients, and others moving through the hallway.

At the beginning of my shift, I made my rounds and checked all my patients, introducing myself and noting their vital signs. Mr. Jones, dressed in the typical blue-and-white hospital gown, gave me a small, welcoming smile and nod as I quickly took his vitals, told him my name, and assured him that I would be back in a little while. Then I hurried off to the next patient.

Following my after-dinner rounds, which included helping patients to the bathroom or to clean up a bit, I returned to his room, suppository in hand.

"Mr. Jones, tonight is the night for your bowel program," I announced.

He gazed at me intently.

"Having a stroke can really slow down your bowels, and it's important that you go to the bathroom every day," I continued. "So, your doctor has ordered that you get a suppository every other evening to help you go."

His eyes never left my face.

"I have the suppository here, and I need you to roll onto your left side so I can give this to you. Then, if you feel like you must move your bowels, I will help you to the bathroom. OK?"

I noticed that he was staring at my lips, not my eyes.

"What?" he asked loudly.

Uh-oh. I had not noticed that hearing impairment was written on the cardex -- a quick-look set of 5×7 cards, one for each patient, highlighting name, diagnosis, treatments, wound care, etc. The cardex helped nurses to quickly become familiar with their assigned patients without having to read the entire chart.

I was standing close to Mr. Jones. But "bowel program" was kind of personal, so I was speaking rather low to maintain privacy.

I pulled a chair next to his bed, sat closer to his face, and upped the volume.

"Mr. Jones, tonight is the night for your bowel program," I said.

He gazed at me even more intently.

"Having a stroke can really slow down your bowels, and it's important that you go to the bathroom every day. So, your doctor has ordered that you get a suppository every other evening to help you go."

He stared harder, his eyes intent on my lips.

"I have the suppository here, and I need you to roll onto your left side so I can give this to you. Then, if you feel like you must move your bowels, I will help you to the bathroom. OK?"

"What?" he asked again, even louder than before.

Oh me. How has this man been functioning in this hospital without hearing? I wondered to myself. He was *really* hard of hearing. I looked at him for a minute and held up my index finger indicating, "Wait, I'll be right back."

I hurried to the nurses' station and retrieved my stethoscope from my lab jacket I cleaned the ear pieces as I returned to his room. Once at his bedside, I mimed how to put on the stethoscope, then pointed to him and held out the device for him to take. He tentatively reached his hands out for the instrument and after a bit of fumbling, maneuvered the ear pieces into place.

I held the stethoscope bell up to my mouth and spoke in a normal tone of voice. "Can you hear?"

He furrowed his brows.

I hollered, "Can you hear me talking?"

His eyes lit up! "Yes," he responded. "What is your name?"

"I am your Nurse Susan," I bellowed into the makeshift hearing aid, adding, "Mr. Jones, tonight is the night for your bowel program."

He tilted his head and said, "What is that?"

By now, my patient interaction had gained the attention of other nurses, visitors, and any patients who happened to be out and about in the hallway. My high-volume teaching had piqued the interest of folks who now wanted to hear how this would play out. I had pulled the bed curtain around Mr. Jones' bed but that was only a visual block. I could not close the room door, as the man in the bed next to him was pushing 100 years old, and the nurses kept a constant eye on him from both the hall and nurses' station.

"I have never been in the hospital before," he says. "I don't know what anything is around here."

Listening to him, I began to see the situation from a new perspective. This man already had been here a few days, and I was not sure if anyone had grasped how hard of hearing he was. Nodding his head was his strategy for survival. It made people go away. How unfortunate and frightening that must have been for him. Armed with this fresh insight, I powered on, realizing I had found a somewhat effective – albeit imperfect – way to communicate.

"Having a stroke can really slow down your *bowels,* and it's important that you *go* to the bathroom *every* day," I boomed, emphasizing certain words I thought would provide clarity. "So, your doctor has ordered that you get a *suppository* every other evening to help you go. That is called a *bowel program.*"

He looked at my open palm holding the suppository, then back to me.

I continued. "I have the suppository here, and I need you to roll onto your left side so I can give this to you. Then, if you feel like you must move your bowels, I will help you to the bathroom. OK?"

"I don't know if I can swallow a pill that big!" he says. "Get me a big glass of water."

I spoke quickly into the stethoscope, shaking my head back and forth vigorously for emphasis. "No, no," I clarified. "You don't *swallow* a suppository."

"A WHAT?" His voice was very loud, compensating for the fact that he could not hear me. I saw that he was becoming fatigued and frustrated.

From the other side of the curtain, giggles bubbled up from the man in the bed next to us. Looking around the curtain I could see a gathering of curiosity-seekers had assembled in the hallway, waiting to hear my next move.

"*A **sah paz zah tory,***" I say as loud as I possibly can.

Mr. Jones and I were both growing weary of this nursing intervention. I sat down on the bed next to him to rethink a better way to proceed, but nothing came to mind. We sat quietly for a few more minutes. I could write it all out, I thought, but that would take forever, and I didn't know if his vision was good enough to read. If not, that would just have been another embarrassment for him.

I was planning a mime show in my mind when he asked, "Well, if you don't swallow it, what do you do with it?"

I peeked out toward the hallway again. Nurses were giving me thumbs-up signs, and visitors had hands clamped over their mouths, chuckling. The man in the next bed had covered his head with a pillow, pressing it tight to muffle his mirth.

I had no choice but to continue. Undaunted by the distraction, I delivered the news about where a suppository goes. "It goes into your rectum."

"WHAT?" he asked, his brows furrowed yet again.

I put my mouth right over the stethoscope and yelled full force. ***"It goes into your rectum. Your bottom. Your anus. The hole where you go Number Two!"***

I mimed the spot, pointing to my butt with an exaggerated index finger stab.

He stared at my expectant face, his eyebrows slowly coming together. He took in a measured deep breath and said, *"Are you talking about my asshole?"*

"Yes! Yes, yes. Your asshole. Yes, sir. You've got it!" I was nodding as I spoke into his stethoscope hearing aid. Relieved, I broke into my inner Snoopy dance of victory.

As my patient's eyes widened, I heard the other bed in the room shaking. I peeked around the bed curtain to see the man laughing behind his pillow. I was worried he would have a stroke.

Unheard by my patient, the entire hallway had erupted into applause for my success. Members of our "audience" wiped tears away and slapped backs. I looked out there and saw nurses giving me thumbs up and nodding in a "she did it" way. Show pretty much over, the crowd began to disperse.

My patient sat quietly, propped up in his hospital bed. The process of a bowel program becoming clear.

As my hallway fan club thinned, my patient – more informed and better relaxed -- posed one final question that made us both laugh out loud.

"Does your husband know what you do for a living?"

12

LETTING GO

Over the years, I have watched as patients writhed in agony, no medical intervention yet developed or discovered to ease their suffering. Sometimes we have no known way to relieve the pain, ease the labored breathing, or stop the raging blood infection that will consume them by the end of my eight-hour shift.

Amid such hardship and heartbreak, I have learned that what I can do is stand and hold space. I must do this even as a mother asks why, why, why did this happen, as she pleads for help to bring her beloved and perfect child out of a coma. I must do this as a husband, willing to sacrifice a vigorous newborn if it would bring back his adored wife, begs for the clock to be rewound just 20 minutes so they can return to the place where the family had been whole. I must do this as people, young and old, try to make sense of a future that doesn't include a loved one or a not-too-distant tomorrow in which they themselves will no longer exist.

Each such moment, while blessedly infrequent, has carved out a deep and unforgettable abyss into my memory.

"I'm so sorry to tell you…"

That is how it most often begins. I have been at bedsides when a physician utters these six words. Despite the questions that follow, I know that whatever the doctor says next is not heard or remembered by patient or family. When you are the "you" given this devastating and personal news, the struggle to grasp the reality of what is happening consumes your thoughts, as well as those of your loved ones. Nothing else gets through.

A good nurse, one who understands that her job is a calling to compassionate care, can and will escort both patient and family forward, no matter how difficult the journey or how dire the prognosis. A good nurse does not run or look away.

We lean in.

My own nurse stories have returned to bring me courage and perspective when facing a crisis involving my own health or that of a family member. Not in an it-could-be-worse way, but more of an everything-always-works-out-and-you-will- get-through-this way.

One truth nursing has shown me is that there is always a greater picture, even if we do not open our eyes and hearts to it amid our pain and sorrow, even if we are unable to see it until much, much later.

I hold fast to the memory of a small boy named Robin, whom I met in the mid-'70s. Looking back, I have come to believe that part of his purpose in life may have been to awaken my awareness to the truth that not everything can be fixed. And to make me aware of other facets of this truth: that doctors tell tales about the possibility of a cure because they have to keep hope alive, that grief will swamp and pull you under, that it may be the patient's mother or father or entire family who will offer you consolation in that moment and for months to come.

Yet no one wants to collect these life lessons for fear the difficult memories may linger in a place in our hearts and minds that time cannot touch, let alone heal.

Children living with the disease of cancer are still children first -- adorable, funny, and emotionally able to cry a gale when it really hurts.

Caring for little Robin was, for me, like having a baby birthed in my heart rather than by my body. I came to feel a deep attachment to him and his mother. The three of us met at my oncology clinic in Denver's Children's Hospital when he was just six. His growth spurt to kindergarten size had not yet come. He was a bundle of tiny bird bones with dark circles under his eyes and a gaunt yet adorable face. When chemo took his hair, his look was exotic, never ill or defeated.

During his frequent visits to the clinic for chemo, blood draws, or procedures, we never ran short of stories to tell. We reveled in one another's company, sharing giggles and hugs.

When Robin was asked, "Does this hurt?" during an obviously painful procedure involving a needle being stuck somewhere, his face would slowly morph into a sardonic mask, an eyebrow raised, nostrils flared, upper lip slightly curled. Tilting his head sideways with his eyes slowly rolling, he'd wait for his mom to burst into laughter. Robin managed to endure physical pain but could not bear to witness his mother's thinly disguised anguish. It was obvious his greatest joy was to make her laugh.

She always obliged, somehow able to mask both her fear of loss and the deep pain of seeing her child undergo agonizing medical procedures. At every silly face, she guffawed before smothering him with kisses.

Sometimes when the doctor came in to the exam room to report on Robin's most recent lab work, his mother and I would stand with an arm around each other's waist to hear the news. It was not a conscious comforting technique on my part. I just found myself there.

Slowly and unrelentingly, the neuroblastoma and chemo consumed Robin. Despite aggressive therapy, the cancer spread everywhere, and after reaching toxic levels in his body, the chemo was stopped.

His mother hoped for a merciful death to remove his pain.

I waited for him to pull through. I felt certain it would happen. The protocol called for it to transpire that way. "Remission anticipated after three months of chemo." That's how I thought it read, anyway.

I continued to champion the treatment protocol that I hoped – even believed – would help Robin while answering his mother's probing questions during our private talks about what death looks like as it approaches and makes its call. Even though I could see his declining condition – his ribs emerging and weight sinking, the hollow spots at his neck, and his hands becoming transparent --I persisted in my delusional, hopeful state. As he ate crumbs and drank sips, I privately could not, or would not, plumb the inevitable coming of his death.

* * *

It is bright, sun-filled morning in 1976. I am a 24-year-old nurse with an open, aching heart, bathing Robin's tiny body as he lies dwarfed by blankets in the center of his hospital bed. My oncology clinic nurse supervisor and co-worker knows Robin's condition and frees me from my duties so I can spend time in the adjacent hospital to be with my little love. I have become accustomed to his shallow sips of breathing and soldier on, staying in the moment of joy that I have caring for sweet Robin. His eyes watch me as I chat about my dog, Fat City. She loves tea bags and steals them from the trash,

I tell him, describing how the strings that dangle from her floppy Labrador jaws expose her bad girl, trash-picking ways. Robin loves dogs and knows all my Fat City stories. He whispers her name so he can hear them again. But there is no smile on his face today. He is too weak to hold his head to center. I use a soft folded washcloth to prop up his head so he can see his mom sitting next to the bed. I am bustling around the room in some ridiculous, this-needs-to-get done, rote nurse dance when I hear him speak.

"Hmm?" I say, coming close to his face.

"I want to look outside, and then I will rest," he says softly with effort, breathing between every other word.

"Okie Dokie," I respond, louder than intended. *This is great,* I think. Due to his pain, he has not wanted to be moved in some time. Getting him out of bed will be good for his lungs and skin.

His mom nods her permission as I move to the side of the bed. I bend forward and slide both arms under the sheepskin pad that cradles him. As I lift, Robin groans and grimaces. Drawing him close to my heart, I stand erect and walk around the end of the bed to the window. His steel gray eyes widen as he scans the Denver rooftops. I gently tip his shoulders higher to see the cars and people below walking around the hospital. He exhales a sigh of wonder. I rattle on about the blue sky, my gaze caught by one small, perfectly white cloud, a silent tribute to the beauty of the day.

Robin's mother steps close to me and gently wraps her arms around the two of us. I think how wonderful this moment is. Then she whispers in my ear, "He's gone, Susan."

I look down. His open eyes are empty, and his body is limp. Although he is in my arms, I realize I feel nothing. Whatever weight he contained seems to have left his body to fly out the window. In the space of this instant, I struggle to take in what has happened, remembering the sigh of wonder that was his final breath.

I cannot move, and his mother does not make me. From depths I do not recognize I feel a surge of incomprehension welling up. *Robin is gone? Then, who is this in my arms?* A tremor creeps over me from head to toe. I begin to quake.

"Lay him back on the bed," she says softly, and I do as I am directed. I pull the stethoscope from around my neck. *My God, he has no heartbeat. But I just bathed him for the day, right? He wasn't struggling to breathe then, was he?*

I pull the blanket up to his chin and stare.

Again, his mother whispers. "He is gone, Susan."

My knees go spongy, and I sit in the chair that had just been holding his mother. My forehead rests on the mattress, and my arms hang at my sides.

"You prepared me for today, Susan," she says. "You told me this would come, remember?"

I did?

"Robin was ready, the pain is gone," she continues. "Remember, Susan, we knew he would die. Right?"

I am lost. All that was just talk, I did not mean it. *Babies don't die, do they? My baby?* The baby of this brave woman standing next to me, reaching out from within the well of her own grief to comfort me.

Other nurses perform the post-mortem care. There is no way I will attach a name tag to Robin's toe and wrap him in a white plastic shroud. There is no possible way I will wheel him to the hospital morgue and put him in a cooler.

Robin's mother sends me away to go for a walk as she prepares to leave the hospital alone.

There is a patio off the second floor of the hospital where employees sometimes eat lunch. I sit out there, alone in the warm sun. My chest feels tight, my heart thudding inside of it. As the metal chair beneath me warms my bones, I review the last 30 minutes of my life. There are dozens more children with cancer here. A tsunamic wave of awareness compresses me. I had told Robin's mother that his body would take only so much cancer and chemo. I know I will tell that to other parents, over and over and over to many, many parents. Now I believe it myself.

After the funeral and in the subsequent weeks, Robin's mother and I would meet or chat on the phone. She thanked me for holding her little boy up to the window and letting his spirit jump to the blue sky. She said Robin would have loved that I was chatting along as he jumped into the arms of Jesus instead of crying like I did later. I accepted the compliment.

During my time at the oncology clinic following Robin's death, I witnessed many more final sighs of wonder, which I came to see as a profoundly sacred aspect of nursing. I became skilled and at ease with praying in many faiths or none, with comforting parents and spouses and friends.

At those times when a patient dies with no loved one touching their face or holding their hand, nurses hold the gap there, in that space of wonder. In the enormity of that feeling, post-mortem care becomes a solemn and sacred ceremony, never just a procedure.

***

Many years later, when I worked as a home health nurse, I attended Grandma B's last day of life. When I arrived for my early morning visit, she was propped up in the center of a king-sized bed surrounded by her four sisters, all lying next to her -- in the bed. Multiple flowered quilts were tossed over everyone. It was an array of tinted gray heads, pinkish to bluish. Five people in the bed, and many around it. Grandma was unresponsive, but I imagined she could hear and feel the loving energy cocooning her.

To check Grandma's blood pressure and pulse, I had to lean over two people. "We got ya," her bedmates chorused as my hips and chest rested unavoidably on top of them. I asked them if they wanted to move so I could check vital signs, and they said no. I told the crowd in and around the bed that Grandma's pulse was weak and her blood pressure very low. They shrugged, no news flash here. She was 95 years old and dying. They were respectful, aware, accepting. They knew her time was drawing near. They planned to stay with big sister, talking and recounting childhood stories, until the end. I apologized for having to leave to see other patients but explained Grandma could linger for hours yet.

"Oh," they said. "Go on. We'll call you when she goes."

Five hours later, I received a page to call the family. "She's gone," was all that was said to me over the phone.

I drove back to the house to pronounce her dead, offer condolences, and see if I could help with calls to the mortuary. I parked in the yard, already full of vehicles, and entered the back door. Walking into the large country kitchen, I saw a dozen people seated around a bountiful feast and many more wandering through the house, plates in hand. The old wooden table was laden with enormous bowls of food, platters of turkey, and all the fixings. It smelled like a holiday.

"Hey! She's here," the crowd greeted me as I entered the kitchen. I tried to scoot by the chair backs crowded around the table when Uncle Buddy said, "Sit down right there, girlie, and have some food. Grandma ain't going nowhere. You can see her after you eat."

* * *

As my nursing career progressed, caring for hospice patients in their homes granted me space to teach, answer questions, and help the whole family. Often, the patient is not the only person you care for during this time. I could walk down the path to death with the patient and the family and answer questions in the moment about what has now become uncommon -- the witnessed death process. I would share my home phone or pager number to call in the night if they needed me. I did not want some unfamiliar nurse answering their questions or coming in the night. Nor did they.

This home care practice is neither routine nor expected. Typically, the on-call nurse would be the one to respond. But I found it important, even personally necessary, to be available to come when called. My patients and their families and I agreed to it, and that was that. It happened so infrequently that it was not an all-consuming practice. The other nurses in my office felt the same way.

* * *

I met Mrs. Forge when she was a hospice patient, her lung cancer already run amok. It was cancer of the everything, her daughter telling me, "that's what the doctor said." Due to Mrs. Forge's shortness of breath, lying down was out. She sat in a gold velvet arm chair with an ottoman for her lower legs when needed. She lived with her 30-year-old daughter, her son in law and their 6-year-old son. They all adored Mrs. Forge. Each weekend morning, I would visit, both Saturday and Sunday.

Comfort was the point of her care. During my half-hour visits, her grandson, Danny, would assist me, putting the blood pressure cuff on his Grandma, checking her pulse, and listening to her lungs. I'd go first, then after cleaning the ear pieces of the stethoscope, hand them to Danny to do his own assessment. He mimicked me precisely.

As Mrs. Forge's health failed, she slipped into a mostly unresponsive state, rousing only every few hours. Entering her living room early one Saturday morning, I could see my patient's color was quite gray. The oxygen cannula was in place under her nose, the soft whoosh of flowing air barely audible. Her eyes were closed, her breathing shallow but not labored. Her spidery hands stayed folded in her lap, and her shoulders drooped forward but looked relaxed. She had roused enough, hours earlier, to swallow her liquid pain medicine. Her daughter reported that her mother had not eaten for days and only drank minimally. I pulled the ottoman close to her armchair and sat, putting my knees up against the seat of the chair, between her knees.

Standing next to her shoulder, little blonde-headed Danny said, "Isn't she beautiful?" He traced one small index finger over the top of her bald head.

"She is," I said as reverently as he did.

He beamed, adding, "She's in heaven you know."

Uh oh, I thought. *What does he mean by that?* I looked up to his mother standing behind him.

"Mom has been talking out loud to her mother and sister this morning," she explained. "They are both dead. We feel she is already there. In heaven."

Gently, I tried to pull Mrs. Forge's frail arm toward me to check her blood pressure. Her wan face registered a wince, but she did not rouse. Slowly, I eased her arm back into place. I charted that blood pressure was not taken, due to apparent discomfort. An unnecessary number at this point. There was absolutely no need to cause pain to get it. I leaned forward and gently held her right hand in my left palm, my right index and middle fingers searching for her pulse.

Unexpectedly her eyes opened, and she peered straight into my eyes. Her eyes grew bigger and bigger. She leaned slightly toward me and opened her mouth, softly whispering, "Are you my angel?" Wide-eyed, her penetrating gaze locked on me.

I did not know what to say, as no air seemed to move in or out of my lungs. I felt a shifting of sorts, like gravity might not hold me in the chair, like she was emitting heat lightning around and through me.

"Ohhhh", she breathed out softly with awe. "I see your wings." She took in a shallow breath and slowly added, "*They* are beautiful."

With careful and deliberate focus, her eyes scanned around my head and shoulders. It appeared she could see something just behind me. I felt a profound pull of energy toward her but no movement. A drawing in. A lifting. A blindness to anything but her face. My mouth dropped open, but no words escaped. Then she closed her eyes and sagged gently back into her chair.

"See, that's what he means," her daughter said calmly and assuredly about her little son.

"Huuuhhh." I finally let out a breath while remaining motionless. *What was that?* I thought to myself. I turned my head slowly to one side and then the other. I could not see or feel wings. I shrugged gently -- nothing there.

I asked Danny quietly, "Do *you* see anything?"

"Nope, but Grandma did!" he said with a chest-forward smile. Another affirmation that this did just happen. It was otherworldly.

After I gathered my wits, equipment, and chart, Mrs. Forge's daughter and son- in-law walked me to my car. "We think she will go the rest of the way today," her daughter said. No panic or spectacle, an unfolding natural process was occurring, and they were enthralled to bear witness. Goodbyes had been said, plans had been made, and with tranquility they faced their loved one's final and complete transition. Their young and compassionate son was peaceful as he watched his grandma on her final journey, schooled in love and faith that this is how life ends.

They promised to call me when she passed so I could complete the required paperwork.

Later that afternoon, I got the call and went back. The shiny black hearse was already in the driveway, driver standing with folded arms, leaning against the door, waiting for me to release the body. The daughter had contacted both of us.

Before she died, Mrs. Forge, forever the good mother, had left the phone numbers at the ready for her daughter to call . . .after she had gone all the way.

13

MY TUMMY HURTS

The art and artistry of nursing is learned on the job.

There is simply no way any educational experience – even one with rigorous courses and multiple clinical rotations -- can provide a nurse healer with all the permutations of a nursing practice or offer up a complete set of templates from which to respond.

It is not until she receives On The Job training, aided and abetted by a head nurse mentor and helpful co-workers, that a nurse learns how to problem solve in the immediacy of the here and now.

Experience – that ever-expanding mix of knowledge and intuition – is, as they say, priceless. In nursing, "informed" flying by the seat of one's pants often is the most effective means of crisis management. Sometimes it is the only option available.

It took almost no time for me to find this out.

That fateful day came during my six-week rotation in the ER when I was a junior in nursing school. Two policemen had picked up a young black woman for disturbing the peace and transported her to our ER. They released her handcuffs and, relief written all over their faces, walked away leaving her pacing and ranting wildly in our midst.

Once her hands were freed and the cops had left, our newly arrived patient's behavior escalated from agitation into violent aggression. Her arms whirred like helicopter blades moving in all directions. As we five student nurses tried to corral her onto a gurney while bobbing and weaving around her spinning limbs, she broke free and ran down the back hallway of the ER, launching herself onto a nearby nurse's back. The pair spun toward the floor. The patient thudded onto the linoleum first, holding the nurse tightly in a bear hug, pinning her arms at her sides. Arriving moments later, the other students and I snatched and grabbed at the patient, trying to subdue her as a group of ER staff assembled behind us.

The ER nurses sprang into action, instructing the student nurses to get out of the way, using plainly understood truck driver language. One nurse appeared with three sheets, folding two of them into thirds lengthwise. These were used to swaddle the patient's shoulders and knees. With the third sheet, they cocooned her body. As they rolled the ranting, spitting patient side to side on the floor to swaddle her, only one nurse spoke to the patient, and that was a soft-voiced repetition of, "You're OK, you're OK." This same nurse placed a pillow on the floor to protect the screaming patient from injuring herself as she repeatedly banged her head against the hard surface. Another nurse arrived with an injection she administered into the patient's thigh, straight through the sheet and patient's blue jeans.

On the count of three, the experienced ER team log-lifted her onto the gurney, raised the side rails, and put a pillow under her now lolling head. With deftness that comes from repetition, they had the patient wrapped and safely on a gurney within minutes.

One nurse stayed with the now-silent woman as the rest returned to their patients without comment. Our breathless student nurse quintet stood wide-eyed in the ER hallway awed by the quick skill and compassionate care we had seen delivered in the face of uncontrolled, violent behavior. The ER nurse standing with the patient turned to us and explained that this woman suffered from schizophrenia. She told us the patient often could not afford her meds or if she was able to purchase them, did not remember to take them. After a few inpatient days on the psych ward for therapy and treatment, the nurse added, she usually was functional enough to be sent home.

That incident – and others that followed – bleakly testified to the ineffective revolving door that passed for mental health care in our community at the time. This woman was well-known to the policemen and ER nurses – both in sickness and in health. Homeless and jobless due to her illness, without the community resources to be housed, and having no one to monitor the management of her illness, she all too often experienced these repetitive and painful ER visits. It was the only option she had for roping her disease back into submission.

Change is the only constant in the ER. I quickly learned to prepare myself for the unexpected and unpredictable. One moment the unit would be under control, the next five burned patients, half a dozen car accident victims, or someone bleeding from a bullet wound would roll in.

When time permitted, our ER nurse mentors regaled us with stories of patients who had suffered horrific injuries in fires and crashes or about fights that had broken out among families of gang members being treated in the ER. Some nursing students ate that up. Not me. I knew then I did not have the courage, fortitude, or any interest in this aspect of emergency nursing care.

So, when I finished my ER rotation, I bowed with respect and gratitude to the men and women nurses I was leaving behind and never looked back. My developing nursing skills, I was sure, would better serve the world in a different setting.

* * *

Growing up in Philadelphia, I was as street smart as any skinny little Catholic school girl could be. Those skills, however, poorly prepared me to work in a rural setting when I took on the job as home health nurse in central Virginia. Luckily, I knew enough to know I needed to learn more.

Adapt, modify, and invent became my new and oft-repeated mantra as I visited patients in their homes out in the country. It seemed to work like magic. As I learned to bend and lean in, I found myself met with kindness and understanding in almost every home I entered.

Soon I was thriving at on-the-road nursing.

I realized I couldn't control my environment or circumstances, so I worked within their ever-changing framework. I performed wound care on front porches. I assessed a patient's condition in silence so as not to disrupt the Silver Star Religious Quartet's rousing radio gospel music, aired every Sunday morning. I became adept at fielding an array of questions from multiple generations relating to their own health concerns even as I tended to the relative in need of more urgent attention, doctor's orders in hand. I even managed to maintain sterile technique doing wound care in a small kitchen with a dog growling at my heels as he watched me touch his owner's feet.

I had settled in, found my niche, and grown increasingly comfortable in my capabilities. But just like in the ER, I soon found out that danger could lurk in the most unexpected places.

One warm summer Sunday morning, I was scheduled to visit a very elderly woman, Ms. Susan, who lived in a trailer with her daughter, one pregnant granddaughter, and two grown grandsons.

I had called the patient the day before to make sure my planned 9 am arrival was OK. She told me to just come on over at any time. I later became certain she never told her daughter about my scheduled visit or how early in the morning I would arrive.

Driving slowly down a back-country road, I watched for the grouping of mailboxes and the bent street sign that marked the entrance to her deeply rutted dirt driveway. The drive extended 50 yards past the turn in and spilled out into a clump of trailers unidentified by street numbers. Big Wheel bicycles, soccer balls, and empty water bottles lay scattered here and there in the unfenced communal space, one yard bleeding into another. Scrubby trees and shrubs surrounded the collection of trailer homes. Bags of trash dotted the landscape, awaiting transport to the county dump.

All was quiet as I arrived, no one was out and about yet. The patient's chart indicated I was to go to the trailer with the big blue flowerpot out front. I saw it right away and parked.

As I gathered the chart and my bag of supplies and exited the car, I heard a rooster give a robust crow from somewhere nearby. I scanned the yard and saw a vigorous and colorful bird standing on the front stoop of the trailer across from Ms. Susan's. He was craning his neck to give me the once-over, first with one eye and then the other. It was obvious he didn't like what he saw. He puffed up his feathers and crowed again, but this time it sounded more like an angry reproach for entering his territory. Not knowing the mistake I was making, I paid no heed to the warnings of this feathered sentinel. I closed my car door and began the 30-foot walk to the trailer's door.

It was then the rooster let out a blood-curdling call that caused me to jump and look back. I was mid-way between the trailer and my car when he took flight, heading straight for me. I launched myself full speed toward the trailer, ripped open the storm door, threw open the front door, and stumbled into the living room. As the storm door slammed behind me, the rooster crashed into the glass, spurs first.

My heart pounding from the near miss, I realized I had just burst into this home without a knock. I froze in place. Spread out on the gold shag carpet at my feet were four young men, sound asleep. Some were partially dressed, others wore only their underwear. Empty wine and beer bottles and pizza boxes were strewn about the room. Despite the commotion that had heralded my arrival, not a single male body stirred.

But someone in the house had been awakened by the crashing sound of the rooster hitting the door and me bursting in. As I took in my surroundings, Ms. Susan's daughter appeared in the living room while tying the belt of her knee-length bathrobe around her. Lighting a cigarette, she looked at me and silently pointed down the hallway toward her mother's room before turning and heading for the kitchen.

No one on the floor had even twitched, so I softly tiptoed over them and walked back to Ms. Susan's room. "I'm so sorry," I said, explaining the event that caused me to blast in without a knock.

Ms. Susan, who like her daughter was smoking a cigarette, listened without a word as I told my rooster attack story. She looked annoyed.

"It's *your own* fault," Ms. Susan said, exhaling smoke through her nose.

My jaw dropped at her words. "*My* fault?" I repeated in disbelief. "How could a rooster trying to kill me be *my* fault?" I asked, placing the blood pressure cuff around her thin upper arm.

"It's your red pants," she said, leaving an implied "jack ass" hanging in the air.

I looked down at my red capris as if they should have offered up an apology for the offense they had given.

"Ms. Susan, tell me how my red pants made the rooster attack," I said, looking back at her.

She sighed, rolled her eyes. "Everybody knows roosters hate red pants," she stated matter-of-factly.

I let it go at that. Sometimes you don't know what you don't know and admitting it to yourself is your only wise option.

Settling in to the task at hand, I could see that my patient shared this room with her daughter. The room held two single beds with a small path between them. To my amazement, Ms. Susan rested in a full-sized motorized hospital bed with overhead trapeze. That bed must have been disassembled and reassembled to get it down the narrow hallway and into this room at the back of her trailer. One small ceiling fixture dimly lit the room.

I removed the gauze dressings from Ms. Susan's heels, measured and cleaned the wounds, and applied clean gauze and tape. Without direction from me, she rolled to her side so I could tend her low back wounds in the same manner as her heels. Wounds in the tailbone and heels are common in patients confined to bed, and Ms. Susan had been fighting them for years. I changed the sheets and gave her a mini-bath while she chain smoked and complained about her lazy grandchildren.

The physician's orders for this skilled nurse's visit was to change the dressings over her bed sores. Ms. Susan had a nurse aide come to bathe her three days a week. She directed me where to find her wash basin and towels, making it apparent she and the family had been accustomed to the visiting nurse providing more personal care than the skilled wound care the doctor had ordered. I obliged, gave her a pits-and-parts bed bath, changed the soiled sheets, and placed them in the laundry basket by the bedroom door.

The low light of the room, mingling with the smell of a soiled bed, swirling cigarette smoke, and heat had quickly become oppressive. I decided to postpone my charting until I got back to the office, rather than sit there for a few minutes to make notes like I usually did.

Forty-five minutes after exploding into the home, I tiptoed my way out over the still-sleeping party of four on the living room floor. Nervously, I opened the storm door and peered out. No rooster. I stepped out and looked again. Not seeing the feathered scoundrel, I sprinted to the safety of my car and jumped in. The yard was still empty. I scrawled in bold letters across the front of the chart folder, "*Watch out for the vicious attack rooster. He hates red pants.*"

At the end of that day's shift, I went home and threw the red capris in the trash. My then-husband called me ridiculous, saying he had never heard that a rooster could see the color red, let alone be prompted to attack because of it.

I was not surprised. He had grown up in Philly, too. I visited many patients in the country, so I wasn't taking any more chances that I might provoke another temperamental fowl. Ms. Susan's reason – strange as it may have sounded -- had convinced me I was to blame.

I followed up with numerous visits to her trailer, but I never caught so much as a glimpse of that rooster again. Of course I didn't – every time I went there I made sure I was wearing a pair of white, keep-the-peace pants.

* * *

Encountering a feathered, four-legged, or crawling threat in the country is one thing. In the confines of a hospital, it is quite another. But it was while working on the pediatric oncology ward at Denver Children's Hospital that I had one of the biggest animal-related shocks of my early nursing career.

I had been working the oncology ward for a few months and was happy to note a developing sense of skill and expertise contributing to a growing confidence in myself as a professional nurse. From the fundamentals of basic physical care to the more advanced and subtle skills of starting an IV in the tiniest of already offended and traumatized veins, I had become adept with procedures or knew when to ask for help before doing harm or hurt. Whether I was assisting a physician with a bone marrow biopsy or spinal tap or standing with parents in their worst hours to listen, pray, comfort, or cry with them, I had matured into a competent oncology nurse.

Working evening shift had always been a breeze, but the later, nightshift schedule had tended to confuse my body. Somehow, caring for children on the oncology ward both simplified the challenge of an overnight schedule and muted its effects. Watching ill children peacefully sleep during my rounds made me feel I was nursing in a tangible way -- relieving pain, anxiety, and suffering. With no doctors or therapists around on night shift, the ward was quieter. I had more time to offer comfort through healing hands, bringing some small ease to these children in the midst of such serious illness.

It was about 5:30 one morning when 10-year-old Michael called me to his room. He was restless and said he had a tummy ache. Leukemia and chemotherapy had wracked his now-frail body. He was bald and pale. His bones ached from the cancerous blood cells packing his marrow. Finding a comfortable resting position was difficult. He hated the hard hospital bed and asked daily when he could go home. I usually shrugged saying that was not up to me -- a weak and unsatisfactory reply for both of us.

Now his little belly hurt. I thought a nice warm bath and lotion rubdown might bring comfort and help him relax. His mother was resting on a cot beside his bed.

As Michael sighed and agreed to the bath, his mom sat up and rested her chin on top of her folded hands on the bedrail on the opposite side of the bed. I pulled the light chain at the head of the bed once, turning the ceiling light on to its lowest setting.

Michael watched me as I quietly gathered the supplies and warm water. While I looked for the soap, he moaned softly again, "My tummy hurts."

I turned to him, reached for the edge of the sheet near his chin, and lowered it carefully down past his chest to his tummy.

Coiled on his abdomen was a black snake.

"Holy SHIT," I shrieked, instinctively snatching the snake from his abdomen and throwing it across the room. *"Oh my God!* How did it *get* there?"

My heart was pounding. I snapped the overhead light chain again flooding the room with light. I searched his body for a bite or whatever a snake might have done. I was gasping for breath. I am not afraid of snakes but *holy shit,* I thought, *how did one wind up on a child's belly in a pediatric hospital?* I was in full freak-out mode. *How and When and Why had this happened?* were the questions racing through my mind. Hadn't Michael felt it moving over him?

"*For God's sake! What the hell?"* Words kept rolling loudly from my mouth as I tried to comprehend. "*Jesus, Mary, and Joseph on a bicycle!"*

It was then that I noticed both Michael and his mother were literally crying with laughter. Immediately I went rigid, pausing to look from them to the snake on the floor. I pulled the light chain to the brightest setting.

Plastic snake.

My shoulders slumped in relief. Oh yes, I had been completely fooled. In the low light, what I had seen lying on my young patient's tummy had looked like a real snake.

"It was Michael's idea," his mom managed to gasp out between guffaws. "He wanted payback for all the times you nurses stuck him with needles full of chemo."

Shaking the rubbery two-foot imposter at him, I growled with fake anger, "I almost peed my pants, you *kooky* child."

He laughed even harder. He made me swear silence about the prank so he could pull off his "tummy ache" caper with both the dayshift nurse and his doctor.

Once the word was finally out, every doctor, nurse, secretary, housekeeper, respiratory therapist, and visitor got a verbatim rundown of my screams, not to mention the close call I'd had with incontinence. Michael took great satisfaction in repeating the "bad word" I had shouted. He became a superhero to the other patients on the ward. Snakes began to appear on a number of other young stomachs. Nurses were feigning fright and running about with arms raised at the plague of snakes that had infested the hospital. Parents grinned with appreciation that their child also could have a story to share.

Fun is hard to come by on a ward where children are savagely ill and often dying. Bad lab reports bring grief, not only for that one child and family, but to everyone who breathed that same heavy air. The oncology ward was a community of families united by hope and fractured by sorrow. That plastic snake brought temporary respite and delight.

I loved it when the other children eagerly asked me, "Were you *really* frightened?"

Wide-eyed, I would say, "It was *so* horrible," and shiver wildly. And for a few seconds, it really was. For the remainder of that nightshift, between the high-octane coffee and the snake-sighting adrenalin rush, it took hours for my heart rate to come down.

Just a few months later, all the doctors and nurses from the oncology department attended Michael's funeral, as we did for all the children we lost. The small white casket, the profusion of flowers, the fog of anguish and grief billowing through the room . . .it was a crushing sadness.

Michael's father delivered the eulogy over the open casket. One hand on his son's shoulder and one arm around his wife's waist, he told the snake story once again, including all the details about the planning and purchase of the plastic reptile. Michael's mother quoted with freakish accuracy my words from that night, even though most mourners present had heard it many times before. She delivered the lines so precisely; it was obvious to everyone it was me who had spoken them. Those congregated laughed heartily while pointing my way. I feigned embarrassment but inside felt a great honor to have been part of that street theater.

His father's softly spoken and heartfelt conclusion made us weep.

"Michael," he said, "loved all his nurses, and so do we."

* * *

It was during my first hospital job as a staff nurse on a pediatric ward that I encountered true danger and a much different fear.

Women's Medical Hospital, located in the Germantown suburb of Philadelphia, offered general hospital services to the community. Some of our young patients came through Child Protective Services and had custody restrictions on who could and could not visit the child.

One evening shift, it was my turn to be charge nurse, making assignments and managing new admissions. The job entailed coordinating with other departments, taking called-in orders from doctors for their patients, and other assorted administrative tasks. All the new graduate nurses took turns as charge nurse to gain experience and grow confidence in an administrative role.

That night, we had at least six children whose visitors were restricted to just their mother or no one at all. One child, an 11-month-old girl, was being treated for burns on her bottom. To silence her from crying one night, her father had turned on the electric stove burner element and plunked her naked bottom down on the glowing coils. He told the social worker in the ER he was teaching her a lesson -- not to cry so much. Opened burns ringed her privates. Every time this baby peed, urine touched raw, open skin, causing a searing, scorching pain that no analgesic could overcome. Her shrieks made us cringe, cry, and shudder with fury. In private, we hoped a judge would arrange to have her dad's ass lowered onto an electric stove coil.

About midway through the shift, as the last of the visitors were leaving, the little girl's father approached the nurses' station desk and asked where his daughter's room was located. At first, I did not know exactly who he was, only that this child was allowed no visitors.

When realization dawned about his identity, a lump rose in my throat. As calmly as I could, I told him the child was not allowed any visitors by court order. Other nurses at the nurses' station grew quiet and looked up from their charting.

He sneered at me, cursed the court order, and pulled out a long, slightly curved hunting knife, pointing it toward my face. "I want to see my baby girl," he demanded, his voice low and threatening.

I held my breath as fragments of thoughts raced through my mind. *I thought he was in custody. When and how did he get out? How could I stall him until help arrived? And will he kill her or take her? Will he kill me?*

Reluctantly, I pointed to the child's room and watched him stride toward her. With his back to me, I quickly ushered two of my nurses into the med room and had them call security. Quietly, I asked the other nurses to go into rooms with their patients, bar the doors as best they could, and stay there.

Because we were on the fourth floor, I knew my knife-wielding visitor must exit via elevator or stairs. I stood at the desk and watched him through the glass-walled room put his weapon away and gently pick up his little girl. He propped her into the crook of one elbow and cradled her head to his chest with his other large hand. Never looking at me, he left the room with her, walked calmly to the elevator, and pushed the down button.

I said nothing, keeping an eye out for other visitors or staff. Luckily, there were none. My heart thudded as the elevator opened, and he stepped in without a look back. I hurried my nurses out of the med room and sent two of them down the stairs to the main lobby to see what would happen. I waited at the nurses' station. I called security to update them about which elevator the man took and that he had his child. My heart still pounding with fear for the decisions I had just made to let that baby end up in the hands of her abuser. At this point, I could only hope security had arrived on time and would rescue the child and apprehend the father when he reached the ground floor.

Within the seeming eternity of a few minutes, the elevator doors opened in front of me, and my two nurses emerged with the baby, now crying, knowing only that she had just been taken from the comfort of familiar arms.

For a while, all of us sat at the nurses' station in shock as the child cried inconsolably. I couldn't stop thinking about how it could have gone horribly wrong.

The next day, our head nurse met with security, and new procedures were put into place for visitors wishing to come to the pediatric floor. For weeks I had nightmares about that knife, of being stabbed myself, or the baby being stabbed.

I knew in my heart, no matter what security changes had been made, it was always possible for an incident like that to happen again.

14

DIALED IN

By the time I turned 56, I thought I was happily destined to spend the rest of my nursing career working in a jail. Correctional nursing, which I found to be an entirely different animal than any other health field, fascinated me. I encountered new health issues almost every day that challenged my knowledge base, stretched my patient teaching imagination and strengthened my clinical abilities.

For instance, before incarceration many members of the jail community used intravenous drugs. They raised questions, to me, about the use of IV street drugs, what it was OK to cut drugs with, and how best to clean used works -- the needles, syringes, spoons, and other materials used to prepare and ingest drugs of choice.

I learned how to manage IV injection site skin infections, treat the pain and injuries from aggressive or unwanted sex, discuss tattoo ink dangers, and handle other on-the-job surprises as they arose.

My passion for patient teaching was engaged and fulfilled as I pondered everything from the best way to explain why tongue piercing was a risky idea to how to effectively convey the infection risk posed by injecting silicon caulk via turkey basting needle into a breast for a cheap, street-sourced augmentation.

At first, the inmates hesitated to ask the questions they really wanted to have answered, but once they knew they had my ear without judgment, I earned their trust. My job became a true give and take. My incarcerated patients taught me about life on the street, and I taught them ways to stay as well as they could, no matter what choices they decided to make.

The experienced jail nurses explained to me how bullets can migrate from deep muscle out to the skin and rupture out just like a pimple. They helped me discern a true pain issue from a drug seekers persistence. And stressed why I should never prop open a supply closet door to save time, no matter how quickly I thought I would return.

The correction officers taught me how to think on my feet and move about the jail safely. With their mentoring, I learned to spot a con a little faster. They protected me and made fun of me incessantly. "Hey look, Bates, Susan came to work again without her ass."

I never failed to respond to that observation in a certain sign language hand signal that made them laugh -- every time. They called me chicken butt, taking care there were no inmates around to hear their teasing. It was meant to be endearing, and I never tired of it. Everybody in jail had an alias. I was CB.

Despite the dangers and surprises – or perhaps because of them -- I loved my job and would have worked there until I retired. But that was not to be.

Jail medical services are contracted out, and the company that had hired me to do inmate physicals renewed their contract annually until, a little more than six years into my working there, they were underbid by another contractor. My job was combined with that of the Director of Nursing to lower the bottom line.

Essentially, my position was downsized and that put me, unexpectedly, out on early release. Unlike inmates, who may be released early for good behavior, I was not happy about it at all.

There were other surprises in store. The employment search process had evolved while I was a jailhouse nurse. I found myself in a foreign world of online job applications where there was no way to pitch my talents in person. And the "don't call us, we'll call you" format left little for me to do but apply, apply, and apply.

Being older – as in over 50 -- and having a lot of clinical experience were two strikes against me that were hard to hide in a resume that necessarily included my nursing school graduation date and recent employment. Career nurses generally expect a higher starting salary at a new job, commensurate with what they had been making. To save money, companies preferred to hire recent grads or nurses with less experience.

Despite these stumbling blocks, a few months into my search I found a job listing through the State Department of Corrections that looked like my ideal match: state epidemiology nurse. I managed to get an in-person interview before a panel of three state administrative nurses. They loved my experience in corrections, quizzed me about my infection control knowledge, and asked how willing I was to travel the state investigating disease outbreaks or monitoring code compliance. We hit it off instantly. I could see how the job would teach me new aspects of nursing, I already liked the people, and the salary was fair.

But just before leaving the interview, I thought to ask a final question. I was aware that Virginia state legislators would soon be voting on the budget that paid the salary for this job I found so appealing. Would this position be eliminated, I asked, if state corrections funding was reduced?

They all looked to the floor; there was my answer. Their silence and forced smiles expressed a "we hope not" sentiment. I understood those downward glances to mean that if I accepted the position, I would work the four remaining months of the current fiscal year and then possibly be out of work again.

As luck would have it, I also had applied for a job as a telephonic nurse coach with a company that hired nurses to do health coaching over the phone for a major insurance company. I had passed their screening tests for computer literacy and had toured the call center. I had a very vague knowledge about this field of nursing, but I had confidence in my ability to do patient teaching, no matter the circumstance.

I was offered both jobs. I truly wanted to stay in corrections. But having been recently divorced, I needed steady employment to feed myself and pay bills. When I called the nurse administrator in charge of hiring at the state to get her gut feeling about what would happen with the budget vote, she was blunt about the likelihood of the state cutting funds to the corrections system. I told her about my precarious financial position, and she accepted my denial of the offer with grace, expressing gratitude at meeting me. We were both disappointed. A few weeks later, I learned the funding was cut, and the position tasks rolled into an already existing job.

That was how fate and fortune took me from face-to-face nursing and tucked me into a cubicle in front of a computer screen. When I accepted the telephonic nursing job, it had seemed like it would be steady work. The pay was good, and I again felt set to stay in my newfound role for the duration of my career.

But from the beginning, the tight quarters unnerved me. Sitting in my swivel chair with legs extended, my feet touched all four walls in a 360-degree spin. Gray carpeted walls compressed my work environment into a six-foot square. My uniform became a telephone headset and whatever I wanted to wear as long as jeans, flip flips, or tube tops were not part of the day's chosen ensemble.

My tiny cubicle made me feel invisible. For 10-1/2 hours, four days a week, I resided in a "cuber-hood" of 80 murmuring spaces. When I stood, only my head and shoulders could be seen by others. Looking down the long room of the call center revealed the tops of only a very few heads. It reminded me of kennels in an animal shelter.

All day I stared at a computer screen and talked to patients on the phone. Even so, I held onto my hopes that I would get comfortable in my tiny, viewless space. After all, I was doing what I loved best – teaching patients how to help themselves.

The goal of the telephonic nursing program was to coach chronically ill patients about their disease, such as diabetes for example, and help them find ways to remember to take their medicines, visit a doctor, or quit smoking. Our role was to offer whatever was needed to move each individual patient toward restoring health. The insurance companies were motivated to fund the program hoping, as studies had shown, it would increase medication compliance, decrease ER visits, and reduce the complications of poorly controlled health problems.

I spent six weeks in a computer lab learning how to run the multiple software programs that interfaced to support this therapeutic phone call with the patient. Every nurse I encountered there shared the same opinion of the software. It did not work well. The computer program made the major but false assumption that a patient on the phone would answer questions in an artificial, robotic, orderly, and succinct fashion. The programs had been written by software engineers, not nurses.

During the initial information gathering assessment, if a patient reported a bug bite and you wanted to teach first aid, you had to exit the assessment program, open the educational tool, locate and pull up the teaching protocol for bug bite care, teach it, go back to the assessment tool, document what you taught, then go back and resume the assessment. Cumbersome, time-gobbling processes abounded.

I had lists of people to call each day, lots and lots of dialing with either no answer or answering machine responses. It seemed everyone had caller

ID, so when our office number came up as unknown, the person at the other end most likely assumed it was a telemarketer and did not pick up the phone. I left what seemed like a million messages and rarely heard back from anyone. Occasionally someone would return a call, but by then I was likely tied up in a conversation with a different patient. Often, another nurse would answer the call and talk with the patient, which was helpful but meant continuity of care went out the window.

Our guideline performance metrics recommended a total 20-minute timeline to complete the initial assessment, formulate a plan of care, do patient teaching, make referrals to other telephonic health care providers (respiratory therapy for smoking cessation, physical therapy for arthritis pain, etc.), and complete all charting.

Ha!

This is how a call typically went.

"Hello?"

"Hello! This is Susan, a registered nurse, calling from your health insurance company. Is this Mrs. Smith?"

Sometimes there was a click. . .or silence. . or a furious "take me off your list"

Or, Mrs. Smith might say, "Well, yes. What do you want?"

"Hi, Mrs. Smith, this is Susan, a registered nurse from your health insurance company," I say again for clarity. "I'm calling to help you with your diabetes. Would you like help from a nurse to help you feel better?"

Mrs. Smith might say, "What did you say your name was? I can't hear too good."

The first five minutes then are spent establishing I am who I am, she is who she is, hearing that her sister, Evelyn, was a nurse too, back in the war, but Evelyn hated people so she worked in the operating room where people were "out of it." And did I know there were scrub tops at the Goodwill for a good price but mostly in size extra, extra large?

On all calls, I explained the privacy law and our adherence to it. I explained the purpose of the program; that the first call is the longest to get all the health information. I told each patient I then would call once a month to check on his or her health, answer questions, and that those monthly calls would be shorter than the initial one.

Mrs. Smith might say, "How long will it take today, honey?"

I'd usually say, "Maybe about a half hour or a little longer." I'd move my phone mic close to my mouth and speak loudly, as she seemed to be hard of hearing.

The assessment components asked for physical health history, social history, names of doctors, medications taken, recent lab results, and recent doctor's visits -- all the same kind of questions you answer when you see a physician in person.

The call with Mrs. Smith progresses smoothly until we reach the most challenging portion, medications.

Think about it. If you are taking medications, can you remember when you started taking each pill and exactly why you are taking it, the dose, and who prescribed it? It's hard for everyone, especially if someone seeing multiple physicians. To make matters even more difficult, the words on a medicine bottle are so small most folks can't make them out. And if they can, they have trouble pronouncing the drug's name. Sometimes I would write down the name, dose, frequency, and reason to then be told, oh, that bottle is empty, and it was too expensive to buy more.

"Does your doctor know you stopped taking it?" I will ask.

"Oh, no," is the general reply. "I don't want him to know I can't afford it." Or they tell me they take a particular medication every other day to save money.

Yikes.

I'd say something like, "Mrs. Smith, I need to write down all your medicines. Can you tell me the names of your medicines, when you take them, the dose, and why you are taking them?"

Mrs. Smith might say, "Oh honey, I take a lot of pills, so does Raymond, my husband. We been married 50 years, we met at church, same one we still go to, well Raymond still goes, my legs won't let me go to church, I watch church on TV."

I'd say, "That is wonderful, Mrs. Smith. Tell me the first medicine you take, OK?"

Mrs. Smith bellows out a name. I jump from the shock delivered into my ear pieces and quickly pull them away. I picture her with her head thrown back like a wolf for maximum volume. "*Raymond?*

Raymmmooonnnd? He can't hear me, he's in the back of the house. *Raymmmooonnnd!*"

I hear a man's voice in the background. "*What?*"

I can tell from my end that Raymond has come to where Mrs. Smith is sitting in her recliner. Mrs. Smith tells me her son bought the chair for her on Mother's Day ten years earlier. Her son is a good man, she says, but his wife is crazy clean and that gets on his nerves, has been that way for years. "But you'd rather have a clean house than a pig sty, right?"

Mrs. Smith says sweetly, to Raymond, "This nurse on the phone wants to know what medicine I take."

"Aspirin," he says without questioning the wisdom of sharing personal medical information over the phone to God knows who. He then apparently returns to the back of the house.

"Aspirin," she conveys to me but I had heard Raymond say it and have already typed it in. I still need the dose, frequency, and length of time she has been taking aspirin.

An Instant Messaging (IM) box now popped up and blinked in the lower corner of my computer screen. It says, "You have been on this call 20 minutes. Wrap it up."

In my call center, there was a room where the active computers of all nurses were monitored. We called it the control tower. All our calls were observed in real-time, and when a time threshold had ticked by, the monitor would send an IM.

"Mrs. Smith, what is the dose of the aspirin, is it the regular aspirin or the baby aspirin? I need the dose and how often you take it and how long you have been on it and why."

"*Raymond? Raymmooonndd?* He can't hear me, he's in the back of the house. *Raymond?*"

"*What?*" Raymond returns to see what she needs. He goes to find the medicine box. Their daughter, Mrs. Smith says, fills it once a week. But there are no pill names or doses on the pills. Their daughter, I find out, took the pill bottles after Raymond and Mrs. Smith were mistakenly taking each other's pills.

I say I can get a current list of meds from her doctor, but she tells me she has multiple doctors and is not sure if each one knows all her pills.

The Instant Message box is advising me that I have been on this call so long that my supervisor has been dispatched to my cubicle to help me end it. Sure enough, I look up and there she stands, arms hanging into my cubicle, palms up, like she is silently asking "What is my problem?" I theatrically shrug and mime that I am uncontrollably twisting in the wind, and she sighs and walks away. Because I am "taking so long," her weekly stats are going to look bad -- as will my weekly performance numbers.

But sweet Mrs. Smith does have important questions about her blood sugar and wants to know what to do about toes that are numb a lot and look dark purple. I slap a blank sticky note on the screen to block out the IM box and teach Mrs. Smith about blood sugar monitoring and foot care, even though I suspect she won't remember much of this call next time I reach out to her. She is very grateful.

Raymond has been listening in on the extension, and he has questions, too. He has been worried about his wife and what he would do if she dies first. I promise to call back in four weeks, and they sound elated. But by the next month, I have been reassigned to another group of patients, and Mrs. Smith is destined to hear from a different nurse, meaning much of the process will be repeated all over again.

Telephonic health coaching is a fabulous concept. In theory, it offers the expertise of a registered nurse to teach a patient about health issues specific to their concerns. In addition, needed referrals can be made to a social worker for community resources, to a respiratory therapist who can help devise a plan for smoking cessation, or to a physical therapist who can formulate a safe program of daily exercises in an effort to prevent falls. The logistics of connecting nurses to patients, however, falls well short of satisfactory.

* * *

I was at the job just a little over a year when one of our company's nurse call centers in another state closed abruptly without notice. My co-workers and I grew alarmed at the news. All of those nurses were suddenly out of jobs, their patient calls routed to other centers. We wondered when our jobs would be downsized.

We were advised that would not happen.

We did not believe it.

Not long afterward, we were shocked to hear our respiratory therapist's position had been eliminated. Our therapist had a stellar ability to navigate patients through the challenges of nicotine addiction. I spoke to several patients – both male and female -- I had referred to her who kicked their smoking habit directly due to her therapeutic approach. They all had tried quitting previously but this time, given the correct guidance, they were finally smoke-free. Of all the positions that could be cut, we found it hard to believe it would be one that had proved to be so valuable. The costs saved by a patient who stopped smoking should have been endorsement enough, but once again, some arbitrary 'cost saving' bottom line ruled.

Many more positions fell as the months passed. It became increasingly more difficult to get patients the referral help they requested. Within 18 months of being hired, I witnessed many senior, higher-paid, nurses' positions eliminated. Several senior team leaders were downsized and out of a job. Our initial patient assessments were outsourced to nurses outside the country, bringing more cost savings to the insurance company, a company that we all knew paid its CEO more than $9 million a year -- plus stock.

Then the call center administrator was terminated, and we were managed by a district administrator through online webinars or via group telephone meetings -- on mute at our end. They talked. We listened.

New software was rolled out to eliminate the no answer/leave a message issue that wasted so much time. The software came and went so often it seemed we were constantly in the computer training lab.

The persistent tumult of uncertainty fatigued me. Each Friday night at 9 pm, I would walk weakly to my car, drained physically and emotionally from the stress of the metrics, the malignant harassment through IMs, and the fear of wondering when our call center would close. Knowing it takes months of applying for jobs to identify even a possible replacement, I began to troll the employment postings once again.

But even in the midst of persistent doubt and darkness, I was able to find a little light. Despite the uncertainty and change that permeated our organization, I continued to feel useful teaching the patients who maintained their connection to the program. I even managed to get to know a few of them quite well.

Late one afternoon, I called a man in my client queue who had been speaking with his previous nurse coach about depression. He was reassigned to me when she was reassigned to another area. He answered the call in a low-energy tone. I identified myself and said that I had read through his chart, which was a lie. I had read the last nurse's note while dialing his number.

He was reluctant, he said, to start all over again with me. He had really liked his last nurse, and she knew everything about him. I could not dismiss his apathy and frustration and bluntly shared that I thought it was unfair for him to be reassigned and that I would not blame him if he was not interested in talking with me. I sent an IM to my nurse manager to see if there was any way to get his previous nurse on the line right now.

A one-word reply from her blinked back immediately: *no*.

Slowly, he began to tell his story. I stayed silent. He explained that he had just had a terrible day of pain . . . emotional pain. He felt hopeless and bleak. Long pauses punctuated his quiet monologue. I did not hear crying. I heard effort, exhaustion, and deep sorrow. Every breath exhaled a quiet wish to be gone.

A lightning bolt rocketed up my spine when I suddenly realized my call had intersected an active suicide plan. The call center had a protocol to follow if we suspected a potential suicide situation. I had no idea how to access it, having learned it during orientation along with a billion other procedures and having yet to use it. I grabbed a sticky note pad and wrote, "*Help*, suicide."

I snapped to a stand and looked at the three adjacent cubicles. All the nurses were occupied on calls. I slapped the cubicle wall to get the attention of Helena, the nurse closest to me. The look on my face made her jump up and grab my note. My voice remained quiet and slow while I spoke to my patient, but inside my heart pounded in my ears. My patient told me he had enough pills in a bottle in his hand to go to sleep and never wake up. This made my throat tighten.

In her cubicle, Helena quickly concluded her call, entered my cube, and grabbed the procedure manual from my hands. As she searched for the protocol, she listened, wide-eyed, to my side of the phone interaction. She leaned over me and pulled up the emergency 911 number for my patient's location. All I needed to do, if I needed to do it, was to open an additional phone line and call.

Despondent but still talking, my patient told me he had rehearsed how this day would end. I IM'd my nurse manager to listen in on my call and shoot me suggestions of what to say through IM. Luckily, she was at her computer and able to do what I asked.

I could not tell when a manager listened in, as any one of them could do at any time, unannounced, as a quality control measure. I did not disclose the additional nurse on the line to my patient. I don't know that I even considered doing so. This privacy issue had been covered on the first phone contact with each patient. They must consent that calls could occasionally be monitored for quality assurance.

In that moment, I was extremely grateful for the support. When I saw her comment "good job" or "that was perfect" following my words to my patient, I calmed. She suggested I ask if he had anyone else in the house. I had already asked that earlier. I told her that he was alone. She continued to advise me as long as he talked, reaffirming that I was doing fine and stressing that if he hung up, I would need to activate 911.

My patient talked another 20 minutes with very little prompting from me. Helena scribbled a few words on a notepad for me to use in my conversation and got back to her work, occasionally peeking over the carpeted wall, miming thumbs up or thumbs down and waiting for my response. My thumb stayed cautiously up.

My heart rate began to settle as my patient drove the conversation to more reflective topics. He had suffered with clinical depression for years, he told me, and visited a psychologist he trusted. His weekly appointment just happened to be scheduled for the next day. I asked if he wanted me to have an ambulance take him to the hospital right then, and he declined, saying he was feeling more stable. He acknowledged he felt that he would not take the pills today as planned and contracted with me not to harm himself for one hour. I asked if I could call back in one hour, and he agreed. I called back hourly, four times. Finally, my nurse manager and I left the call center late after making as sure as we could that he would keep his appointment the next day.

It was difficult for me to sleep that night, thinking about this 40-year-old man, so alone and despondent. When I arrived at work the following day, I called my patient back. He answered with a brighter voice. His visit with the psychologist had gone well, he said. He had given her his stash of pills, as I had suggested the night before. Our conversation was brief, and he ended by saying if his other nurse could not call anymore, he would be willing to let me call every couple of weeks. I hung up and wept with relief, allowing all the stress I had carried with me since the previous day to drain out.

* * *

Over the course of my time with the headset herd, I learned just how much health information I absorbed through my sense of sight. The eyes, skin, and gait all relayed stories of their own as I watched my patients' approach or walked into their hospital room. Despite the handicap of being sight unseen, I found a relationship could still be forged over the phone and effective teaching could bring about positive results.

This was especially true in the case of Bert, who, through sharing his health journey with me, profoundly proved to me the power of intention over statistics.

I called Bert one evening to invite him into the health-coaching program to help him manage his diabetes. A warm, kind voice poured into my ears saying that he would welcome any help he could get, as long as he could tell me his story so far. He and his wife had just finished dinner. They usually took a walk at this time, but he checked with his wife, and she agreed they could still go after our phone call. I told him I would be delighted to hear about his health journey.

After my obligatory HIPPA law blather, Bert begins. My back rounds into my chair and my hands slip into my lap. My eyes half close as I am transfixed by his smooth country tone and engaging storytelling style.

He began driving a cement truck right after high school, Bert tells me. He and Muriel met young, and the job and marriage happened right around the same time. Sitting all day in a truck added weight to his linebacker frame, and as the years went by, his belly just got bigger. High blood pressure and diabetes became his companions. He went to the doctor's office regularly like you're supposed to do and took all his pills. Many days Muriel fixed his lunch for him, two big sandwiches and some sodas. They both loved Little Debbie snacks but tried to only eat them occasionally due to the diabetes. Insulin injections twice a day became routine.

When he was in his early 50s, Bert began to have pain in his left leg. He had ballooned to 404 pounds. It was hard to get in and out of his cement truck cab, but once he was seated, he could drive just fine. He saw the doctor for the leg pain and was given pain pills without so much as even a look at his leg. Over a few weeks, the left leg swelled larger. When the tingling and burning pain became more intense one evening, Muriel drove him to the small local ER for help. The doctor gave him an injection of pain medicine, stronger pain pills, and sent him home. That night, he says, was one long stretch of excruciating pain.

"The doctor looked at me with disgust, Susan," he sighs. "I knew I was fat and gross looking."

The next day back he went to the ER in so much pain he could no longer bear it. The doctor accused him of drug seeking and told him to leave. But Bert begged for help. The doctor looked at his leg and relented, agreeing to order a test to check the circulation in his groin, thigh, calf, and foot. The test showed that at the site where the biggest artery to the leg enters the groin, there was an enormous blood clot compromising the circulation to his entire leg.

According to Bert, the doctor told him to go home and wait for the clot to kill him, which was what he deserved for being so fat. But Bert begged. He pleaded with the doctor to remove the clot. The doctor told Bert the anesthesia alone would end his life. Bert pleaded more, adding the resolve to lose weight if given this chance.

"That is what all fat people say," Bert remembers the doctor retorting.

Bert says he could tell the doctor wanted to help because he kept standing there in the room arguing instead of stomping out. Even if he could get the clot out, the doctor said, Bert was too huge for the OR table and too high risk to survive surgery no matter how great the need.

Bert says he asked for a piece of paper. On it he wrote that he consented to be duct taped to the OR table. That he realized he might die just lying flat. That if they would just do the surgery now he would leave the hospital right after the surgery and not come back. He wanted no more pain pills. He signed the paper. Muriel agreed with everything Bert wrote and signed it herself.

Miraculously, the doctor relented.

The hospital staff groaned when they saw Bert, he says, and poorly disguised their feelings of disgust, fear of injury, and obvious thoughts that doing surgery on Bert was a waste of time. He says that right then and there he felt they might be right. He knew he was likely to hurt someone as they hefted him around and that he might die wrapped in duct tape

The *instant*, Bert says, verbally punching the word and picking up his story telling pace, the *instant* he woke up from the anesthesia, his pain was 100 percent gone. The staff let him lie right there for a few hours while the incision sealed.

The doctor was relieved Bert survived but told Bert snidely that he expected him to be fatter than ever when he saw him in a month for his post-op check.

Muriel and Bert were elated the long-endured pain was gone. The day after surgery, Bert says he and his wife came up with a plan to lose weight together. Bert wanted to lose 200 pounds, and Muriel felt 70 pounds would be a good goal for her. The clothes and Christmas decorations piled on the treadmill pushed up against the wall of their living room were removed, and space was made for Bert to navigate between the machine and his recliner. "My first day on the treadmill I went very, very slow and lasted four minutes," he specifically recalls, having become profoundly short of breath.

Each day he lasted a minute or two more. By his one-month post-op checkup, he had lost 40 pounds. It made Bert grin big to see the stunned look on the doctor's face. He says he told the Doc, "You ain't seen nothin' yet."

At first, he and Muriel made no changes to the food they ate, merely reduced portion size. Their once-a-week date night treat had been to go to Burger King, where each of them consumed two Whoppers. They cut back to one apiece and now, he says with a chuckle, "We cut one in half." The couple reduced the amount of soda they consumed and drank more water. Once back at work, Bert revised his lunch-break routine. After he ate his one sandwich, he would get up and walk around his truck for the rest of his break. Upon returning home, he got on the treadmill, increasing the height and speed gradually until he reached the maximum for both. After dinner, he and Muriel went for a small walk.

"We still hold hands, you know," he adds with boyish delight.

One by one, his physician eliminated his medications, including the insulin shots. Bert's co-workers were transfixed by his determination and ongoing transformation. In one year he had lost 100 pounds. His lunch break exercise routine gathered members, all of them walking around the parked cement trucks. He laughs about people staring at a bunch of men going round and round the parking lot, all teasing and joking with one another.

Over the next six months, the length of time designated for participation in the health coach program, I speak to Bert or Muriel every four weeks for an update. Muriel reaches her weight loss goal before Bert.

They keep a piece of paper by the phone to write down comments or questions for me. "Bert is tellin' me to write that for Susan when she calls," shares Muriel, who tells me Bert really looks forward to my calls. We talk about oral care, eye care, depression, and whatever else comes up. Bert remarks how he would no longer need to be duct taped to the OR table if he needs surgery. I tell him I wish he could work in the call center with me and share his story with other people who think it is impossible for them to feel better.

Of course, Bert is unique. He always has loved being active and working around the house, but the leg pain and routine of sitting in the truck had made his conditions go from bad to worse. Once the pain was eliminated, he returned with vigor to his determination to be healthy.

On our last phone call, Bert reports he has just crossed the 200-pound weight loss goal. I was elated and whooped so loud the nurses around me jumped up to see what had gotten into me. I holler out, "Bert lost 200," my hands clapping over my head. Bert can hear the whoops and cheering from the nearby nurses, who have no idea who Bert is but celebrate his accomplishment, nevertheless.

As I conclude my final paperwork and say goodbye to Bert, I hear him stutter and stammer. He thanks me for being a good cheerleader and for all the things I have taught him. I told him he has taught me way more than I have him. I can hear Muriel in the background urging Bert on about something.

Finally Bert says, "Muriel wants to tell you something. Goodbye, Susan. Here's Muriel."

"Oh my lands, Bert. She's a nurse." Muriel feigns exasperation while taking the phone from Bert. Then to me she giggles, "Me and Bert's havin' sex again. That's great, right?"

"That *is* great news, Muriel," I tell her, without missing a beat. "The best."

This is the highest of all honors for me as a nurse, to be a part of and bear witness to these steps toward wellness. To walk this healing path with patients facing challenging health issues. To observe how their extraordinary successes come from determination and a willingness to modify old habits, one at a time. And, maybe, pick up one or two new ones.

That is what nursing is all about!

15

TEAMWORK

In 1981, I was working on a plastic surgery, medical/surgical and psych combo unit at Stuart Circle Hospital in Richmond, my first job in Virginia.

One afternoon, the call bell toned at the nurses' station monitoring box next to where I sat with several other nurses charting end-of-shift notes. At the same moment, the light above the patient's door directly across from me turned on. I glanced up. It was *my* patient calling for help. I left what I was doing and walked into her room, all the while looking down, pondering my charting.

I stopped at the foot of the bed, making me visible to the other nurses busy at the desk.

"What can I help you with, Mrs. T?" I asked, turning my eyes toward the bed she occupied. Instantly my jaw dropped.

"Oh," I said in shocked surprise.

Mrs. T was lying on her side, her naked bottom shining out of the sheets.

"Scratch my rear end," she purred demurely, gazing at me over her left shoulder. I looked at her in disbelief, then glanced out to the nurses' station. Seeing the look on my face, Nurse Venus stood up and came into the room.

"What did she say?" Venus asked me.

My mouth stayed open. No words found their way out.

"Scratch my rear end," Mrs. T. cooed to Venus.

Standing beside me at the foot of the bed and wearing a calm expression on her face, Venus asked my patient. "Can you do this?" Venus lifted her arms out in front of her, palms down, hovering parallel to the floor.

"Oh yes," said Mrs. T, putting her hands out in front of her, imitating Venus.

"OK then," continued Venus, "just take it on around." Venus let her hand float around to her back. She gave her own butt an exaggerated scratch. Then she snatched my sleeve and pulled me out of the room, leaving the patient speechless, wondering what had just gone down.

Mrs. T's four words lived on in infamy.

In the weeks following the bare-butt encounter, "Scratch my rear end" echoed across our unit, becoming the greeting and response we used on both the doctors and one another.

All levity aside, Venus gave me a gift that day. She showed me – yet again -- that not all patient teaching is spelled out in a nursing textbook. Sometimes a nurse instructs by scratching her own rear end while identifying it as an independent activity of daily living, or IADL, and chalking it up as part of that patient's learning for the day.

Prior to the scratch-my-rear-end episode, Mrs. T had been demanding attention all morning. When I entered her private room at 7 am to introduce myself and check her vital signs, she barked, "Get me orange juice." She was sitting regally with the head of the bed elevated, clutching her delicate silk bed jacket around her throat. Her bright orange hair, an inch of gray roots showing, stuck out in all directions.

Wow, I thought, taking her in, *this is one spoiled 80-year-old lady*. Rather than pointing out that her breakfast tray, arriving momentarily, would have juice on it, I headed down the hall to the patient snack refrigerator and retrieved a four-ounce plastic cup of orange juice. I popped a straw through the foil top and handed it to her with a cheery, "Here you go."

"I want ice in it," she commanded as though I should have intuited her preference. She did not say damn it, but I could hear it in her voice.

You're welcome, I thought, and went and got ice. That was just the beginning.

Throughout my shift, Mrs. T. pressed her call button incessantly, making one demand after another. I managed to maintain my composure, making nice, trying to get her to see me as a professional nurse, not her handmaiden.

Mrs. T. had been admitted on a Friday afternoon for "evaluation of an unsteady gait." In other words, she was what we called a drop off. Her family, with whom she lived, needed the week off for a planned vacation and wanted their mother in a safe place where she would neither terrify nor fire the household staff in their absence. One of her children just happened to be on the hospital Board of Directors and called in a favor on behalf of their generous donations to the hospital. During her week-long stay, Mrs. T never had a blood test, an x-ray, or a screening by a physical therapist.

It was not unusual for my Richmond hospital to cater to old Virginia families in this way. But we nurses resented these "guests," as they drew our time away from the ill patients who needed our trained attention. We took turns caring for these divas to maintain our own sanity and save a physician from writing "death by nurse strangulation" as the discharge diagnosis.

Throughout the years of my professional nursing career, there have been many days when I answered multiple calls for help from the same patient. But those individuals had medical issues that required my assistance. Mrs. T was just mean and arrogant and desperate for attention. All the nurses felt sorry for her family. We truly hoped they were having a good vacation.

As exasperating as it was to care for these patients, it could not compare to the frustration, aggravation, and rage we felt for a family we dealt with on this same unit a few months after Mrs. T. left our care.

Early one afternoon, Mrs. Rudacille, our wonderful head nurse, called us all together to alert us that the hospital was about to admit an elderly obese woman suffering with multiple bedsores.

During the day our unit – known simply as 2A -- was staffed by six or seven nurses. A new admission typically would be assigned to one nurse. We all knew that when Mrs. Rudacille took a team approach to a new patient, something out of the ordinary was about to happen. We could never have guessed the magnitude of the nightmare that was about to unfold.

A home health nurse had contacted Mrs. Rudacille to give a report on the patient who was on her way to us by ambulance. A month or so earlier, a community health physician had sent the nurse out to the patient's home to evaluate her skin status and communicate what she found. The trip was necessary because the patient was no longer able to get to her doctor's office due to her large size and weakened condition. The doctor then ordered twice-weekly nursing visits for wound care to the heels, buttocks, and sacrum, areas where the patient had developed pressure sores from being confined to bed without being turned every couple of hours. After several visits, the nurse reported that the wounds had become medically unmanageable in the home. The doctor decided to admit the patient to the hospital for more aggressive wound care.

Mrs. Duke, our soon-to-be patient, lived with her son, a colossal 40-year-old who apparently invested little time in his own personal or dental hygiene. He was arrogant, obnoxious, foul-mouthed, bigoted, and just plain nasty. We met him before his mother arrived as he strutted off the elevator, his enormous belly straining over the top of a saucer-sized Confederate flag belt buckle. The troops – a brother and a sister -- trailed behind him. All three shocked us with their odorous presence and angry demeanor. The brother looked younger; a skinny, greasy-haired, snaggle-toothed man jittering his way toward us. The hefty, big-busted sister – dressed in a tube top and spandex leggings – swaggered down the hall as though looking to start a fight with anyone who stood in her path. I felt like we were a pack of beached seals watching a pod of killer whales swimming straight for us.

We stood at the nurses' station and stared. It was hate at first sight for all parties concerned, and we had not even met the patient yet.

"Holy shit," we mumbled among ourselves, all of us leaning back slightly, collectively eyeing the approaching train wreck. What a clusterfuck (a word nurses save for the worst of the worst) we muttered to one another, the epithet softly sliding out between fiercely gritted teeth. If ever a nursing staff instantly united against a common enemy, this was it.

Just as the patient's family slid up next to the nurses' station, the other elevator door opened. The young ambulance crew flashed us a warning look of "here comes a shit storm" and rolled the litter quickly on past the nurses' desk in the direction of the finger Mrs. Rudacille was pointing down the hall.

The patient was howling, "*I need ice cream.*"

We followed Mrs. Rudacille and the litter down the hall. I noticed Mrs. Duke had aprons of fat that bulged around the litter straps. The odor of infection and feces wafted behind her.

"*I need ice cream,*" she hollered a second time.

Her enormous son bellowed back, "*Shut up, ya fat bitch.*"

Visitors appeared in open doorways, as wide-eyed and open mouthed as the medical staff. We all made "yikes" faces at one another.

I was only a few minutes into this nightmare, but my mind was already desperately seeking a way out. I seriously considered snatching my Virginia nursing license out of my purse – the license that I had earned through three years of hard and disciplined work – and tearing it up in front of Mrs. Rudacille. Then I would grab this belligerent, bellicose excuse for a son, drive him to the zoo, and shove him right up the nearest elephant's ass. Or I could push him in the lions' cage and let them eat on him for a month. No, I thought, I'll just beat him to death with the meat cleaver the home health nurse reported he had hung over his mother's bed to threaten her with when she refused to shut up.

"Susan?" I heard Mrs. Rudacille calling me.

"Huh?" I snapped out of my reverie. The first few minutes with this family had been unbelievable, and now we were in the patient's room.

"Get on this side of the bed," she directed. The litter had been positioned tightly against the bed. Three nurses stood next to the litter, three positioned themselves on the other side of the bed. One person was stationed at the head of the bed, another at its foot. The sheet edges that the EMT's had used to get Mrs. Duke onto the litter were pulled out from under the patient and unrolled. The nurses on the litter side and those at the head and foot of the bed grabbed the sheet. They would be the lifters. The nurses on the bed side leaned over the bed to grab the sheet edges. They would be the pullers. All seven of us looked at Mrs. Rudacille.

Quietly she said, "On three we will lift her onto the bed." We made sure both bed and litter wheels were locked, securing them next to each other. We grabbed the sheet as close to the patient as possible and spread our feet for maximum balance.

Mrs. Rudacille waited for all of us to nod that we were ready. "One, two, three," she said softly. I pulled with all my might, as did everyone else, if their groaning testimony was any indication.

"Stop!" she said, this time in a louder voice. The patient had not budged one inch. Mrs. Rudacille turned to me. "Susan, go look for some men to help us." I found a respiratory therapist and a male nurse's aide on the unit and had them follow me to the patient's room. The young men from the ambulance team came with us.

As I passed by the patient's children in the hall, I heard the daughter stage whisper, "This is taking *forever.*"

I snapped my head around to glare at her, noticing that visitors had congregated in front of other patient doors behind her. They met my gaze and shook their heads as if to say "poor nurses." *Good*, I thought, picking up my fantasies where I had left off. Maybe these visitors would smother the three children while we were tending to the patient. Never before or since have I taken such an immediate and intense dislike to any patient's family.

While I was out of the room recruiting help, Mrs. Rudacille had reconfigured the nurses. Now we had five people to pull and five people to lift. I was at the foot of the bed to lift the feet. Three large trash bags were spread out on the hospital bed to decrease friction and help slide the patient into the bed once we got some momentum going. Upon my return to the room, I looked at our patient to see how she was tolerating the hub bub of moving her from the ambulance litter to the bed. Mrs. Duke's eyes looked about the room with a disaffected air, neither offering to help nor asking questions, other than wondering when the ice cream she had repeatedly demanded would be brought to her, or at least that is what I imagined.

Again, Mrs. Rudacille called, "One, two, three." This time the patient slid two-thirds of the way onto the bed. The lifters handed off the sheet to the pullers and quickly moved the litter out of the way. They shoved their hips against the patient and as Mrs. Rudacille counted again, we pulled and lifted her to the center of the bed. To pull up the siderails, we had to manipulate Mrs. Duke's aprons of fat to avoid pinching her between the rails and the mattress. We all were breathing hard. This was dangerous for the patient and for us. We did not want to drop Mrs. Duke, nor did we want to risk a back injury. Thanks to Mrs. Rudacille's careful planning, we all made it safely through the ordeal.

Within seconds of our shared accomplishment, the ambulance crew vanished. "Keep the sheet," we heard them holler from down the hall. It had taken us 30 minutes to get this patient off the litter and into the bed. Now we needed to remove the trash bags and transfer sheet.

Mrs. Rudacille asked us to tip the patient toward her right side using the transfer sheet. Then we would hold Mrs. Duke on her side while the sheet and bags were tucked way up under her. We could then tip her in the opposite direction to pull everything free. At the same time, we could also assess the patient's back to see how extensive the bed sores were and place clean pads under her.

Hovering over our new patient this closely, the odor of urine, feces, and sweat was intense. Out in the hall we could hear an escalating argument among her three children as to who would get what when their mother died. It seems her car was the possession most coveted. We rolled our eyes, shook our heads, and turned to Mrs. Duke, who was again insisting we bring her ice cream – *now.*

There was no time to address her demands. We still had plenty of work to do to get her settled. Five of us shoved our hips into the bed's siderails and pulled the patient toward us and up onto her side.

"A little more," coaxed Mrs. Rudacille. The sheet and bags were stuck. We barely had the patient tipped up. Her large size wedged her between the siderails; there was simply not enough room. We needed a bigger bed. Our hospital would have to rent one from a medical supply company. We could not care for the patient in this bed.

But first things first. We still needed to remove the bags and sheet. We yanked again – even harder. The patient moaned. The trash bags pulled free. The sheet pulled free. Then a wheel at the foot of the bed bent, snapped, and shot out across the floor. The bed frame slammed onto the floor at a tilt. The patient screamed. We gasped. We pushed with our hips against the siderail. Mrs. Rudacille sent a nurse out to call maintenance personnel. The nursing supervisor arrived, took one look at the scene, and fled to call for a larger bed.

All the commotion threw Mrs. Duke's son into a rage. "I'm gonna sue this place if my mother is hurt," he threatened. He thought he could smell money in that room, but that was the smell of all of us sweating as we tried to keep our patient safe.

We assured Mrs. Duke that all was well, and we would have the bed fixed soon. The maintenance man came with wood blocks. He helped lift the bed while the blocks were positioned under the frame.

Mrs. Duke's son was now at the nurses' desk hollering at our supervisor. "I insist my mother get the best medical care money can buy," he shouted, while his brother looked furtively for what I felt pretty sure was a possible source of whatever pharmaceutical product he would normally be using at this time of day. I saw him head for the elevator. I knew that two blocks from our hospital was a street corner where he could find whatever substance he needed. I was certain he would be back in 15 minutes or so. The daughter told her super-sized brother – still standing at the nurses' station berating our supervisor – that she would find the cafeteria and bring back food for all of them.

By then, every nurse could have used a break. But none of us had a minute to spare. We still had the admission paperwork to fill out, the wounds to assess, and several call lights were on. Other patients needed attention.

With the family sideshow split up, however, we were able to regroup. Mrs. Rudacille called a pow-wow in the nurses' lounge right next to the nurses' desk. We gathered around her. First, she pointed out that things could be worse. All our other patients were somewhere between wonderful and manageable. By now they all knew what was going on. We only had this one nutty family to deal with. We could do it. She was right. We'd dealt with worse. Well, maybe not worse, but just as bad.

The nursing supervisor stayed to answer the phones, respond to call bells, and retrieve what was needed that was not already on the unit.

Next on the agenda was bathing Mrs. Duke. Four nurses stepped into her room. Normally a bed bath is not done as part of an admission, but this was no normal admission. It was obvious the patient had not been bathed in some time. She had been incontinent for who knows how long and had wounds on her heels, back, and rear end.

Mrs. Lightfoot, a member of our nursing team and a champion bed-bath giver, prepared the bath supplies. Her years of clinical experience made her efficient and competent. Her skills were well respected and highly regarded by the rest of us. She was an A-team nurse all the way, and each and every one of her patients always sparkled with cleanliness.

Another nurse assisted her with the bath, while the two other nurses helped to hold up the folds of skin so they could be examined, washed, and dried. The bath team worked in silence, knowing what each other needed by a nod or a pointed finger. Yet another nurse took vital signs and asked the admission questions. From the foot of the bed, I unwrapped Mrs. Duke's knee-high foot dressings. The home health nurse had left all the three-day-old dressings intact. She knew we would be getting wound care orders here at the hospital and would remove whatever dressings she would apply. Our hospital employed a nurse who had been trained in the latest advancements in wound management. I was told she was on her way to help me.

"How long have you had this rash under your breasts?" I heard Mrs. Lightfoot ask our patient. I looked up to see a bright red fungal rash covering the chest and underside of Mrs. Duke's large breasts. It was not surprising. Such a combination of heat, moisture, and darkness is a breeding ground for fungal infections.

"I want ice cream," was the patient's response. We assured her that her dinner would be there as soon as the doctor ordered her a diet. It was mid-afternoon, and we knew from what she had told us that she had eaten lunch at home before coming to the hospital.

I tucked pillows under the Mrs. Duke's legs and knees to raise her feet off the bed. "I need to see your feet," I told her. Just as I was removing the last bit of dressing on one foot, the wound care nurse arrived. The pungent odor from the drainage-soaked dressings filled the room. I introduced the new nurse to Mrs. Duke as I unrolled the last row of gauze from her foot. We all looked at the newly exposed foot and went silent. We shot glances at each other.

The patient could tell something was up. "Is everything alright?" she inquired.

Mrs. Lightfoot resumed the bath and told the patient everything would be fine as the assistant nurse helping with the bath left the room. We could hear her gagging as she ran down the hallway toward the bathroom.

Maggots swarmed in the tennis ball-sized heel crater. The wound nurse left to get peroxide. I piled the soiled dressings into a trash bag, tied it up, then placed it in another bag and tied that one tightly. I washed my hands and put on new gloves, two pair. I forced a neutral expression onto my face.

"Mrs. Duke, do your feet hurt?" I asked.

"Not really," she replied. "Can't feel them."

Thank God for that, I thought. Once we flushed the maggots away, the wounds would fill with dead tissue and infection. The maggots were doing a marvelous job of keeping the wound pink and pristine as they consumed the necrotic debris. But medical maggots were not in vogue at this time, and these had certainly not been acquired from a sterile laboratory. Mrs. Duke's substantial and deep back wounds had no maggots; flies had only reached dressings that were exposed to open air.

Once she had been bathed and her sheets were changed, the bed scale was positioned, and Mrs. Duke was placed on it and weighed. She did not believe it when told she was 380 pounds. She said the last time she remembered being weighed she was 220 pounds. But it doesn't take a nurse to know how quickly the pounds add up on a steady diet of ice cream. Thankfully, the extra-large hospital bed arrived the next day.

Every day it took six nurses to bathe Mrs. Duke, perform wound care, and change the sheets. It took the same number to change the pads under her whenever she was incontinent.

Despite such constant care, our patient's condition worsened. Her veins were deep and fragile, making it impossible to keep an IV in place to properly administer antibiotics. Due to the raging wound infections, her diabetes resisted control. She refused food other than ice cream, and she screamed for it nonstop.

During her first week in the hospital, Mrs. Duke's older son showed up daily. Sometimes the others came, but usually not. During her second week there, we got daily afternoon telephone calls from the same son.

"Hey, this is Frank. Is my mother dead yet?" he always asked.

By the third week, the infection had traveled to Mrs. Duke's blood and consumed her. She was unresponsive, and her kidneys and liver failed. Her lungs filled with fluid.

Doctors summoned the children.

They entered the room together as several of us were tending to her care.

Frank poked one finger into his mother's shoulder. "Ma!" he barked. "Ma." She lay there motionless. He shrugged, and they all retreated to the hallway. Visitors peeked out from some rooms.

"I want her house and car," Frank announced, continuing the discussion they had started a few weeks earlier. A hullabaloo ensued. Hospital security tried to usher them out. Appalled visitors whispered to each other, and patient doors slammed in disgust.

Mrs. Duke died that afternoon. The funeral home people came to pick up her body. It took a crew of us to help them secure her body onto the thin litter. We wondered how they would fare at the funeral home once they got her there.

Looking back on this time – past the mean-spirited family of a difficult patient – I feel so much gratitude for everyone else involved. So many of our other patients on the unit had helped us cope with Mrs. Duke. Her stay had affected them because it took multiple nurses to participate in the care of just one patient. Every day my patients assured me they would only call if they absolutely needed help. They were part of the team that it took to care for this patient and her children. Visitors told new patients or new visitors about what we were dealing with. They filled water pitchers and helped themselves to the fresh laundry if they needed a towel or sheet for their family member.

Throughout those long three weeks, both patients and visitors never stopped caring for us and nurturing us. Our hospital was small with small units. Staff members had all been there for ages, and everyone helped everyone else. That is not always the case. We had a head nurse who kept us going with words of encouragement and little treats of candy or cookies. She often put aside her own work to help at the bedside. It was true team nursing, and it was exhilarating, even during the ongoing difficulty of carrying for Mrs. Duke and dealing with her family.

Finding a place of employment like this Richmond hospital was a rare treasure.

* * *

A few years after my time there, the hospital was purchased by a real estate developer and turned into condominiums.

16

ZERO TO TEN

The moment your butt hits the hospital bed, normal life disappears. You are stripped of clothes, shoes, jewelry, make-up, and, for the most part, your identity. Your world view is from your back, which struggles to make friends with the overused, unforgiving mattress that has become the center of this strange new universe. It doesn't take long for your hair to begin pointing in odd directions. Your mind soon follows, and you start to wonder if anyone has ever died in the very spot in which you now find yourself. It's no surprise that you wake up confused every morning you remain in this tight, unwelcoming space.

Nothing here is simple or easy. Even the act of donning the standard hospital garb, ironically called a gown, requires assistance. With three arm holes or three head holes -- hard to tell so flip a coin – the "gown" never fits. It is always too big or too small. Does it open to the back or front, you ask yourself, as has every patient who has ever preceded you.

You are graced with a few sundry possessions -- a comb, a toothbrush, maybe a magazine. Unspoken rules and that ill-fitting gown keep you stuck in your adult-sized bassinette. Don't bother with "but I don't want the side rails up" or "I just want to walk around the halls for a few minutes." You are not in charge of those – or any other – decisions. Whether you like it or not, someone else is now the boss of you.

Your body, once your own, has become an object of interest to roaming groups of color-coded, scrub-suit wearing young adults. As the sole occupant of your mattress planet, you are orbited by constellations of badge-wearing aliens, all seeking your blood, urine, stool, or sputum (aka phlegm). Someone bearing a clipboard asks you what you want to eat the next day. Someone else arrives to draw tubes of blood. Another someone asks that you take a deep breath and cough as he leans close, holding a stethoscope against your back. Hmmm, he might say, but before you can even formulate a question, he makes a mysterious note in your file, turns, and disappears.

Your wrist band is where all these eyes focus, not your face.

Words roll through your mind in a desperate mantra that is some variation of "Get me the hell outta here."

Having been on both sides -- looking up from the bed as a patient and looking down as a nurse -- I know exactly what it feels like.

As a patient, I questioned the supposed "clean environment" when I examined the hospital bed itself. Rails and cords, buttons and mattress, all in all, a complicated tangle of nooks and crannies. I couldn't imagine that every one of those surfaces had been carefully and thoroughly cleaned before I arrived. And sitting in that very same bed, behaving like a patient -- compliant and consenting -- I waited to be told which body fluid I should offer next for analysis.

As a nurse, I saw my patient's stress: mentally, emotionally, energetically, and physically. I wanted to connect and comfort, be supportive and respectful. But that took time. And time was often in short supply for reasons beyond my control.

But as both patient and nurse, I learned that good relationships and positive outcomes required keeping the lines of communication open in a way that everyone involved understood what was being said.

For example, the accurate use of the pain scale has been one component of medical care with which I have struggled from both angles, looking down onto the hospital bed, or looking up from one.

The pain scale is a tool designed to help estimate and then communicate how pain feels to you -- the patient -- in this particular moment in a concrete and measurable way. Based on your responses, physicians then gauge whether you are feeling better or worse and adjust your medications to better manage your pain. Your nurse relies on the same scale to determine if the prescribed pain med is working or if further adjustments are needed.

Problems with this scale abound. If you say you are at a ten because you are in the worst pain you have ever experienced, but the physician does not feel your physical appearance reflects a ten, then that's trouble. If the pain scale wall chart numbers with the smiley/grimacing faces designed to help you decide between a five or a six make no sense to you, then that's more trouble. But perhaps worst of all – since it can affect the quality your care – is when you blurt out a number just to get this prying doctor or nurse out of your room.

Here is how it typically goes.

"On the scale of zero to ten," I may ask my patient, "describe your pain level right now, zero being no pain and ten being the worst pain you have ever had in your entire life."

At this point, the patient either will look perplexed or roll his eyes. He may furrow his eyebrows and make a tentative stab at an answer. "Three?" he'll say, voice trailing off into a question as he looks toward me to validate his response.

I had one patient who didn't even hazard a guess. He just flipped me the bird and rolled over, closing his eyes. End of assessment. My nurse's note for the shift said blandly, "The patient refuses to answer with level-of-pain number."

Other more typical responses are, "I feel bad/ terrible/ awful/ like death warmed over/ queasy/ achy/ logy/ crappy/ like shit." Then it is up to me to figure out where those fit on a scale of one to ten. Which I am not supposed to do. No guessing permitted.

Often, I will persist, determined to get some number -- any number -- out of my patient. "I must write down in my notes what your pain number is", I'll say for the third or fourth time and wait until my patient fills the silence by blurting out "five."

"Oh good," I might say, looking at his chart. "That's lower than yesterday."

"No, no," he then protests, not remembering what it was he said yesterday. "I feel worse than yesterday." I can see we are heading nowhere fast.

But necessity, as they say, is the mother of invention.

One day, I begin the drill as usual, asking my patient to describe his level of pain on a scale of one to ten. Already frustrated by his hospital stay, exhausted from listening to his roommate puke all night, and hopeless about ever having a real conversation with his surgeon -- whom he had glimpsed through the bathroom door crack that morning for a total of ten seconds while sitting unproductively on the toilet – he barks out, "I feel like shit."

He is sitting in bed with the head elevated, restlessly shifting his legs about as he tries to get comfortable. He rubs his hands over his face. The white bed sheets do nothing to improve his color. His gown has broken neck snaps so one bare shoulder hangs out, not in a sassy way.

I pause. God, I hate that damn pain assessment box on my nurse's notes that must have a number scribbled in. The pain scale is a big pain in the ass.

I think about taking a stab at what number "shit" would be so I can put it in the box and stop badgering this poor soul. But I am very much aware that shit has a range of its own. My patient looks up to see me standing there looking dispirited.

"What?" he asks, sighing deeply, annoyed that I am still in his room.

"I can't figure out how your 'shit' fits on the pain scale so I can write it down in your chart and leave you alone," I answer. He remains mute, his silence emphasizing the fact that this is my problem, not his.

I remember back when I was little how Nannie, my grandmother, would say, "I feel like a bucket full of shit, but don't tell your mother I said that." I think how my friend, Rusty, uses "shit sandwich" to make a point and another friend, Tom, who once told me, one morning after a partying hard, he felt like "hammered shit on a stick."

I sit down in the chair next to my patient's bed and quietly start to write out the shit scale.

"What are you doing now?" he groans in resignation, eyes half closed.

"I am writing a shit scale of pain assessment, matching kinds of 'shit' to the numbers so I can write a pain number down in your chart," I say. "You, sir, are not the first to say you feel like shit. I just need to quantify it."

I had the feeling this man was depressed and exasperated. A small diversion along with a sympathetic person sitting next to him for a minute or two rather than speaking through a door crack might do him some good.

My pen moves along the page. The room is quiet. My patient's roommate is asleep behind the pulled bed curtain.

"All right," he says, surprising me. "What have you got so far?" Trying not to perk up too brightly, I hold back a smile.

Joining forces, we decide that "hammered shit on a stick" would be number ten, about as bad as it can get. We attack the list and debate what goes where. My patient becomes slightly more animated as we engage in this creative endeavor and sits up to dangle his feet over the side of the bed. I reach up and pull his gown up on his shoulder. Our discussion heats up over seven and eight, and we get a little loud. The paper soon is covered with scratch outs and rewrites. My patient taps the paper at times with his index finger as we sit knee to knee. Someone from the hallway pulls the door closed. I assume it's another nurse who has decided to spare the rest of the unit from overhearing our "not suitable for all age groups" discussion and realize I should have closed the door myself.

In five minutes, we compile a workable list.

Zero would remain as No Pain.

One: dog shit on your shoe. Annoying, but you can clean it up.

Two: shit under the fingernails. Gross to clean up, plus nasty.

Three: shit sandwich. No one wants this.

Four: bucket full of shit, in honor of Nannie.

Five: ten pounds of shit in a five-pound bag, intense pressure.

Six: flaming dragon shit, nerves on fire.

Seven: ten days without a shit, the entire body is in revolt.

Eight: holy fucking shit, help me. Exactly.

Nine: hammered shit, beaten down by so much pain.

Ten: hammered shit on a stick. Horrible. You'd rather die.

At one point we get stuck on the idea of shit circling the drain. I think it symbolizes death if the shit goes down the drain, while my patient thinks it signifies the lessening of pain. We can't come to a compromise, so we agree to leave it off the list.

Based on this new framework, my patient says he is clearly feeling like ten pounds of shit in a five-pound bag. I write five in the pain assessment box in his nurse's note for that shift and stand up to leave.

His roommate, who apparently has been listening in, says he feels like flaming dragon shit. I advise him to answer "six" when his nurse asks him about his pain level.

I tell my patient I will get poster board and markers from home, and he can draw the chart for me the next day. But I had forgotten I was off the next day, and when I make it back to the unit for the evening shift two days later, markers in hand, he has been discharged. I ask the nurse who had cared for him on my day off how he had been that night.

She said he had slept most of the evening and she heard, all through the night as well. She says she discharged him the next morning, adding, "The man was a little weird. Before he went home, he told me he felt like shit under the fingernails."

Hmmmm, I think upon hearing that. He must have been feeling better. But I just shrugged and let it go at that. I never said anything more about the shit list. That was between the two of us – nurse and patient.

* * *

Alcohol is legally permitted in the hospital, but only through the pharmacy by doctor's order with a specific dose and time to be administered. As a freshman nursing student working on the men's ward, I was assigned to a patient who was a bouncer at a downtown Philadelphia taproom. Doing his job one night, he evicted a drunk from the bar. A short time later, the drunk returned with a length of 2×4 lumber and smashed the linebacker-sized bouncer smack in the mouth, fracturing his lower jaw and ejecting many teeth. Surgeons realigned the lower jaw and wired it to the upper jaw to heal. 'Six weeks' healing time', is what they told my patient he would have to endure, with his jaws wired together the entire time.

I met him three days after surgery. He was awake, in pain, hungry, and shaking from the sudden withdrawal of his daily intake of alcohol. He begged me to help him get a beer. I asked his surgeon for an order for alcohol but got a snort of disgust instead -- a he'll get over it, it's his own fault for drinking so much snort. But, I argued, alcohol withdrawal symptoms can be fatal for a heavy drinker. What about meds to manage his anxiety and blood pressure, I continued. The doctor was not negotiating. *Incompetent ass,* I thought. I told the head nurse. She did nothing. I told my instructor. Still nothing.

With my options exhausted, I procured several cans of beer on the down low, as I was underage at the time, and stuffed them in my uniform waistband. Awkwardly, I made it out the front door of my dorm, down a block to the hospital entrance, and up five flights of steps to the ward, all the while holding my folded arms across my belly, looking like an acute appendicitis case. My movements were even more awkward as I removed the cans at the bouncer's bedside, first demanding he close his eyes even though I stood behind him and out of his line of vision. This was a man who worked at a strip bar and saw pasties and G strings nightly, but this cradle Catholic would not be exposed while delivering contraband. I wanted to make sure there were no witnesses to my "sin."

I hid the beer and can opener in his bedside table behind towels and washcloths. I grabbed a few straws and advised him to parcel out the beer carefully, as that was all he was getting from me. I wrapped one can in a washcloth, opened it, and popped in a straw. With the curtain drawn around his bed, I washed his broad back and bandy legs while he sipped the beer, some of it dribbling down his chest. At the end of my shift, I carried the empty can in my waistband back to the dorm to discard in the foyer trash can. Alcohol also was prohibited in the dorm, so there was no way I would have allowed a can to be found in my room.

Several days later, my bouncer patient was discharged without incident.

One afternoon a few months later, I was surprised by a loud "hey" as I walked to my after-school, department store job in downtown Philly. I paused and turned, nervous until I recognized my former patient, his jaw no longer wired shut, striding toward me.

He reminded me of our hospital encounter and told me as soon as he was discharged he had cut the wires restricting his jaw and just sipped through a straw for a few weeks. He said he had limited himself to one beer a day in the hospital, thinking no one would "help" him like I did. He probably was right. I doubted if any other nurse would have provided beer delivery. Still missing a number of teeth, he moved his lower jaw slowly up and down, to show me that he had healed "good enough." As he turned to leave, his large palm patted me on the back, twice.

"Thanks, gal," he said.

* * *

Farting loudly near a stranger can be an embarrassment and farting unexpectedly and loudly is even worse. For most people, passing gas is a silent affair of releasing and hoping no one can trace the odor to its source. Holding in gas is harmful to the body, but personally I have held it in many hours when in a group of people. A loud expulsion can mortify most people, prompting them to hide their face in their hands while wishing they could just disappear. Most excludes my late Uncle Tom, who reveled in asking us young children to pull his finger whenever he had the urge to let one go.

Mr. Shores was in his mid-70s when I met him in the tidy ranch house he shared with his wife in a river community in New Kent County, Virginia. As his home health nurse, I was there to follow both his nutritional and pain status as he endured chemotherapy for colon cancer. We got along famously, and he brightened when sharing stories about his grandchildren. His wife doted on him and worried about every detail of his care. She carefully administered his daily meds and kept track of his food intake and bladder and bowel function with the exactness of a researcher. He lovingly teased her, and she hollered at him in a mocking tone to stop.

Early one Sunday morning, I arrive for my usual visit. This encounter follows a week that, according to Mr. Shores' chart, had not gone well. My patient had been having pain, and his appetite was poor. When I get there, he is sitting at the round kitchen table, his usual spot for my visit. I had called the day before and set the time, so he is expecting me.

Right away, Mrs. Shores tells me with some agitation that their son had been there the night before. He had brought marijuana and had taught his dad to smoke, she says, hoping it would improve his appetite. Apparently, it had worked. For breakfast this morning, Mr. Shores ate two scrambled eggs and toast, his wife continues, adding that is more than he had eaten all week. Mr. Shores' eyes go from mine to his wife's. I know his doctor has been trying to get him a pill form of THC but an act of Congress would be faster. I say it is too bad they must resort to this under-the-table therapy, but I am glad he ate well. As I check his blood pressure and pulse and complete my necessary nursing visit paperwork, Mr. Shores chats animatedly about his grandchildren, laughing about their antics. He seems relaxed and calm.

This is great, I think.

Suddenly, a loud, wet-sounding fart explodes from Mr. Shores. I mean *loud*. His eyes pop open, and he looks mortified. Mrs. Shores gasps. The three of us look at each other. Instantly, I rocket to standing and snap my right hand into a crisp salute. Shocked, Mr. Shores leans back and knits his brows in confusion.

"Oh, was that you?" I ask. "I thought it was an honor guard somewhere nearby giving a 21-gun salute!" I stand there holding the salute. In a flash, Mrs. Shores bolts up to join me.

Mr. Shores exhales and begins to laugh. He grabs his stomach and laughs harder. The deep movement of his diaphragm causes more explosions of gas, which escalates his laughing, tears running down his face. Suddenly he realizes he must get to the bathroom . . . immediately. He stands shakily and, still laughing, makes his way down the hallway toward the toilet. His wife escorts him, holding his arm to steady him. Together they hurry, both of them shaking with the laughter that I know has been pent up for ages, tamped down by the stress of dealing with his serious illness.

Because of the gas and the laughing and the long walk, the next words I hear from Mr. Shores are a booming exclamation from the bathroom. "I didn't make it in time, Susan. I just shit my pants, and it's all your fault! I got to my age without needing a diaper until you came along."

Their continued laughing is infectious, and I laugh, too.

Mrs. Shores hollers from down the hall to me that they can manage, to let myself out of the house, and they will see me soon. I chart about the improved appetite and bowel status but not about the salute. This mocking of an uncontrolled bodily function is not a practice I am in the habit of performing, but because I knew this family and their enjoyment of kidding, the inspiration that arrived in that moment had worked. It could have been disrespectful and embarrassing, just like the fart, but it wasn't. Instead it served to lighten the mood.

The following Friday, when I check in with the home health office for a report on the patients I will see that weekend, I discover Mr. Shores has been sharing our salute story. Laura, the nurse who sees Mr. Shores during the week, tells me that he could not wait to describe to her what had happened during my weekend visit. He and his wife have been plotting to have him on the toilet for my next arrival, just in case I "acted up" again. I was not to know about their plan, so I react with shock when I find him just where I had left him the previous Sunday. On the toilet.

It is apparent they have spent the morning readying for me. Newspaper sheets cover the hallway floor and kitchen chair. Mr. Shores sits enthroned on the toilet, pants up, waiting for me. When I tell him, hands on hips, he is the one acting up this time, he beams. We all shuffle back to the kitchen. Once settled, I hear how he has shared our story with his son, brother, sisters and neighbors, warning each of them to be prepared for visiting nurses that cause you to poop in your pants.

Mrs. Shores sits grinning, elbows on table and chin in hands, watching her husband intently and enjoying this moment of happiness. When my visit is over, she follows me out to my car, hugging me firmly. "Thank you, thank you," she whispers in my ear.

As I drive away, I inwardly salute both my patient and his wife for reminding me that laughter, when shared in the presence of love, is perhaps the most potent medicine of all.

17

HEALING TOUCH

A little more than a hundred years ago, in Florence Nightingale's day, common wisdom held that a good nurse was either a woman who had been disappointed in love or one who had few abilities and even fewer options.

Throughout her life, Florence worked tirelessly to change that perception.

A nursing pioneer, she set new standards and opened a school to teach nursing as science. She kept rigorous records and made astute observations. She studied concepts and ideas such as sanitation, nutrition, fresh air, and quiet in the context of healing. Her insights and theories continue to inspire today.

Among Florence's much-noted pet peeves were doctors who stood in the hallway talking grimly about patients within earshot. Also, the volumes of terrible food left to congeal at the bedside of patients too sick to tolerate more than a bite or two.

Sadly, despite Florence's lifetime commitment and the persistence of leagues of nurses who followed in her footsteps, not much has changed over the years.

Much of the common-sense patient care for which Florence advocated generations ago remains sorely missing from today's health care. Money, the bottom line driver of patient care, drives nurses away from the bedside. So goes the power of therapeutic touch. Physicians are pushed by time parameters, and nurses are restricted by understaffing and increasing emphasis on manipulating technology -- pumps, monitors, computers, and bar-coded supplies to be scanned.

All of this may have become necessary as the medical world modernizes, but showing empathy is as simple as it always has been:

A good doctor or nurse is one who gives attention by looking into a patient's face and not at a screen while providing personal care.

Each body is unique with its own wisdom. Empowered health care recognizes this truth and supports wellness in a nurturing, positive, and respectful way. Excellent nurses learn to consider their patients' mental, emotional, physical, and energetic components. Listening to this unspoken language, they work to squeeze in "healing" care one second at a time. This awareness can be good enough. It can even be great.

As a nurse, once you step into this unseen river, you recognize both its power and how naturally it begins to flow. This was something that became apparent to me early on and in the most unlikely setting.

For two years of my nurse's training, I worked after school and on weekends at a cosmetics counter in a downtown Philadelphia department store within walking distance of my hospital nursing school. My nursing classes ended at 3 pm. I then would change into street clothes and walk the eight blocks to work. My route took me down Arch Street, past shabby old center city buildings. My favorite was the raunchy, rundown burlesque theater known as "the Troc." The Trocadero was an old Victorian building, its former grandeur now covered with billboard-style signs featuring provocatively posed ladies wearing only pasties and a G string. The marquee below touted the performers currently onstage. I was particularly amused by the pronouncement, "Lynn O'leum, she'll floor ya."

A sandwich board propped on the sidewalk next to the ticket window proclaimed, "No longer obscene!" Despite that assurance, I never went inside. Even the front sidewalk smelled like stale beer and urine. Not a calling card I wished to answer.

Besides, looking at naked people was part of my job, and even at the beginning of my studies, I couldn't shut the nurse thing down. Proof of that occurred at a 40th birthday party for my friend, Robin.

There were about 50 people – both women and men -- attending Robin's garden party celebration. As entertainment for the event, her husband had hired a stripper, who arrived costumed as a policeman. I happened to be seated near another nurse when the dancer ripped away his Velcro-modified uniform to reveal his buff, muscular 20-year-old physique. I leaned over to my nurse friend and remarked that I did not see a pimple, mole, or scar anywhere on his skin. And, of course, my view was excellent -- the G string allowed for maximum assessment.

She thoughtfully agreed, adding she could not see evidence of scoliosis or any other orthopedic injury. We both observed how his skin was flawless and his muscular coordination stellar, as evidenced by his ability to balance, hover, and grind around on a super long flashlight and nightstick he had set down in the grass. We could have gone on -- there was so *much* to see -- but the other women around us had heard enough. In unison, they yelled at us to *shut up*.

But back to where I was before I got sidetracked.

Working at a department store cosmetics counter turned out to be a plus for an aspiring nurse. My part-time job allowed me to meet saleswomen who had spent decades selling beauty products from the very same spot and to learn the fine art of interacting with other women in an intimate, caring way. One saleswoman, in particular, made a lasting impression that carried over into my nursing career.

I originally was hired on as Christmas help but after the holidays was invited to stay on part-time. Marie was charged with training me at the store's Coty and Francis Denny cosmetic island, and it didn't take long for me to admire her devotion for helping make women feel good about themselves. Marie and the other saleswomen I met understood their clients' motivation to stay young looking and glamorous, which they thought would keep their man happy. With consummate skill, these make-up professionals directed women through the gauntlet of day creams and night creams, cleansers and toners, foundations, fragrances, and lipsticks. This was no small feat. There were hundreds of different products on that beauty island, each one promising its own touch of magic. And Marie and her co-workers somehow seemed to know all their secrets.

When I met Marie, I knew about blush, period. Shift by shift, my new mentor schooled me on the technical and psychological aspects of beauty products. Her customers adored her because she cared about how they felt and looked. For many, her makeover sessions were that day's much-needed therapy. Marie knew every woman as an individual, remembering what products she used, making suggestions as to what she might like to try. Her ability to fuse marketing with humanity was spellbinding to a neophyte like me. Her sales numbers were phenomenal. They were surpassed only by her obvious compassion.

I remember one late afternoon when a woman approached our gleaming, glass-topped cases in tears. Marie spied her coming and waved her to the rear section of the square of waist-high cases. Each square framed an open space where the saleswomen worked the counters. Outside there was considerable browsing room for customers. There were five of these glass islands in an aisle that stretched from the front door to the escalators at the store's center. While Marie and the woman spoke, I busied myself stacking dozens of new lipsticks by color-coded number. Kneeling on the floor, I would pull out the old lipstick inventory, wash the glass shelf, then rearrange the display to fit both old and new inventory in an inviting way. Marie loved how precisely I arranged the tiny boxes. It was a task I enjoyed -- creating order that stayed that way.

I listened as I worked, eavesdropping while Marie's customer revealed the source of her distress. Apparently, the woman's husband had seen her without her makeup for the first time in their marriage, now more than a decade long. I held in a gasp. I had no idea some women wore foundation, blush, eye shadow, eyeliner, mascara, and cologne 24 hours a day. Seems that she washed her face at bedtime and reapplied all the makeup fresh to sleep in. Her husband had unexpectedly walked into the bathroom during the in-between phase, she told Marie, looked in the mirror at her, and called her "a pasty-looking thing." It had crushed her. Marie listened.

During the telling of the tale, shoppers came and went. I handled the occasional new customer and when the line grew a little long, a saleswoman from another counter ran over to help. Just as in nursing, the sisterhood of this professional cosmetic sales staff watched out for each other.

Marie focused intently until the woman finished her story, then gently pointed out that of course she looked pasty without her makeup. The woman appeared shocked that Marie was on "his" side. But after a Marie lesson in how the skin needs time to breathe, she was willing to consider keeping her face clean overnight. Marie continued; her skin would enjoy the break and the nourishing new night cream from Coty Cosmetics would give her a natural glow and ease away fine wrinkles. The customer – no longer distraught -- purchased the night cream and hugged Marie goodbye. I found it all amazing

Listen carefully and tell the truth kindly. Next, offer a workable solution or two. That's what Marie added to my nursing education and clinical expertise.

Marie's generous spirit embraced me, her young apprentice, wholeheartedly. She was proud of me being in nurses' training and shared my health care ambitions with the other store employees.

Within months – mostly due to Marie's unbridled enthusiasm -- I would have at least one or two store employees waiting as I arrived at 4 pm to begin my evening shift at the cosmetic counter.

"Say, can you look at my toe and tell me what is wrong?" someone might ask, giving me no opportunity to decline before hoisting a bare foot onto the glass-top cosmetic case. I would see a thick black toenail, sort of semi-attached or semi-detached, green around the edges and think to myself, *This is very, very bad.*

Every time something like this happened, I would look at Marie, hoping she would chase my would-be patients away. Instead, she took pride in my medical prowess, which at that time included a smattering of anatomy and physiology and competence at giving someone a bath while they were confined to a bed. Nurses don't diagnose, yet these people held onto my every word as if I had the knowledge and skill set of an experienced physician. Knowing my own limitations, I always advised them to go see their doctor. Most of them did.

It took a little while, but I finally discovered why my arrival at work was greeted by co-workers clamoring for medical attention. Apparently, Marie had been bragging in the department store lunchroom about my being a nurse and had invited the ill and feverish to meet me between four and five each evening I worked for a consult. Marie left at five. She wanted no one to invade my space after that.

Marie also taught me the therapeutic approach to selling cosmetic products. "What do you need and why?" she would always ask. Sometimes it was just a replacement lipstick. Sometimes there were heart-wrenching stories of domestic abuse or a life lived in fear. Many times, it was a search to halt the natural changes that take place as a woman ages.

Marie was tiny but had a powerful presence. She was five feet tall, heavy chested, and beautifully dressed. Her dyed hair was always in a French twist with never a strand out of place. Her demeanor was calm and respectful. It was easy to see why she was perceived as a trusted adviser. No one ever left Marie having bought just one item. They left with a bagful. They also left smiling, peaceful, and rejuvenated. Marie was not just a saleswoman. She was also both confidante and therapist, a truly kind, caring woman and master of her craft.

I had no problem becoming passably competent at selling cosmetics under Marie's able guidance, but most of my department store co-workers told me they could never switch roles. When my career choice became known, I often heard a variation on this response. "God," they would say, shaking their head, "I could never be a nurse. Too much blood and guts and disgusting things. Ew!"

Nurses are pigeonholed as universally tolerant of all that can happen to the human body. It is an interesting viewpoint. It assumes that all nurses are immune to the inherent unpleasantness of bodily secretions and excretions, do not flinch when they come upon a limb facing the wrong direction, and can calmly abide both hideous burns and wrenching screams of pain. It assumes that all nurses can stand with courage at the foot of the delivery room table and know what to do with the new life entering the world, regardless of what they will confront. Or that we know how to meet the needs of a psychotic and physically dangerous patient, no matter how crazy the behavior.

But every nurse is an individual, and each of us has situations in which we excel, and those that make us want to turn and run away as fast as we can.

Take me. I am a very good nurse when the patient is lying in the hospital bed with all body parts in their anatomically correct position. Small amounts of active bleeding I can tolerate, but a clot the size of Nebraska -- I'm outta there.

The delivery room suites terrify me. I weep with joy or sorrow at the delivery of a child, making me no help to the obstetrician or mother. No operating room for me, either. It's way too cold. I loved neurosurgery, but the long procedures in that necessarily frigid environment would leave me frozen for hours. I can't do the ER with its never-ending train wrecks. Those nurses are saints. And newborns, well, they terrify me. Feeding tubes and IVs in a tiny two-pounder . . . no thank you.

* * *

Just like nurses, lay people have strengths and weaknesses when it comes to helping the ill and dying. Many want to contribute in a meaningful way. Groups raise money to support research, volunteer time in hospitals, or knit caps for the tiny babies. Occasionally though, despite such good intentions, their efforts miss the mark.

During my years on the oncology unit at Denver Children's Hospital, I met many citizens who were devoted to easing the suffering of children. One volunteer focused her energy on collecting donated wigs for our children once chemo claimed their hair. As a result, our unit had a storage closet full of adult-sized cast offs. All the wigs had been carefully washed and stuffed with paper by our dedicated volunteer before being brought to the clinic. She was elated, and we could not say no. Dolly Parton and Farrah Fawcett big blonde hair wigs predominated.

One rainy day, I noticed that the dark moods of the dozen or so folks in our oncology clinic tanked further every time I called a family back for their dreaded turn of lab tests and chemo. Children sitting quietly – too down to even complain -- is not a good sign. Something was needed to break through the gray pall of the day.

A mini-brainstorm drew me to the wig closet, where I threw the box lids open. I found two curly, layered wigs with tresses that trailed down to the waist. I approached Mary Jo, my esteemed nurse boss and the only other nurse that worked the oncology clinic with me and shared my plan. She told me no to her part but to go on ahead myself. *Poot,* I thought. A pair of bombshell, blonde nurses would have been a hoot. Oh well, I was on my own.

Disappointed but undaunted, I put my plan into action.

I wadded up two 5×9 dressing gauze pads, stuffed them in my bra, and donned the wig. Not to digress but honestly, the transformation was mind blowing. I looked fabulous. Big chested and blonde really was my look. I realized I had been robbed at birth.

This was my moment. I strutted, chest first, into the waiting room and called for my young teen patient, Mary, and her family to come on back. As they approached me, a nurse they knew well, I pivoted so they could get a good look at my waist length "do" and my enhanced figure.

Bam! Mary shrieked with laughter. She insisted I grab her a wig and some bra stuffing before her oncologist came in for her exam. I already had the wig I had hoped Mary Jo would wear. I found two washcloths, and Mary's mom tucked them in place. Instead of sitting on the exam table, our teen patient struck a bent knee, sideways-looking pose in front of the exam door. I grabbed an emesis basin with one hand and placed the other hand on my hip, imitating Mary.

To my surprise Doctor H, head of the oncology department, appeared in the doorway. I had not expected this. Mary's usual doctor was on site. I knew he could take a joke. But yikes, the department chair?

Mary lowered her voice and let out a sultry, "Hello there."

Dr. H's widened eyes volleyed between Mary and me. Without missing a beat, she threw her hands to her hips and sashayed into the room with her own chest thrust forward. Looking at Mary, she responded, "Well . . . hello there. Don't you look marvelous."

In the oncology clinic, no one ever is told she looks marvelous. Now that the ice had been broken, more marvelous lookers appeared.

Before long, both girls and boys were sporting provocative coiffures. A few moms and one dad participated. Mary Jo sighed and shook her head, holding fast to her 'no' as the kids begged her to wear a wig. Her teasing assessment was that they were the silliest things she'd ever seen. That delighted the kids even more.

Decorum disappeared in the clinic hallways for the rest of the day, which soon were filled with hair flipping, strutting floozies of all ages. I was all in.

Alas, my newfound glamour was not destined to last. Later in the afternoon as I completed cleaning up an exam room and walked out into the hallway to call the next patient, I encountered the prune-faced, by the books, no sense of humor nursing supervisor. I jolted to a stop. Her icy stare, pursed lips and crossed arms revealed how she felt about my unprofessional manner without a word coming out of her mouth.

When the kids saw me facing this Cruella, they vanished like songbirds in the canopy of a tree when a hawk is flying overhead. I was directed to tidy myself and expect disciplinary action if I was caught doing such nonsense again.

I shrugged it off. She had her job, I had mine. She did not know my patients like I did, so I could see why she wouldn't get the therapeutic value of a stuffed bra and exotic wig. Her redirection was not all bad. My scalp was on fire from the heat of the synthetic hair, and my head itched wildly until I got home and took a shower. *No wonder those wigs were piling up in the closet,* I thought. Hot and sexy has a painful price.

***

Another lesson in the power of feeling beautiful occurred even before my time with Marie, when I worked as a nurse's aide at the Catholic Nursing Home in Philadelphia. Every summer the facility Director hired teenage help so her staff could have time off for vacations. There were plenty of us looking for nursing experience to beef up our applications to nursing school. My head nurse, Mrs. O, had a herd of us teenagers on her unit – as many as seven or eight every day shift. We would complete our baths, change beds, and tidy rooms by noon. After that, there was not much to do other than an occasional clean-up from an incontinent patient.

Looking for ways to pass the time, we asked Mrs. O if we could bring in curlers and nail polish for our patients. She readily agreed, knowing we would be more easily managed if we were occupied. Shirley, the only African-American in our crew, carted in a portable record player. Cranking up the sounds of Smokey Robinson and Martha and the Vandellas, we gathered our wheelchair-bound ladies at the dead end of one hallway and operated a beauty parlor a few afternoons a week. We used brush curlers, pink plastic curlers, and spoolies -- a kind of rubber spool with funnel ends. You roll the hair around the spool then flip one funnel end over the other to hold it in place. These torturous curlers pulled hair right out of your scalp if rolled too tightly. The spoolie fad came and went rather quickly, and I am certain it was because of that.

Denise painted fingernails and Jerry, our only male aide, transported patients via wheelchair from their rooms to our salon and back to their rooms when their makeover was completed. We used a portable domed hair dryer and hairspray -- an ungodly amount, enough to trigger an asthma attack.

The goal was to doll up everyone for the upcoming church service in the facility's chapel. Our plan worked. Every Sunday, we would proudly roll our pimped-up ladies to Mass in our chapel. Our favorite hairstyles were French twists, French curls, and cornrows – long before Bo Derek made them a white-person thing. Our ladies beamed and managed to stay awake or mostly awake during Mass. And we could see that family members who tended to visit only on Sundays were shocked at how marvelous their loved ones looked and how much better they obviously felt.

As one of only a few nurse aides who continued to work during the winter months, I witnessed a remarkable decline among my ladies in mood and cognition when summer's beauty sessions ended, and the other teens left. Slowly the chipped fingernail polish grew out. In the interest of time and expediency, hair was either combed straight or pulled back in a rubber band. As social interactions declined, many of the residents withdrew into a shell, talking very little. The summer bustle of teenage aides had brought fresh faces and new activities. The dismal routine of bed, wheelchair, bed, and the dull and repetitive sequence of taking pills, eating, and sleeping crept back into their world, dulling the senses. For three months they had enjoyed music, manicures, and a little magic every day. Cleanliness and proper medical management may be essential in a nursing home setting, but the wonders of personal touch still need to find their way into the standard protocols of many custodial care facilities.

***

During my work as a home health nurse I learned the truth of this in a close-to-the-bone way. My co-worker, Laura, was driving to a patient visit when she was hit by a speeding car passing her on a wet road. The impact spun her car into the woods, where she struck a tree head-on. Laura maintained consciousness long enough to call the office on her bag phone, the very early pre-cell phone version of portable phones, they plugged into a car's cigarette lighter port for power. She screamed to us that she was dead. We immediately notified police with her likely whereabouts, and they found her quickly. She was covered in blood from a large forehead laceration and had multiple injuries of the orthopedic variety, none life-threatening. She was transported to the hospital, and her patient assignments for that day were split among the rest of us. I did not get to see her until two days after the accident.

It was mid-morning when I entered Laura's hospital room. Her eyes were shut, and she looked pale. Her lips were noticeably dry, and she had two IVs running fluids and antibiotics. A row of stitches crossed her forehead just above her eyebrows and over to one ear, marking the spot where her face had hit the windshield.

Laura's breakfast tray lay untouched at the foot of her bed, a soft diet of pureed food. As I got closer and debated about waking her, I noticed one dirty arm, then the other. Then I saw dried blood crusted above and below her blood-splattered neck brace.

While I was taking all this in, a nurse came in to check the IVs and replace the bag of fluids. I said hello and told her how I knew Laura, that we were both nurses. The nurse remarked that she had an impossibly heavy workload that day and said if I could help Laura in any way, she would appreciate it. She added that the neck x-rays had come back, and the collar could come off. With that, she was gone.

Laura opened one puffy eye. The other looked stuck shut from drainage.

Softly, I told Laura my name and asked if she knew me. She said she did and that she remembered the accident but most of all, right now, her neck hurt. I offered to take the brace off and bathe her. She readily agreed and closed her eye.

As I removed the brace, I discovered a blood-caked ponytail scrunchie pressing into the back of Laura's head. It was cemented in place. I found a plastic trash bag and spread it under her head. I ran hot water into a basin and slowly was able to saturate the scrunchie and remove it with Laura propped over on her side. Two whole days she had been lying there with head and neck pain, and apparently no one had thought to look behind her head under the EMT-applied neck brace. I scrubbed away the dried mud, tree debris, and blood from her back, arms, and legs, cleaning her from head to toe. Then I raided the hallway linen closet and changed her bed sheets.

Laura had been too weak to wash her own cheeks and chin, but she was able to feed herself a few spoons of applesauce. I went to the cafeteria and got fresh coffee to help with what I knew was a caffeine-withdrawal headache. She savored a few sips before she fell asleep.

I returned the next morning armed with shampoo and lotion. I entered her room and found an empty bed. For a moment I panicked, thinking she had died during the night. Her nurse from the day before saw me and said Laura had been moved to another floor. I let out a sigh of relief.

When I finally located Laura, she again had her eyes closed, one IV running. She was now in a two-bed hospital room, but the second bed was stripped and empty. Laura heard my footfalls and opened her eyes. She said she'd been up most of the night moving to a new room. Once settling into her new bed, her new roommate, who had since been moved to ICU, had cried out most of the night keeping Laura awake with the racket.

"You're getting your hair washed and your legs shaved today, so close your eyes and rest," I told her. She smiled, said thank you, and closed her eyes.

Washing the hair of a supine, bed-bound patient is a difficult, messy business. I had done it a few times as a student nurse, so I knew the drill. You need a plastic barrier, lots of towels, and a very small amount of shampoo. I filled the basin with super-hot water and spent the first 30 minutes softening and picking the caked blood from her hair. Laura's head lolled from side to side as I worked. She was drifting in and out of sleep. I washed her scalp, massaging the final bits of blood out. I rinsed, dried, and combed out her shoulder-length hair. I changed the sheets, deciding she had had enough for today. The hairy legs could wait. It took nearly two hours, but she looked like Laura again, or more like Laura who had gotten the crap knocked out of her.

I know neither of us will forget that bath. How many other patients, we have asked one another from time to time, lie in bed without a nurse friend to help with these minor but profoundly important healing touches?

They are a deep hug from the soul. Something a born healer – like Florence or Marie or any good nurse – knows all about.

18

UNBEARABLE

Self-induced abortions/ methods

- Douching with substances believed to induce miscarriage, such as turpentine, clorox bleach, or lye, all of which could cause intense chemical burns (beginning in the 1960s, many women used Coca-Cola for this purpose, although its utility is at best dubious)
    - Wikipedia contributors. "Self-induced abortion." *Wikipedia, The Free Encyclopedia*. Wikipedia, The Free Encyclopedia, 4 Feb. 2019. Web. 4 Feb. 2019.

Unrelenting moans.

The most difficult patient encounter of my career came at its' beginning when I was a 19-year-old nurse in training. My patient, Connie, was 15. More than 40 years later, I still can see and hear her.

Connie's' mother had brought her to the ER a day after an at-home self-induced abortion attempt had gone horribly wrong.

Connie had become pregnant from a sexual assault by an uncle. Attempting to help her daughter end the just discovered, unwanted reminder of violence, her mother had prepared a combination of lye and Coca-Cola. The "procedure" had been researched on the street then concocted and delivered by the mother at the willing consent of Connie.

Through shaking sobs, the mother told me how she had Connie lie on her back in bed, hips propped high with a pillow. The fluid, meant to be an irritant to trigger a miscarriage, had been poured into the vagina.

It was one of many methods used to induce a miscarriage in the poor communities in Philadelphia during the 1960s and 1970s.

Openmouthed and wild eyed in unspeakable pain, Connie turned her eyes to me as I checked her blood pressure. Watching as fear twisted her porcelain face, I had the sickening sense of a beast consuming this beauty from within.

Her guttural moaning ripped through my bone marrow. Every two hours throughout that endless day shift, I injected her with an intramuscular narcotic and changed the blood-soaked bed pads beneath her hips as lye slowly burned through her pelvic organs.

The physician making morning rounds stopped at the foot of the bed, looked at the chart and then at this suffering child in intractable pain. He shrugged. I couldn't tell if he was acting superior, felt she had brought it on herself or if this was simply his coping strategy. He mumbled a variation of, "There is nothing we can do," eyes downcast as his shoulders faced Connie's mother. It was clear he had nothing left in his repertoire of healing tools. Only Connie's moans broke the silence.

It was Connie's mother who had learned from the street that a coke and lye douche could terminate a pregnancy.

Connie did not want a baby from "him." Connie's mother meant to spare her daughter the shame and health danger of bringing a child into the world as a young, unwed mother. She meant to help her daughter forget the consequence of an unwanted violent assault from the pedophile uncle. She meant to spare the already large and poverty-stricken family another member, one that was especially unwelcome.

Standing at the bedside as her daughter endured the wrath of lye dissolving her body tissues, the mute mother shrank from the moans but never abandoned her sacred child. In my presence or that of the other nurses who cared for her, Connie never uttered one word of blame against her mother.

Standing witness . . . that was all I could do. It is what nurses do, we bear the unbearable with our patients and their families.

Keep the sheets clean and the patient dry. Stand in recognition of unfathomable pain. Swallow emotions -- my own, the mother's, the doctor's. Store it in my mind's cellar, in the bottom drawer of an imaginary dresser that, once closed, nearly never sees the light.

Standing at the bedside, useless to stop this chemical catastrophe, my mind sought revenge. I dosed the uncle with lye down his throat.

I delivered lye into his bladder with a foley catheter. I administered lye eye drops. My jaws squeezed, my tongue pressed against the roof of my mouth.

From time to time my classmates came to the doorway, staring. They did not speak but their body language asked if I needed anything. Eyes fixed on theirs, my head did not move. They walked away.

As day shift came to an end, I gave my end of shift nursing report to the oncoming nurse who would care for Connie. As I walked down the hall to the elevator door, I could hear Connie's cries until the door closed behind me. During the ride from the 14th floor to the lobby, I prayed that death would take Connie overnight.

As the elevator doors opened the next morning, I walked toward the nurses' station listening for but not hearing moans of pain. I sighed with relief. Moments later, I was shocked to see my name listed as Connie's nurse again for the day.

Entering the room, I saw her mother looking desperate and exhausted. Her daughter, although unresponsive, remained restless in the bed. Her muted voice no longer was able to signal pain, yet her tortured body squirmed.

I placed my hand on Connie's arm and slid my fingers gently to her wrist. I felt for her pulse. Thready. . .. fast and faint.

I gently bathed her and carefully changed the sheets, trying not to add to her agony. By noon her restlessness began to settle. Blood, now mixed with stool, seeped from between her legs.

When the lye breached the abdominal aorta, the beautiful, gray girl exhaled.

She grew still.

Limp.

Gone.

In the moment following her last breath, everything changed. I could see only the sacred, still body of a child. There were just the three of us. The motionless mother, her daughter and me. I could hear soft roaring in my head. The acrid smell of blood enveloped us in a private fog. I did not feel my body. I felt suspended in time, in unreality.

Slowly thoughts began to surface, in single phrases. Time of death. Morgue pack. My nurse sensibility returning first.

I considered placing my stethoscope over Connie's heart to verify death.

What for. . .

Connie had been defiled enough. Defiled by her predator uncle. Ignored by a healthcare system that is blind to the needs of each individual woman and the challenging health issues they face. Abandoned by a culture that allows women to be blamed for and endure the consequences of sexual assault.

My stethoscope stayed noosed.

With her mother beside me I bathed Connie again, performing post mortem care. Her mother sobbed quietly and prayed. She hugged her deceased child, stroking her hair.

Trembling, I left the room to ask a staff nurse to please help me wrap this child in a shroud. I had covered the faces of older women with a shroud, never a child.

My instructor joined us.

Standing silently around the bed, hands folded on the siderails, the three of us nurses stood reverent vigil. Waiting. Breathing. Silently praying.

I still trembled as tears slid down my face.

Connie's mother released her arms from around her daughter and, without looking at us, gave a small nod.

We attached the toe tag and wrapped the white shroud tenderly around the child, a ritual that nurses perform humbly and with respect. We tied the shroud about the neck, waist and ankles, then covered her with a sheet.

The morgue gurney came, triggering stares as two orderlies conveyed Connie to the service elevator, then to the basement morgue.

My nurse helpers went back to their patients.

Connie's mother watched as her daughter was carried away. With sagging shoulders, we leaned into each other and silently hugged. . .a lifeless, defeated hug.

In the space of two terrible days, Lye had ended life for both of them.

Connie and her mother would live in me.

Forever.

19

ABSOLUTION

"Happy Father's Day," I say to Dad, who answers my call on the fifth ring. At 86, getting out of his recliner and walking to the dining room, it takes him a while to maneuver to the phone. After all, he only answers it twice a year – on Father's Day and on his birthday. Otherwise, Mom picks up the phone.

"How are you, Dad?" I ask.

"About the same," he says, then casually mentions that mom has broken her leg.

"Wha-a-a-t?" I stammer in shock. "When did *that* happen?"

"Oh, maybe a week ago or more, she won't go to the doctor's, you know how she is," he says in a resigned, whatta-ya-gonna-do-with-her kind of way.

It is hard for me to contain myself. At this point in her life, Mom suffers from rheumatoid arthritis and has had her mobility impaired for years from a combination of her affliction and a minimal amount of activity. She weighs a mere 88 pounds, and her muscles have wasted away from lack of use. In addition, her chronic depression feeds a tendency toward drama, which she has refined into an award-worthy routine during her adult life. It has always frustrated Dad and my sister, brother, and me.

For example, years back Mom decided that due to her arthritis she could no longer walk up and down the two flights of steps in our Philly row home, one set that led to the second floor bedrooms and bathroom and the other to the basement to get into the garage. When the need to go upstairs to the bathroom would arise, she would drop slowly to the living room floor – moaning the whole time -- then scoot, with tortoise speed, up the steps on her backside. If I pointed out it took the same muscles to scoot as it did to step, and that holding onto to the railing provided safety, Mom retorted her standard response, "I knew you wouldn't understand."

Then at 72, she used a walker on the main floor and shuffled her feet. "My hips are locked," was another of her refrains. All her muscles have contractures from lack of use. This problem could be resolved with regular movement but sitting and crawling has become her only game.

"Well, how is she able to cook and what have the two of you been eating?" I ask Dad.

Dad says he has been walking to the Italian restaurant at the end of the block for takeout twice a day -- pizza or a sandwich for lunch, pasta and salad for dinner.

"How does she get to the bathroom?" I dread the answer but already know, if she hasn't moved from the sofa for an unknown period, what it will be.

"She goes in her pants," he says, as if it was a completely acceptable thing to do while sitting on the sofa. He explains that he carries the trash bags of diapers away once a day for her.

"Has she had a bath?" I am flummoxed as to why Mom has not called, why Dad has not called or why, when I find out their saintly neighbor helped her back on the couch after the fall, he has not called, either. Apparently, a broken leg is my mother's self-diagnosis. Mom generally calls my brother, her favorite, with such news. I wonder if he knows.

I live in Virginia and my sister, Joan, lives in Denver. Our brother, Paul, also is in Denver, but his work as a long-distance truck driver takes him all over the U.S. I see my parents twice yearly. We are not -- if it hasn't become obvious by now -- a functioning family. Joan and Paul visit our parents in Philadelphia about as often as I do.

At the news of Mom's broken leg, my mind begins to whirl with the fervor of a would-be savior, my default persona in this complicated parent/child relationship. I have worked as a nurse in home health and with disabled seniors for decades. I know the medical needs of the elderly and can provide the necessary care.

Now my parents need that care, and since I am the one nearby that can provide it, they will finally see that I am "good." Or, so says my, still trying to please, inner child. At long last, I get a chance to prove that I am a good thing, not a mistake, a causer of pain. I think I smell redemption.

"I'll be there tomorrow," I tell Dad. "You and Mom are coming here to live with me until she can walk again."

"Oh, we don't want to be a bother," Dad says, but I cut him off. I am not interested in what he wants. The grown-up memory of Little Susan has taken charge, pushing reason and reality out of the way.

This is going to happen, and I am going to make it work, I tell myself. I will take care of my parents, my sons, and work full time. This is my golden opportunity to repair the ruin I caused in Mom's life by being conceived out of wedlock, to vanquish the words boiling in my head since I was a small girl: "If it wasn't for you, I would be happy."

I feel exhilarated. I call Joan and Paul. They know nothing of this broken leg. I tell them my plan, and they are relieved I am willing to act.

The next morning, I leave home at 5 am and drive five hours without stopping. When I arrive in Philadelphia, I find Dad packing one suitcase with clothes. He has Mom's bag on the bed, open and empty. I give a quick hello kiss and sideways hug to Mom and Dad while I take in the situation. I do a physical assessment of Mom's leg; circulation is good, and she can move her toes. Mom refuses to see a doctor before we head south, and in my mind, I echo my father's "whatta ya gonna do." She does agree to see my family doctor once we get back to Virginia.

Preliminaries accomplished; I roll into action. I have the rest of the day to clean and prepare the house to be closed for an unknown amount of time, notify the neighbor, cancel paper delivery, and get mail forwarded. I have a list.

Mom smokes her Newports and naps intermittently. Dad helps with the tasks. He gets the trash and garbage cans out, checks his car, locks the garage, and putters around to see if he can find other things he may want to take. When he stalls out, I give him more to do.

I check behind him and find him bringing the trash can back in because it is not trash day. "Bob will bring the can in tomorrow, Dad," I say, reminding him the neighbor will be watching the house.

"Oh yeah," he says tentatively.

I stuff several bags with Mom's clothes, grab a few more items for Dad, make sure all their prescriptions are packed, clean the bathroom and kitchen, and do laundry. By late evening, I declare we are ready to leave the next morning bright and early. I send Dad upstairs and bathe Mom. She seems relaxed and comfortable if she remains still. The sofa reeks, and carpet stains abound at the place where she has taken up residence. Her stool-crusted fingernails disgust me. I bring her a sudsy basin of warm water to wash her hands, but she declines saying a wet washcloth is good enough. I cave.

Up early the next morning, I fix Dad breakfast, pack him and Mom a lunch for the road, and ponder how to get Mom into the back seat of my Windstar minivan. Thinking ahead, I had removed the middle two passenger seats before I left home. There is plenty of space for her either to sit in the rear bench seat with her legs up or to lie on the floor. I have two foam sleeping mats from camping, just in case she chooses to lie on the floor. If need be, I can use all the bed pillows from her house.

Downstairs in the basement, I find one of the old webbed folding chairs we took on family picnics in nearby Wissinoming Park when I was a child.

Back then we had no car, so on family picnic day we'd load up the big red wagon with the Hires cooler, basket of food, and the two aluminum folding chairs, Mom would take a happy pill, and we would parade the 10 blocks to the park. At some point – I don't remember exactly when or why -- these faked fun family get-togethers just evaporated.

With all systems go, I walk next door and ask Bob to help me load Mom up. I figure we can lift her to the folding chair, carry her out the door and down the eight cement front steps to the van, and lift her onto the back seat.

Bob is my brother's longtime friend. The two grew up together, boys into men. Bob lives with and cares for his elderly mother. To everyone's great relief, Bob's father is long dead. He was a brutal, abusive alcoholic who routinely beat his wife, mother, and son. I know this because – given how rowhouses are built -- my bedroom wall also served the same function in his grandmother's room. I often would hear her beg her son to stop beating her. I remember telling Dad about it as a little girl; he said we had to mind our own business. It was terrible to lay in bed at night and listen to the commotion in the bedroom next door.

Everyone in the neighborhood had feared Bob's dad. The man's hulking build and violent demeanor fused with his alcoholic rages discouraged intervention of any kind. He was perfectly cordial each morning as he came out his front door and headed for work. Boozed up, he was maniacal.

But Bob always has been a kind and generous soul and has kept an eye on my Mom and Dad, unbidden, for years. Mom was good to Bob when he was a young boy, and he would often tell me how he enjoyed coming to play with Paul in our house.

Bob now fills me in on what has been happening in my parents' home. He tells me of Dad's many falls in the past month. I find out Bob had transported Dad to the ER after one of those falls. I had no idea. It occurs to me that Bob is the reason my parents have been able to function alone in their own home, though minimally, for these past few years. I ask him why he didn't call one of us. He says he really doesn't mind helping them, and it has never been any trouble.

As we prepare to move Mom from the sofa to the car, I think about how, for someone who is deconditioned, being transferred by lifting can be quite uncomfortable. Because of Mom's osteoporosis and arthritis, I worry about the risk of moving her, knowing it will be painful. Like a dutiful nurse, I explain to Mom that I will place a large towel under her, and Bob and I will lift the towel instead of grabbing her. She shrugs and says nothing. In her lap, I notice her 90-count prescription bottle of oxycodone with the lid barely secured. Oh, great. She is ready to travel, all right. I have no idea how many she has taken with her breakfast. All I know is that her morning "meal" had consisted of coffee, a cigarette, and oxy.

Knowing that Bob suffers from severe work-related back problems, I coach him to keep his knees bent and spine straight as we prepare to lift Mom. Dad watches without comment from his threadbare recliner as if this was all just another day of retirement. On his first day of retirement 19 years ago, he sat in this same chair to read the *Philadelphia Bulletin* newspaper, watch the Phillies play on TV, and fart. He has kept up this routine faithfully.

Mom shrieks as Bob and I begin to lift her. We lower her back immediately. She says we jerked her broken leg. I add another towel under her calves, Bob takes her upper body, and I take the legs, and we smoothly move her to the lawn chair. Uneventfully, we carry Mom like Cleopatra to the van and install her on the van seat. As I fasten her seatbelt and prop pillows around her, her head lolls and eyes close. Her lower jaw drops. I am relieved she has thought to dose up. The trip is sure to go more smoothly for me this way.

Dad takes the passenger seat next to me with the soft cooler between his knees, and we are underway. With his lunch in his lap, he can reach it anytime he chooses. I stop the car only once at an interstate rest area to let Dad use the bathroom. Mom still is knocked out, so I check her pulse. It is regular and strong. I wait for Dad at the restroom door. Two minutes, five minutes, eight, then ten. A young black man strides toward the bathroom entrance. I tell him my dad is in there and ask would he please check on him, "His name is Joseph," I add.

The young man hollers to me from inside that Dad is not at the urinals. I hear him call out, "Joseph? Joseph?" I holler in that Dad is hard of hearing.

"Joseph?" Bang, bang, bang, he pounds on the stall doors. "Joseph?" I remain at the white-tiled bathroom entrance listening, now certain Dad is dead in the rest stop bathroom.

"What?" Dad finally responds, curious that someone knows him in Maryland.

A few minutes later, Dad exits the bathroom. He looks fine. He tells me he has been constipated recently, so he had taken a laxative the previous night and feels better now that he "emptied out" and that the commode was so comfortable, he fell asleep. As we walk back to the van on this already hot summer morning, it dawns on me how Mom has been in the car 20 minutes with only the front windows open a crack. When I check on her, she is sweating but asleep, her pulse and respirations steady.

Unfortunately, this rest stop incident is a mere foreshadowing of what is to come in the days and weeks ahead.

Grateful for no other incidents between Philly and my Virginia home, I back down the driveway to the basement door of my house so the van side door will open right there. My home has a full finished basement with kitchen, living room, bathroom, and bedroom. The laundry room adjoins. It is the ideal setting for what I have planned. Mom and Dad will have a place of their own, and I will be right upstairs.

I get out and open the van side door. Mom's head, bent at an odd angle, rests against the back of the seat. On the floor around her are dozens of Darvon capsules. The open bottle and cap lay in her lap. *Jesus.* I check her pulse, which is fine. I shout, "*Mom.*"

Finally, she mumbles, "Huh?"

Where this Darvon stash came from, I do not know, and I have no time to dwell on it.

By now Dad has gotten out of the van, walked up the gravel driveway to the garden, fallen against the post holding the pea vines up, and cut his hand. Thankfully, my husband appears and helps me decant Mom onto the unfolded sofa bed, bandage Dad's wound, and unload the van.

That evening after I cook and serve dinner, do dishes, and bathe Mom, I realize that she cannot stay on the sofa bed in the living room. My back is aching from all the bending --bathing my mother on my knees, changing her diaper, putting fresh sheets on the bed. I am exhausted but phone Joan and Paul to report the swell job I am doing. They laugh at the rest stop story. I am delighting my whole family. I swell with pride. This is grand.

The next day, I carry Mom and Dad to my saintly young family doctor using the same chair transfer technique as before. Doctor Naumann obtains a full set of X-rays of Mom's leg and happily reports there are no fractures. He says she likely has a torn knee ligament and orders a brace for her leg. After I describe my plan to care for her at my house, he also orders a hospital bed, over bed table, commode chair, Hoyer lift, and wheelchair. He orders a physical therapist to come to my home and assess Mom and design a treatment plan of exercise to help her to build strength, mobility, and balance.

Mom wonders out loud if this physician can really read X-rays, as this feels like a broken leg to her. "Doctors just don't know everything," she mumbles.

I ignore her and prepare to follow the doctor's orders. In two days, my husband and I have moved the sofa bed out and have had a fully motorized hospital bed delivered. It is situated by the living room window facing the woods. I put a hummingbird feeder outside the window for Mom to have something to watch.

We settle into a routine. At 4 am I bathe Mom, change the bed, start the laundry, and give her breakfast. Then I go upstairs to prepare breakfast for my sons and do chores. Afterward, I head back down to feed Dad his breakfast. Using the Hoyer lift, I transfer Mom to her wheelchair so she can wheel outside to smoke.

Mom is hostile about this turn of events. She wants to smoke in bed, but I do not cave to this. I tell her if she wants to smoke it is OK with me if she bathes first and gets into her wheelchair and smokes outside. Visions of my house burning down with all of us in it haunt me. I police her matches, cigarettes, and pills. I am a therapeutic gestapo daughter determined that Mom will be safe, clean, med compliant, and eat healthy, whether she wants to or not.

All day, Dad sits in a chair, as we do not have a recliner for him, staring out the window. When I have time, we go for a walk down the quarter-mile driveway and back. I notice his gait is unsteady, so I don't ask my sons to make this trek alone with Ahpu, their pet name for their grandfather, fearing a fall. That is all that I need.

Things seem to be settling into an acceptable pattern – for all of us.

One morning, about two weeks after my parents' arrival, Dad beckons me over to his chair and whispers with excitement, "Look! Look, it's a parade. It's the Boy Scouts dressed in uniforms walking behind the Gold Star Mothers." He is pointing into the woods outside the house, but there is no parade happening there. His eyes sparkle with animation. Slowly I realize he is recalling his Pennsylvania hometown, Hazelton, and the Memorial Day Parade from his childhood. My stomach sinks.

Oh my God, I think to myself, *Dad's mind slipped away while I was too busy to notice.* He knows who I am but has no idea where he is or how he got here. But he is calm and follows instructions. His slacks bear stains that reveal he is no longer continent. My chest feels heavy, and my jaw tightens.

Still I soldier on, determined to be my parents' savior – wanting them to see me as such – no matter what it takes.

Each morning my two sons pop downstairs to hang out with Nana and Ahpu before leaving for school. One day I happen to follow them in and hear my Mother say to them, "You resent us being here, don't you?" When they do not respond, she asks it again, louder.

They stand there in shock, and I angrily say, "No, no they do not." I watch as they run back upstairs, confused that they have done something wrong. I do not insist they ever go back down for a visit. A stew of fury begins to bubble. Pick on me, Mom, OK. But do not pick on my children . . . ever.

As for my husband, he has become tired of all of us squeezing around the small dinner table in the basement apartment and asks for dinner upstairs. To accommodate everyone, I now try to eat with my parent's downstairs, then again with my husband and sons upstairs. Two meals to prepare and clean up. Dad does not do dishes, never did, too old to learn, he states. He really means it is women's work, and he will not do it. He agrees to stack the dishes in the sink. Mom is bed-bound and can't help. My sons set and clear the table and do dishes upstairs, but there is always a final pass for me to make to clean up the kitchen. I fear food left out may attract cockroaches, though I haven't seen one since I lived in Philadelphia. Eating parts of two dinners is good, I think, since I have no time for breakfast and lunch.

Just a few days into my parents' stay, Mom's physical therapist, a kind, patient, and gentle young woman, performs a thorough exam and tells Mom she must do exercises for five minutes, three times a day, to build up her strength and flexibility. If she is disciplined and follows through, she will be back walking in no time. Mom tells the therapist about her frozen hips and horrible pain. The therapist reassures Mom she will do just fine after two weeks of therapy and returns three times a week to help Mom with the bed exercises.

It is apparent that Dad considers this his ticket back home to Philly and begins directing Mom through the exercises, at least the requisite three times a day. Before long, Mom possums up for at least one of those exercise times. She musters little to no enthusiasm for the other sessions.

There are some aspects of care that I find are beyond my scope due to lack of talent and schedule constraints. Mom's hair is dirty, and she hasn't had a haircut in forever. I call my beautician friend, Shawnette, and ask if she can come over to wash and cut Mom's hair. Shawnette sees several shut-ins regularly and agrees to come, visiting the next morning. Before I can fill her in on the details of my mother's condition, Shawnette asks Mom, who is sitting up on the side of the bed at my insistence, to walk over to the kitchen sink. "I can wash your hair over there," she tells Mom.

Without missing a beat, Mom stands and *walks*, with a shuffle but without a cane or any other assistance, slowly to the sink, about ten feet away.

I am freaking speechless. I have been using the Hoyer lift to transfer Mom from bed to wheelchair since she has arrived here. I have been changing the hospital bed with her in it. I have been pushing her in the wheelchair. And *this* is what she can do. I am near tears when I ask, "Why don't you walk for me?"

She looks over her shoulder at me and snaps, "Because *you* never asked."

She is correct, I never asked, I assumed she could not do it. I boil inside. Mom feigns pain and has pain, but I can't tell which is which. Some damn nurse I am turning out to be.

In four weeks, with a heroic amount of encouragement, the therapist gets Mom walking with a walker. I tell the therapist about the hair shampoo episode and how Mom walked and stood unassisted. Mom says it took everything out of her to do it and led to her not being able to walk again.

For the therapist, Mom goes up and down the steps, slowly but safely. Along the way, Mom pulls out all her drama stops, from "I can't" to "I am afraid" to a spit flying "You are trying to kill me."

For those who doubt the existence of angels, I can tell you the physical therapist who came to my house to care for my mother had a halo and wings. No matter what Mom said or did, I never heard a fat sigh of exasperation from this young woman or observed her rolling her eyes.

Well into our second month of blended family life, I find I need to be out of town for one day -- from early in the morning until early evening -- to attend a mandatory educational conference. Typically, my husband would agree to hang around the house while I am working my regularly scheduled shifts, but on this day, he, too, is otherwise engaged. I hire a personal care agency to send an aide to prepare meals, bathe Mom, and supervise Dad. The woman visits ahead of time to meet all of us and do the paperwork. She is capable and kind. I like her vibe and years of experience caring for folks in their own homes.

Mid-afternoon of the day I am out of town, I get an emergency call from the agency telling me that Dad has threatened to kill the aide with a knife, Mom will not stop screaming, and the aide has left in fear of her safety. The agency refuses to send another aide due to risk of bodily harm.

I lose it. *What in the hell are they doing,* I fume, *trying to kill me? Couldn't they give me one freaking day without World War III?* Fortunately, my husband agrees to get home as soon as he can.

At 7 pm I walk into the house and run down to the basement.

Dad takes one look at me and bellows, "We cannot live like this. It is 7 pm, and we have not eaten dinner. We eat at 5 pm."

He threatens to kill Mom for all the trouble she is causing him, and she shrieks that he will do it, just watch him. Dad storms out the door and stumbles up the hill to the gravel driveway. He says he is walking back to Philadelphia. I gather that he thinks walking to Philadelphia may take a few hours. He refuses to entertain the fact that he is 350 miles from home. I cannot get him to slow down or stop. He is stomping, and I am full out shouting, demanding he get back to the house.

I threaten police intervention. He thinks that is a great idea. He can tell the police he has not eaten anything today and get me arrested. I call my sister, fill her in on the crisis, and ask her to speak to Dad. She is crying and pleading. No good. I am sobbing, pleading, begging Dad to turn around, but he plods on. We almost get to the four-lane road at the end of our long driveway when my husband pulls up with our van and screams at my Dad to get the fuck in the van. It works.

Dad and I get back to the basement living room, and I fix them dinner. Mom refuses to eat. She expounds on how they hate it here with nothing to do. She hates me bossing her around.

Dad starts to cry and says simply, "We just want to go home."

I face reality and admit failure. My dream of redemption crashes and burns.

Early the next morning, we head north. My 12-year-old son, Nick, is my helper in the back seat with Mom. Once again, Dad sits next to me. The radio reports heavy traffic but no major incidents. There is nothing to chat about. I am even too spent to beat myself up on the inside.

We stop at a McDonald's about two hours into the trip. Dad takes diuretics for his blood pressure management, so I know he must pee.

He says no, he doesn't. I say get out and go to the bathroom. Nick helps his Ahpu get out of the front seat of the van, and I stay in the car with Mom. We are silent. She is looking around and chewing gum. As Nick and Dad return to the car, I can see that Nick looks frantic. He tells me Ahpu did need to pee but forgot to open his fly. Dad's pants tell me the tale before I hear the words. I tell Nick that it's OK, just get in. My vast skills as a registered nurse have gone unnoticed and have had no effect whatsoever on my parents. I am done. It is what it is.

We stop for lunch at the Maryland House, located at an Interstate 95 rest area. It is busy with summer travelers, and the parking lot is full. I park in a handicapped spot, even though I do not have a tag authorizing me to do so. I don't care. I get Mom's wheelchair out, and Nick and I lift her from the van to the chair. Slowly we process toward the restaurant, so Mom has time to have a smoke. Dad seems invigorated by the thought of eating out and oblivious to his urine-stained slacks. He and Nick walk arm and arm for safety.

Mom needs to go to the bathroom, so I send Nick and Dad to grab a table in the restaurant, which is already hopping. I offer to go in the stall with Mom, but she firmly declines. I remind her through the closed door that there is no smoking in the restroom, and I hear her sharply sigh with disgust. The back of Mom's gathered denim skirt falls into the commode as she slowly stands up, soaking it, and she is furious. I see it but say nothing.

All the tables are full, but there is plenty of wait staff. Our lunch arrives quickly despite the throngs of people eating. Dad and Mom have ordered BLTs. Nick and I get burgers.

I glance at Mom as she lifts her sandwich top and counts the bacon strips. She lunges toward Dad's plate and jerks the cover off his sandwich before loudly proclaiming to the restaurant crowd that Dad got one more piece of bacon than she did. The attentive waitress runs over to help Mom and offers to get her more bacon. Mom shouts at the waitress to just bring the check and a takeout box for her sandwich. She announces that she will not eat her BLT now because they cheated her out of bacon, adding for emphasis that we will never be eating here again.

Most people in the restaurant will never eat here again, I think to myself. It's a restaurant for travelers, for God's sake.

Dad, Nick, and I ignore her and choke down our sandwiches, mine sticking in my esophagus, or so it seems. We also ignore the staring people around us. I leave a generous tip for our waitress, and we depart through the double-glass doors and wind our way down the flower-lined cement sidewalk toward the parking lot.

I am pushing Mom's wheelchair. She is busy striking a match to light up for a smoke before we get back to the van. I look up to see Dad leaning over to pick up a penny from the sidewalk. I yell, "*No*," but it is too late. He pitches forward and lands on his nose.

Nick did not know what I intended by yelling "no," so he lets go of Dad's arm to come to my aid. As I run forward to help Dad, Nick screams, "Nana is *on fire*!"

I whip around to see Mom still trying to strike a match, not noticing that the previous match has ignited her BLT Styrofoam container, her skirt, and the rented wheelchair.

I race to her side, grab the container, and pitch it. I toss the cigarette pack into a trash bin right next to me, snatch the matches from her hand, and pitch them, too. I flatten my hands, then slam them against the flames on her skirt and wheelchair, trying to smother the fire. Unknown to me, and to Nick's obvious horror, I am repeatedly screaming "*Fuck! Fuck! Fuck!*" the entire time.

Within seconds, the flames are out, and somehow my hands are not burned. Dad is standing with his hankie over his bloody nose. Mom is demanding her cigarettes back, and dozens of people are staring in silence at my meltdown. Luckily, they don't intervene, call the police, or offer to help. They turn away and mind their own business, which is exactly what I want them to do.

Nick seems like a young man who has just been struck by a bolt of lightning from the blue. Wide-eyed he looks at me and says, "We're not going to make it to Philly, are we Ma?"

This statement snaps me back into the present moment. "Oh, *yes* we are," I say with determination. "We are 90 minutes away. Let's get in the van." I roll Mom to the van at warp speed and throw open the door.

Mom continues to pitch a holy fit because she needs her smoke after lunch, she always has a smoke after lunch, and she wants her *BLT and a smoke.*

I have turned to a pillar of stone. No words remain. I left my voice and all its fucks behind in the rest area. We load Mom and Dad in the car and head north.

Curbside at my parents' home, I open the van's side door to find Mom has mostly slid off the seat. Darvon capsules litter the floor. Again. I have no idea where she is stashing these pills, nor, at this point, do I care. Nick looks terrified and holds his palms up in a gesture of helplessness.

Good old neighbor Bob comes out and helps Nick and me. In an hour, we are unloaded. Dad, who positions himself in his familiar recliner holding an opened newspaper, already seems like his old self. Mom is passed out on her stinking sofa. I set up her walker, diapers, trash bags, and smokes. I update Bob and tell him to call the police when Dad falls again.

Nick puts the slightly scorched wheelchair back in the van, and we head out. I don't look back to see if anyone is waving.

The late August heat is oppressive. The AC is blasting, and Nick and I travel in peace, listening to "his" music on the radio. I admit defeat to myself. I did what I thought was my very best, even if my goal was not met. I say to myself that my parents are who they are. I feel a weight lift.

Just across the Delaware state line, six lanes of I-95 South funnel into four, and we slow roll to a stop. Nick sighs a deep "Oh, no."

As we sit there contemplating how much time this back-up will add to our trip, we notice the driver of another minivan about a half dozen cars in front of us hop out and frantically jerk open the side door. He is a white man, maybe in his 30s, wearing khaki shorts and a white T-shirt. He reaches into the van and hurriedly pulls out a 10 or 11-year-old girl, rips down her panties, and helps her squat next to the guardrail. She is in full view of dozens of vehicles, and she is wailing. Torrents of explosive diarrhea pour from her. We gasp. The father is holding her, but her clothing still becomes soiled. We can't hear the conversation with the windows up, but he seems to be talking calmly to her during the entire episode. We watch as the shaking girl steps out of her panties and into the van. The man appears to be wiping her down, but all we see are his arms moving. Just as the man returns to his driver's seat, the traffic begins to crawl forward.

As we pass the pile of poop, I don't look. Instead I turn to Nick and say, "No matter what has happened to us so far today, we are now headed south toward home, the AC is working, and we are not having explosive diarrhea on the interstate."

We share a wan smile and enjoy the music all the way home. The durable medical equipment company comes to retrieve the bed, Hoyer lift, potty chair, and wheelchair. No one ever contacts me to ask for an explanation about the puck-sized burn hole in the wheelchair seat.

A few months later, my brother comes off the road to valiantly deal with my parents. Despite living with them and providing care, their 'round-the-clock needs exceed his abilities, and he gets them placed in a shared room in a long-term care facility. I return to Philly to help him empty the house of 50 years' accumulation. It all goes onto the sidewalk on trash day. Beds, dressers, cabinets. Everything. Within a few hours' time, neighbors with young families have come, helped themselves to the household items and gone. Only the shit-stained sofa is left behind. A woman raising her three-year-old twin granddaughters takes grateful ownership of the bedroom set that Joan and I once shared. The little girls hug me and thank me for their new furniture.

In his new and unfamiliar environment, Dad's dementia progresses. Within a few months of moving to the nursing home, he suffers a stroke, which leaves him unable to swallow. He spends three months unable to eat. His weight drops from 205 to around 100 pounds before his heart gives out. It is horrific for him. He had been admitted to the nursing home with a "Do Not Resuscitate" order, but the night of his stroke an agency nurse who does not know him nor see the DNR posted on the headboard finds him unresponsive and begins CPR. Dad makes it to the hospital in time to be placed on a ventilator.

A physician calls me to inform me of Dad's condition. I fax the DNR to the hospital, and the physician removes Dad from the ventilator. The physician advises me that due to the massive stroke he has had, Dad will not live long. I call a random funeral home in Philly near Dad's hospital and connect with a very kind and competent man named Lenny. I tell Lenny what has happened to Dad and explain that Dad is a veteran. I say Dad may be ready for funeral care soon. Lenny tells me not to worry about any of the details, that he will begin to process a request at the veteran's cemetery in Hazelton, Pennsylvania, to bury Dad there. I am relieved and make plans to head to Philly the next day. I relay what Lenny has said to both Joan and Paul.

The doctor calls me again that evening. Shortly after Dad was removed from the ventilator, he opened his eyes and asked the nurse if he could please have scrambled eggs. Yep, Dad was alive, and he was hungry. But he has no gag reflex, and eating is a choke fest. He returns to the nursing home on a pureed and heavily thickened diet, which he hates. He begs my brother for a hot dog day after day. After weeks of listening to his pleas, my brother relents, buys a tiny food processor, purees a hot dog and takes it to Dad, who rolls the mushy paste in his mouth, relishing the taste. Then he coughs and sputters and out it comes. The nurses are furious with Paul, but Joan and I agree with his compassionate desire to give Dad what he so wanted.

Dad stops breathing for good three weeks before his 90th birthday and six months after the first time he died and was brought back to life. Or whatever you call an existence where you can't swallow without choking. No matter what is listed as cause of death on the death certificate, I know Dad died of starvation.

We have no viewing for Dad. Lenny takes care of all the rest.

The poignant graveside service is choreographed by the veterans' cemetery staff and includes a flag-draped coffin, "Taps," and a 21-gun salute. Dad would have loved it. His time in the army was the happiest time of his life, he often said. Now he is back with his military brothers and in peace.

There is no eulogy.

For her entire married life, Mom barely tolerated Dad and was blatantly rude, mean, and angry about being stuck with him. I have a feeling Dad's funeral will not change the sentiment. I pull Lenny aside before the ceremony and say I fear a scene.

Before the service begins, Lenny, in his gorgeous, polished, tight-fitting black suit, strides over to Mom as she takes her place at the head of the coffin. His black, precisely combed hair gleams in the sunshine. He leans toward Mom, seated in her wheelchair. He tells her that after the 21-gun salute – seven guns fire simultaneously, three shots each -- the flag will be folded by the service members and presented to her.

She tells him, spit flying, she does not want no damn flag. Composed and unflinching, Lenny leans closer to Mom and slowly stage whispers to her that she will respectfully *and* silently accept the flag from the service member and will then be free to give it to anyone else *after* the ceremony. To her credit, Mom does as Lenny directs. Thank you, Jesus, for sending me another angel, a take-no-shit-from-anyone Lenny.

Mom, who seemed to have spent her whole adult life wishing Dad was dead, finally gets what she wants. At the time of Dad's death, Paul and Joan still live in Denver; I am still in Virginia. Mom is given the option of moving into a nursing home in Virginia to be near me or relocating to Denver to be near Joan and Paul.

She chooses Denver. Joan is happy, and so am I. Joan visits her every day after work, carrying her food treats and, most importantly, bringing her cartons of her favorite cigarettes. Mom builds friendships with other residents, and the nurses coax her into bathing and getting in her wheelchair by insisting she smoke outside. Joan has a lightweight wheelchair custom-made for Mom, which is a breeze for Mom to wheel.

Mom soon develops a routine. She likes to hang out in the all-you-can-eat taco bar dayroom with the staff and her new friends. She goes outside to smoke on the patio, oxygen tank in the back pocket of her wheelchair. She never remembers to remove the oxygen cannula from her nose while she smokes, but she never catches on fire or blows up. On a day with a gusty stiff wind, Mom blows halfway down the block on the sidewalk before an aide catches up with her, but she is none the worse from her adventure.

Mom is happy. She has her cigarettes and coffee and access to all the oxy she wants. She is relaxed and loves being waited on by her aides. She does not need to cook or clean. She plans her cremation and pays for it. She writes her will.

Occasionally, she goes out to restaurants with Joan and Paul. At mealtimes she hoards food to feed to the two resident therapy dogs that wander the nursing home halls, even after she is told not to. Paul takes his black lab, Dyna, to the home to visit. Dyna loves Mom and everyone there. Dyna gets free food and to the chance to savor the smells on the floor that are only obvious to her Labrador nose.

Mom lives at the nursing home for a year and a half. As the months pass, the effort to breathe with advancing COPD slowly but surely reduces her appetite, which was less than vigorous in the first place.

I go to see Mom in Denver, one time. I do not really want to go but am forever grateful I did. I finally get to see her truly happy. She has no domestic responsibilities and no hateful in-laws to badger her. Her physicians do not insist she do therapy, and there is no husband to agitate her. She has daily visits from Joan and plenty of people to hang out with to smoke. Paul and Dyna visit and entertain Mom and all the residents with her friendly black lab antics. Mom is contented and with her kind of people. She has, at last, found comfort and ease.

Every time I visit Mom during my five-day stay in Denver, she looks relaxed, smiles, and shares funny stories about life "in the home." One day she tells Joan, Paul, and me about "getting stuck" in the dayroom when a group of "holy rollers" came in to sing for and pray with the residents. Mom is not into praying, and she is not into worshiping through song. She says she slid down into her wheelchair, rested her chin into her chest, and began to drool. Worked like a charm, she comments. An aide came and rolled her back to her room and put her to bed. She mimes her strategy for us while recounting the story, her eyes closing, and her bottom lip hanging down. We laugh until our sides hurt. Anyone looking on would be jealous of how well our family is getting along.

Not long after my visit, Mom begins to slide into and out of consciousness. Joan stays by her side and is present to hear Mom whisper her final word, "Coffee."

Even though we still had harbored hopes of a "thank you" or "love you," not one of us is surprised by this final request.

Mom lasts three more days. My compassionate and benevolent sister is there for every long minute, which includes Mom's final earthbound breath. At age 44, Mom said she would not make it to the next Christmas. At 78, she has made it for many more than she thought.

Long enough to find happiness and peace.

OFF RAMP

I walk this earth as a nurse. Not just when I am face-to-face with my patients. It's every minute of every day.

At restaurants, I can't help but hear someone wheeze and think, *That guy needs to use his inhaler.* Or I'll see a woman with hugely swollen ankles at a nearby table and comment to my dinner companions, "See that lady's ankles? She has 4+ pitting edema, and she'll be in ICU by 10 o'clock tonight. Oh, no. Look at the salt she is pouring on her fries. Make that 8 o'clock."

If my companions are nurses, we ponder out loud whether to run to the lady and do a bit of patient teaching. If I am with my husband, he glares a mute cease-and-desist order, and I keep all further comments to myself.

***

In 2018 I attended my 46th nursing school reunion. Out of fifty four that graduated from Hahnemann Hospital School of Nursing, thirty of us came to Philadelphia for the reunion. The clinical experiences we had during those three years of training prepared us to enter the highest levels of nursing expertise around the world. Many of us still work as nurses, some in advanced levels as Nurse Practitioners or Nurse Anesthetist's.

As Hahnemann nurses, the scope of our healing hands across the decades must have touched hundreds of thousands. Smart, glorious and loving. I am honored to keep these women close to my heart.

* * *

My satchel of stories is far from emptied out. Yet to be shared: An old country farmer named Fuzzy; a 400-pound eleven-year-old; and a jail inmate with a blood infection progressing so rapidly he was dying right in front of me.

I want to share with you the story of a nine-month-old baby so sensory deprived she lost her will to live. And details of my own accidental encounter with a contaminated needle stick that resulted in me acquiring hepatitis B.

The patient encounters that delivered upon me a broken nose, a forearm bite, a kick in my jaw, deep fingernail scratches down my back and a near sexual assault.

And more of my one-of-a-kind home health nurse encounters -- with a pig and a pug, a ferret and a beagle.

Wishing you happiness, health, and a passion to tell your own stories. Perhaps those that came to mind while you visited my one nurse universe.

2014- current — Nurse Susan Yoga
Position: Nurse entrepreneur

Duties: Certified YogaNurse®, local community therapeutic yoga teacher, holistic wellness speaker

2011- 2014 — Hand n Heart Home Care Services
Position: Director of Nursing

Duties: Medicaid Personal Care case management, aide training and supervision. Part-time position eliminated by Company owner July 23, 2014

2009- 2012 — Anthem Care Management
Position: Telephonic Nurse Coach

Duties: Chronic disease patient assessment, teaching and case management

2001- 2007 — Henrico County Jail East-Barhamsville, VA
Position: Corrections RN

Duties: Perform History and Physical Assessment on all newly committed inmates. Identify and refer for treatment inmates with chronic illnesses, infections, STD evaluation.

2001 — Integrated Benefits Corporation
Position: Medical Record Reviewer

HEDIS (Healthplan Employer Data and Information Set) medical record reviewer for Trigon Healthkeepers, Inc. through IBC. Performed medical record reviews

1998- 2000 — Virginia Commonwealth University-School of Pharmacy
Position: Skills Lab Instructor

Duties: Provide classroom and clinical laboratory instruction to third year pharmacy students in PharmD program in physical assessment and operation of medical diagnostic devices.

1993- 2001 Brookside Home Health Care
Position: Visiting Nurse
Duties: Assessment, treatment and teaching patients in their home environment

1984- 1993 Cumberland: Hospital for Children
Position: Charge Nurse
Duties: Pediatric Acute Care Coma Recovery Unit

1991- 1992 Sheltering Arms Hospital
Position: Rehabilitation Nurse
Duties: Care and treatment of medical and surgical rehabilitation patients

1982- 1984 Stuart Circle Hospital
Position: Charge Nurse
Duties: Care and treatment of medical- surgical, plastic surgery and acute psych patients

1980- 1981 Family Practice MD office
Position: Office Nurse
Duties: Assessment of patients, assist physician in exams and minor surgeries, draw labs, perform EKG's

1977-1978 Poudre Valley Hospital
Position: Charge Nurse
Duties: Night shift charge Nurse, Acute Care Psychiatric Unit

1976- 1976 Drs. Avner, Buckley & Perlman
Allergy Specialist
Position Office nurse
Duties: Allergy skin testing, shots, labs

1973- 1977 Denver Children's Hospital
Position: oncology nurse
Duties: Inpatient and outpatient clinic pediatric oncology nurse; draw labs, administer chemo, end of life care

1972- 1973 Women's Medical College Hospital
Position: pediatric nurse
Duties: staff nurse 40 bed pediatric unit

CPSIA information can be obtained
at www.ICGtesting.com
Printed in the USA
FFHW011933170819
54371249-60071FF